POLITICAL ANTI-SEMITISM IN ENGLAND 1918–1939

Political Anti-Semitism in England 1918–1939

Gisela C. Lebzelter

HOLMES & MEIER PUBLISHERS, INC.
New York

First published in the United States of America 1978 by
HOLMES & MEIER PUBLISHERS, INC.
30 Irving Place, New York, New York 10003
Copyright © 1978 by Gisela C. Lebzelter
All rights reserved.

Library of Congress Cataloging in Publication Data

Lebzelter, Gisela C
   Political anti-semitism in England,
   1918–1939.
   A revision of the author's thesis,
   St. Anthony's College, Oxford.
   Bibliography: p.
   Includes index.
   1. Antisemitism – Great Britain. 2. Jews in Great
Britain – Politics and government. 3. Great Britain –
Politics and government – 20th century.
   I. Title
DS146.G7L42   1978
323.1'19'24042   78-16795

ISBN 0-8419-0426-X

Printed in Great Britain

Contents

List of Illustrations

Acknowledgements

The object of this book is threefold: a documentation of manifestations of anti-Semitism between World War I and World War II; a portrayal of organized anti-Semitism; and assessment of the impact of attempts to instrumentalize anti-Semitism in political campaigns. Throughout, the approach is selective rather than exhaustive since the aim was not to accumulate 'more of the same', but to trace and discuss the patterns of anti-Semitism as they emerge from the English example, a case which hitherto has been given little attention.

The origin of the present work is a DPhil thesis which I wrote as a graduate student at St Antony's College, Oxford. I am grateful to the Warden and Fellows of St Antony's College for enabling me to pursue my studies at such a stimulating place. I should also like to thank the Volkswagen Foundation for its generous financial support.

While I am deeply indebted to many individuals, too numerous to list, who took an interest in my work and offered advice, particular thanks are due to Professor C. Abramsky, who supervised my dissertation from the beginning. Above all I wish to thank Mr A. J. Nicholls, without whose constant help, encouragement and valuable criticism it would not have been completed. I am also grateful to Mrs Maureen Tayal, who read the entire manuscript and patiently discussed it with me at various stages. Any errors that remain are, of course, entirely my own responsibility.

During my research I received much assistance from archivists, librarians and research officers. It is a pleasure to acknowledge my gratitude to Mr N. Higson, who helped me with the records of the National Council for Civil Liberties; to Dr B. Kosmin who guided me to the minute books of the Board of Deputies of British Jews; and to Mr G. Phillips, who allowed me to consult documents in possession of *The Times*. I am particularly grateful to Mr Tindal-Robertson for his hospitality and for enduring my requests regarding the material preserved by the Britons Publishing Company; to Mr Hamm for his kind reception when I consulted the Mosley Secretariat; and to the Council of Christians and Jews for allowing me to examine their records.

I wish to record my gratitude for having been granted permission to consult the Astor Papers at Reading University, the Baldwin Papers at Cambridge University, the H. A. Gwynne Papers at University College, Swansea, the J. S. Middleton Papers at Transport House, London, the Maxse Papers at the West Sussex Record Office, Chichester, the Mount Temple Papers at the Hampshire Record Office, Winchester, the Nicolson Papers at Balliol College, Oxford, the Trenchard Papers at the Royal Air Force Museum, Hendon, and the A. White Papers at the National Maritime Museum, Greenwich, by courtesy of His Grace, the Duke of Bedford. In addition to the keepers of these records, I should also like to thank the staff at the Bodleian Library, British Library, Marx Memorial Library, Mocatta Library, Parkes Library, the Public Record Office and the Wiener Library. Transcripts of Crown-copyright records in the Public Record Office appear by permission of the Controller of H. M. Stationery Office.

Finally, I wish to express my deepest gratitude to my husband, on whose love, devotion and understanding I could always rely.

G. L.
January 1978

List of Abbreviations

BoD	Board of Deputies of British Jews
BUF	British Union of Fascists
CAB	Cabinet Papers
CPGB	Communist Party of Great Britain
HO	Home Office
FO	Foreign Office
IFL	Imperial Fascist League
JPC	Jewish People's Council
MEPO	Metropolitan Police Files
NCCL	National Council for Civil Liberties
NSDAP	Nationalsozialistische Deutsche Arbeiter Partei (National Socialist German Workers' Party)

Introduction

Much has been written on anti-Semitism since the end of World War II. Once the scope of the holocaust in the middle of Europe became known, the urge for explaining this unbelievable page of 20th-century history began to occupy historians, sociologists, political scientists, theologians and psychologists alike. While the people at large turned away from the difficult task of coming to grips with the shocking reality of Auschwitz, Dachau, Theresienstadt and other extermination camps, and embarked upon the more rewarding and equally urgent task of rebuilding what lay shattered in pieces, it remained the responsibility of academics to trace, analyse, understand and explain the mechanisms which had led to the extermination of two-thirds of European Jewry.

Understandably enough, the focus of study was Germany – mostly the anti-Jewish policy and ideology of the NS regime, but also the periods which preceded it and provided a continuity of anti-Semitic sentiment. However, one cannot reduce the subject of anti-Semitism to its German variant alone if one wants to assess its rank within modern history in general. Difficult as it may be, one has to abstract from the event of the 'final solution' and look at the potentials that lay buried in the ideology as such. Once its inherent dimensions have become intelligible, its impact upon different societies at various times can be discussed and it becomes possible to expose its social and political function at certain historical junctures. An analysis of anti-Semitism in England, where it was of limited importance, should therefore be regarded as an attempt to comprehend the nature and dynamics of anti-Semitism from a theoretical angle.

Since there is no precise understanding as to who is an anti-Semite and what constitutes anti-Semitism, the topic has to be defined. By common usage, anti-Semitism is generally meant to describe any hostility against Jews. For historical reasons, and for the sake of analytical clarity, however, it should be differentiated between an age-old hostility against the Jewish minority, a distinct body of foreigners pleading for political equalization and integration into Christian societies, and the qualitatively new anti-Jewish movement which emerged in the 19th century.

The former anti-Judaism can be traced throughout history since the dispersion of Jewry after Titus's conquest of Jerusalem. Their strong religious bond, constantly reinforced through pressure from the host societies, prevented the Jews from being absorbed like other minorities. Christian thought, which governed the Western hemisphere unchallenged for nearly two milleniums, provided an ideological framework for the formulation of stereotypes and hostile attitudes against the Jewish minorities. Jewish communities, visible enclaves in the Christian environments, were ready targets whenever the antagonism between Christian and Jewish faith was stirred up. The vulnerability of Jewish communities was increased by the fact that legally and economically they were reduced to special status, mainly engaged in money-lending and trade. Thus they depended entirely on the benevolence, tolerance and need of their respective masters.

With the reform of civil life in the age of bourgeois revolutions the Christian value system was challenged: the rapid development of commerce, industry, science, technology, communications and education entailed also a fundamental secularization. Traditional structures and norms were questioned and new concepts, based on rational, realistic and democratic principles, were demanded. Together with other underprivileged groups Jews achieved equal civic status in the various countries at some stage during the 19th century. In the wake of their emancipation, anti-Semitism developed as a new phenomenon, a reactionary anti-liberal doctrine directed against the Jewish minority.

While a qualitative difference between pre-industrial and modern anti-Semitism is generally assumed, there is no unanimity among scholars regarding the historical foundations and specific characteristics of anti-Semitism.[1] As primarily a product of the Gentile society, anti-Semitism has to be seen as a phenomenon that developed after the emancipation of Jews. Its features, religious, racial, historical and socio-economical arguments, corresponded to the traditional hostility. The new element was that one no longer assumed that in principle the Jews should and could be assimilated and absorbed. Previously, conversion to Christianity had provided 'an entry-ticket into European culture', but now this no longer satisfied the Jew-baiters. As a group, they argued, the Jews could not be integrated without undermining the host societies. Assimilation, they pointed out, was nothing but a cunning fake to conceal their real identity. No matter how well the Jews adapted to their host societies, it was said, they always retained their identity as a people distinguished through their bond of blood.[2] Therefore, it was concluded, they constituted a state within the state, and invariably aimed at a judaization of the world, controlling the social, economic and political life of the nations while subjecting them to Jewish values. Thus stigmatized as a 'national mischief', the Jews were stylized as the most obstructive anti-group, the source of all evil. Not only were they blamed for the faults and vices of capitalism, modernization and democratization – the 'Jewish question' was hypostatized as a key issue to solve the fundamental problems of modern society.[3]

To differentiate between the old anti-Semitism, which has also been called 'anti-Judaism', and the new variant, as it emerged in the 19th century, the latter is mostly referred to as 'modern anti-Semitism'. It seems less confusing to reserve the very term anti-Semitism exclusively for the new phenomenon and to derive its definition from its historical contents. Accordingly, anti-Semitism can be qualified as a doctrine which attributes to the Jews an exceptional position among all other civilizations, defames them as an inferior group, denies their being part of the nation and categorically refuses them any symbiosis.[4] This definition includes non-violent social anti-Semitism and 'compulsory Zionism' as possible forms of anti-Semitism. It transcends the general understanding of Jew-hatred, or combat of Jewry, and emphasizes the latent totality of a phobia, which represents a secular version of a dichotomous conception of history.

Once the Jews are singled out as the root of all evil, a Manichean *Weltanschauung* is presented and it is there that we find the potential 'final solution'.[5] Once anti-Semitism is instrumentalized by political, economic, religious or cultural power élites who perceive themselves as the defenders of Western culture, it stipulates an uncompromising hostility towards Jewry: if Jews are seen as the source and incarnation of all evil, the salvation of the world depends upon the outcome of the Armaggedon between Jews and Gentiles. Where Jews are not a remote and untouchable supranational entity such as a God, a *Weltgeist* or eternal sin, where they present a visible and tangible target of attack, they constitute an enemy that can actually be overthrown. Political cultures dominated by liberal, enlightened, philanthropical values might mitigate the call for drastic measures for some time, but do not alter the inherent totality of the ideology. The difference between physical destruction of all Jews, their deportation to a place where they are rendered innocuous and their gradual exclusion from society seems to be marginal with regard to the underlying principle – no more than a question of political expediency at a certain time, dependant on the function and relative importance of anti-Semitism in a certain political culture.

Anti-Semitism as a mass-movement originated in Germany, where emancipation was understood not to be a raising to equality of a minority retaining its group identity, but was perceived as a policy whose aim was precisely the opposite of emancipation, namely assimilation. Once the ghetto walls were broken down, the liberal reformers had argued, and the Jews were integrated into society, they would quickly lose their group-consciousness and identify along common patterns. Indeed, their assumptions proved to be correct and the complete assimilation of Jewry seemed in sight when, due to the depression of the 1870s, the opponents of emancipation, who denounced assimilation as an outward camouflage to conceal the tenacious pursuit of Jewish interests, prevailed upon the liberal reformers.

Just as the successful conclusion of the formal emancipation of Jews had depended on the permeation of liberalism, its successful reversal was linked to the general anti-liberal reaction. The widespread appeal of such a reactionary ideology was due to several reasons: while a period of political stability and economic prosperity might have consolidated the emancipation of Jews and their gradual integration into society, in 1873 Germany was hit by an economic crisis which, although part of a world-wide depression, was felt more severely there than elsewhere. It brought the feverish boom that had accompanied the unification of the *Reich* to an abrupt end; it coincided with a structural crisis that emanated from local reforms and the rapid transition from an agrarian to an industrial society; most important however it disillusioned a generation that had shared a profound optimism with regard to its own future and that of the German state. As a consequence, the national euphoria was replaced by a widespread crisis-consciousness, insecurity and dissatisfaction.[6]

The economic crisis was not analysed, and it was not recognized as a cyclical event. Instead, it was blamed upon economic capitalism and political liberalism, which had allegedly inspired the recent developments. Roused by a severe economic slump, those who felt disappointed after an age of reforms which had by-passed their personal aspirations, those who felt left behind and suffered rather than gained from modernization, those who had expected more rewards from the national unification and Germany's advancement as an international power, rejected liberalism and capitalism. The Jews, one of the groups that had gained most from liberal reforms, were now identified as their authors, and served as ready targets for the diversion of widespread discontent. In this period, the very term anti-Semitism was coined and subsequently transferred from German into other languages.

The emergence of anti-Semitism indicates most clearly the change from pre-industrial to modern politics: during the Middle Ages Jews were completely at the mercy of their sovereigns. As long as they proved useful for a state and its governors, they were protected. Their legal rights were manipulated expediently and very often they suffered as scapegoats for various complaints by being out-lawed or expelled. During the 1870s, political agitators for the first time instrumentalized anti-Semitism as a political ideology, the only substance of their claim to power.[7] The hereditary irrational prejudice against the Jews served merely as a foil for a popular controversy about the status of the Jews, their influence and impact on society. No longer was the anti-Jewish policy generated at will by the authorities and more or less readily taken up by the mob, nor was it confined to sporadic outbreaks. It was a doctrine, propagated by its promoters as the magic key to solve the problems of modern society. On the open market of local and national politics they campaigned on the 'Jewish question', in their opinion the most urgent issue. With other parties, inspired by different ideologies, they competed for financial and electoral support and sought for a mandate to subdue the Jewish influence in all spheres of public life.

The backbone of this modern Jew-hatred was the new gospel of racism, which developed and spread rapidly during the second half of the 19th century.[8] The adaptation of Darwin's theory of the survival of the fittest in order to propagate a conflict between superior and inferior people has to be seen in the context of defining the nation-state and validating imperialism. In an age of rapid technological and scientific progress, it supplied an important pseudo-scientific legitimation for the revival of Jew-hatred. Now the Jews were discovered as a race, not only different from but opposed to their Gentile neighbours. Racial differences were explored, measured and quantified and, from the results, the quality and respective ranking-order of an ethnic group was deduced.[9] The desirability of individuals no longer depended on their merits, but on their descent, and Jews in particular were seen as a threat to the racial and cultural purity of their host societies. Dispersed among other nations, they were seen to represent a disintegrating element in the national life. If there was no way to erase the mistakes of the past, at least the future could be planned: eugenics, the cultivation of finer offspring, became a favourite topic for discussion not only among enthusiastic scientists, but among all concerned with the betterment of mankind. The Jews, already stigmatized as a politically perilous element, quickly became one of the groups singled out for 'special consideration'.

In functioning as an outlet for discontent, social envy and cultural pessimism, and providing a common pattern of identification, anti-Semitism proved to enhance German nationalism. All efforts to develop anti-Semitism into a systematic theory of history complemented the endeavours to prove the alleged superiority of the German nation and culture, and anti-Semitism soon became the common denominator of the radical right.

In England, the 'Jewish question' never assumed similar political importance, although it was exploited by right-wing propagandists. One important reason for the absence of a popular anti-Semitic movement in 19th-century England was the extensive integration of Jews into British society during the age of emancipation. Unlike Middle Europe, where the emancipation controversy focused on the repeal of specific Jew-laws, in England the issue was perceived as a pragmatic problem of admitting Jews to full citizenship by removing anachronistic obstacles, rooted in the traditional alliance between state and church.

The official re-admission of Jews in 1656 after their expulsion in 1290 had been the result of long negotiations, whereby Jews acquired the status of non-Protestant citizens or, if foreign-born, aliens. Obligatory religious oaths and declarations excluded them from Crown office, Parliament and other institutions, but no special legislation singled them out and regulated their position in any particular way.[10] The practical dichotomy between a growing economic and social influence of Jews and members of other religious minorities and their exclusion from important political rights posed the 'Jewish question' in terms of civic rights for minorities. In Germany, by contrast, this had never been the issue. Those who favoured the emancipation of Jews had on the contrary argued that it would precipitate their assimilation, and would thus gradually eliminate the distinct Jewish minority.

The British opponents of political equalization of Jews, like their continental counterparts, maintained that their religious separatism, their national identity and their secretive habits set the Jews apart from their neighbours. But the reform movement within Jewry which accompanied their gradual emancipation, and the transition from a predominantly lower-class to a predominantly middle-class community, invalidated this argument. In England, social status proved to be a more decisive factor than religious denomination in determining the degree of acceptance of minorities.[11] In view of the factual influence Jews had already achieved their political emancipation was overdue when it was formally concluded with their eligibility to Parliament in 1858, the Promissory Oaths Act of 1871 which admitted Jews to high offices and the granting of a peerage to Nathaniel Rothschild in 1885.[12]

After the passing of the acts of emancipation, the Anglo-Jewish community rapidly lost its group-consciousness. This development manifested itself in the changing party affiliation of English Jews: those who were elected to Parliament no longer represented the interests of a religious minority. Depending on their general political preference, many shifted from the Liberal Party, the champion of their emancipation, to the Conservative Party. Class and status thus superseded the religious factor in determining Jewish political behaviour.[13]

The test of loyalty was put to Anglo-Jewry in the last two decades of the 19th century when, as a result of the persecution of Jews in Russia, a new tide of Jewish immigrants entered England. The Jewish community, which had increased from 35,000 in 1850 to 65,000 in 1881, increased fourfold during the next thirty years.[14] The influx of Jews from Eastern Europe consisted mainly of lower middle-class and artisan strata, and the immigrants tended to settle in industrialized urban areas, particularly in London, Manchester and Leeds. Their regional and occupational concentration was enhanced by their cultural individuality, their Yiddish language and orthodox faith. This, together with the rejection from the host society and heavy economic pressures, predisposed the immigrants towards Zionism and radical movements, and soon efforts were made to organize the Jewish workers.[15]

The poor arrivals were met with embarrassment and reserve by both the English public and assimilated Jewry. 'The East-European Jews are treated like dirt', one observer wrote in 1908. 'The native population has an unbelievable contempt for them, and their western fellow-Jews are ashamed of the connexion.'[16] Charity to help these undesirable aliens was aimed at removing the stigma which the immigrants imposed on English-born Jews and all efforts were made to re-educate them quickly. The *Jewish Chronicle*, the official organ of established Anglo-Jewry, argued:

> Our fair fame is bound up with theirs; the outside world is not capable of making minute discrimination between Jew and Jew, and forms its opinion of Jews in general as much, *if not more*, from them than from the Anglicized portion of the Community. . . . By improving their dwellings, attracting them to our synagogues, breaking down their isolation in all directions and educating their children in an English fashion, we can do much to change our foreign poor into brethren, who shall not only be Jews but English Jews.[17]

The sensitive reaction of Anglo-Jewry corresponded to the predictable response from English society. Conservatives and trade-union leaders joined hands in their demand for a restriction of uncontrolled immigration. Unemployment was high during the 1880s, and the foreign immigrants served as ready scapegoats for the economic crisis. 'England for the English' became a catchword for the anti-alien lobby around Captain Colomb, Conservative MP for Tower Hamlets, and the jingoistic journalist Arnold White, advocate of a strong navy and upholder of a mighty Empire. It was argued that the immigrants flooded the labour market by cheap labour, monopolized local trade, ruthlessly practised the sweating-system and undermined traditional English values.[18] Although these charges appeared in fact in most cases unfounded, anti-alienist sentiment spread rapidly. It produced a typical anti-Jewish whisper-propaganda, manifested in the rumour that Jack-the-Ripper, the Whitechapel murderer of 1888, was Jewish.[19]

In 1902 the British Brothers League, an anti-immigration league, was founded, and attracted some 45,000 members. It was based in the East End of London and directed all its agitation against the Jewish population. Led by Major W. Evans-Gordon, MP for Stepney, it accused the Jews of being clannish, unwilling to abandon their identity and thus remaining a separate element within society. J. Banister, one of the sympathizers of the League who was to remain a passionate anti-Semite for the next decades, took all foreign Jews for criminals – 'thieves, sweaters, usurers, burglars, forgers, traitors, swindlers, blackmailers and perjurers'.[20] He argued:

> No Jew is more of a hero among his fellow tribesmen than the one who can boast of having accomplished the ruin of some friendless, unprotected Christian girl. Owing to this fact, the male members of what is probably the most lecherous breed in existence have in every country acquired such a vile reputation among working women, that English servant girls who desire to preserve their respectability can seldom be persuaded to take service in Jewish families.[21]

In 1905 the Aliens Bill was passed, which retained the right of asylum. Immigration continued at an annual rate of 4000 to 5000 Jews until 1914. At the same time the immigrants began to assimilate and the interest in the 'Jewish question' ebbed off. The anti-Jewish campaign had, however, a lasting impact in that it instigated a new 'Jew-consciousness', stamped by the awareness of a racial difference between Jews and Gentiles. Jews began to be suspected for their ubiquity and their political and economic influence in various countries, and the revolutionary events in Russia lent the myth of a world-wide Jewish conspiracy a sudden relevance. While Disraeli had been completely acceptable to the English public despite his Jewish origin, a hypersensitiveness against Jews in high offices became apparent after World War I. Churchill drew attention to this mood in a letter to Lloyd George in which he discussed the forthcoming ministerial appointments:

> There is a point about Jews wh[ich] occurs to me – you must not have too many of them. . . . Three Jews among only 7 Liberal cabinet ministers might I fear give rise to comment.[22]

After World War I, domestic and international pressures required adjustment to a world much different from the pre-war era. 'Ours is a time of world-wide unrest and of unparalleled convulsion', one contemporary observed, 'a time of cataclysmic change and woe.'[23] Such a political climate, which resembled the cultural pessimism that dominated Germany after the *Gründerkrise*, proved prolific for the development of mass hysteria which could be directed against the traditional scapegoat, the Jews. The nature and impact of this 'new anti-Semitism', against which the Chief Rabbi protested in 1920,[24] will be discussed in the following chapters.

Part One
Manifestations of Anti-Semitism

1 The Myth of a Jewish World Conspiracy

The theme which figures most prominently in anti-Semitic propaganda is the persistent myth of a world-wide Jewish conspiracy. Even if individual Jews identified wholeheartedly with their respective countries of residence, anti-Semites argued, ultimately they constituted states within the states, chains of an international unit held together by a double bond of religion and blood.[1] In England, this argument was extensively exploited in the debates on immigration and the Aliens Bill of 1905. In the parliamentary debate of 10 July 1905, A. J. Balfour for example, observed that

> a state of things could easily be imagined in which it would not be to the advantage of the civilization of the country that there should be an immense body of persons who, however patriotic, able, and industrious, however much they threw themselves into the national life, still, by their own action, remained a people apart, and not merely held a religion differing from the vast majority of their fellow-countrymen, but only inter-married among themselves.[2]

The apparent 'internationalism' of Jews, their very dispersion throughout the world, made them an obvious target of criticism at a time of growing national consciousness and the emergence of nation states. Various publications appeared to substantiate rumours of malicious Jewish plans, ranging from straightforward fiction, such as Hermann Goedsche's novel *Biarritz*, to presumptive documentations such as the *Protocols of the Elders of Zion*.[3]

What one took to be a conclusive proof for the alleged subversive activities of world Jewry, the notorious 'protocols', turned out to be a plagarism fabricated by the agents of the Tsarist secret police *Okhrana*.[4] Before they were recognized as a forgery, however, they

13

focused attention all over the world. In 1903 they were published for the first time in a newspaper series in Russia. In December 1905 the *Protocols* appeared as an appendix to the third edition of a book by the mystic writer S. Nilus, *The Great in the Small, Anti-Christ A Near Political Possibility*. This version was to become the most celebrated one. It was republished in Russia in 1911 and 1912 and was brought to central and western Europe by anti-Bolshevik officers, the main carriers of anti-Semitic propaganda during the Russian civil war.

The war experience and the Bolshevik revolution served as momentous foils for the eager reception of these 'protocols' in Western Europe. In England, the myth of a 'hidden hand' had already been part of the anti-German wartime propaganda, when the nation was evoked to pull together in a common effort to beat the 'Hun', whose secret influence was suspected everywhere. German residents in England seemed to be potential enemy spies, and the 'hunnish hand' was blamed for poisoning patriotism by pacifist propaganda, causing a food shortage and manipulating international finance contrary to British interests. The former Home Secretary, Herbert Samuel, asserted in the House of Commons that 'there never has been any hidden hand',[5] but such a plain statement could not quell the xenophobia, a common phenomenon in times of exceptional external pressure.

The themes in the anti-German propaganda corresponded closely to the traditional anti-Jewish arguments, and in some cases the two targets of hostility merged into one enemy figure. The Rev. B. S. Lombard, Chaplain to the British forces in Russia, for example, suggested in March 1919 that 'Bolshevism originated in German propaganda and was, and is being, carried out by international Jews'.[6] The argument that the Russian revolution was the work of Jews of German extraction and in German pay was given full publicity in the columns of the arch-conservative *Morning Post* which commented:

The Jews are a great nation, emphatically a nation, and the able statecraft of their secret rulers has kept them a nation through forty centuries of the world's history. In their hands lies the traditional knowledge of the whole earth, and there are no State secrets of any nation but are shared also by the secret rulers of Jewry. . . . It may be doubted whether all that is best in Jewry the world over will not ere long find cause deeply to regret what seems, in the light of the latest revelations, something like a Jewish alliance with Old Testament Germany to regain temporal power upon the earth.[7]

The total identification of the German enemy with the 'Jewish peril' is also illuminated in a piece of amateur poetry evoked by an enthusiastic reader's encounter with A. White's book *The Hidden Hand,* which depicted the alleged German penetration of international finance, trade and politics.[8] It seems significant that a book which did not even refer to 'Jewish influence' could provoke such an outburst, containing all aspects of reactionary anti-Semitic propaganda. Stigmatizing Jewry as the universal agitator stirring all conceivable political and social unrest, the author stressed the historical dimension of the issue by allegorizing crucifixion for the high death-toll in the contemporary war:

Who are the Pacifists? Lets look at their noses
Are they tiptilted like petals of Roses
Or like sausages do they hang down at the ends?
Then they are *Jews,* they are *Jews,* they are Jews,
    my friends.
. . . . . .
No one would guess theirs was 'the Hidden Hand'
Whose Spies cause Disaster on Sea and on Land
And whose we to *crucify* Christian men on the *field*
And to force Christian Women to their *Bestiality*
    yield
There's a list of Christians in *every* town
In the Jews' possession *let that be well known.*
The Play of the Socialist is a play, on the name
Of its *Founder* Rothschild who played th'Revolutionary
    Game
By the net of Free Masonry, they have Englishmen
    caught
And *Socialism, Sinn Feinerism,* Labourism taught!
Dissensions, in the Church, Discontent in State
    and on Land
Every kind of Rebellion *the Jews* in secret have
    fanned. . . .[9]

Anti-Jewish propaganda captured the same sentiments as the

hysterical anti-Germanism which accompanied the English–German rivalry and warfare. But whereas the actual German enemy was anonymous and for the population at large intangible, the fictitious Jewish foe was more perceptible and could easily be identified as 'state within the state'. The juxtaposition of the two seemed all the more natural since the recent Jewish immigrants had all been Yiddish-speaking Ashkenazim and represented German culture. When anti-Semitism superseded anti-German agitation after the war, it was simply argued that Germany too was Jew-ridden and both England and Germany victims of the Jewish yoke.

The crucial event which gave rise to post-war anti-Semitism was the Russian revolution. The degree to which the British government was concerned about the 'peril of Bolshevism' became apparent when it instructed its intelligence service to submit fortnightly reports on 'revolutionary organizations in the United Kingdom', covering among others the activities of workers' organizations, the Independent Labour Party and the suffragettes. In one of his reports Sir Basil Thomson, Director of the Special Branch, characterized Bolshevism as follows:

> People who live under the Bolshevik regime describe it as a sort of infectious disease, spreading rapidly, but insiduously, until like a cancer it eats away the fabric of a society, and the patient ceases even to wish for his own recovery. A nation attacked by it may, if we may judge from the state of Russia, be reduced to a political and social morass, which may last perhaps for a generation or more, with no hope of reaction; whilst civilization crumbles away and the country returns to its original barbarism.[10]

Bolshevism was considered the principal antipode of democracy, its primary object being the destruction of existing states before constructing upon their ruins communist societies.[11] Pressure for continued intervention in Russia remained strong even after the victory over the Central Powers was imminent and it was no longer necessary to press for the reconstitution of the Eastern fighting front against Germany. In their attempt to mobilize public opinion in support of an interventionist policy, the critics of Bolshevism focused less on its political implications than on graphic accounts of alleged Bolshevik terror and ferocity. Thomson noted with satisfaction that 'a good deal is being done by private enterprise to combat Bolshevism, and the newspapers have been giving much space to news from Russia'.[12] The press indeed reported extensively about the 'horrors of Bolshevism', and the people were again called upon to rally behind the forces of 'good' in defence of Western civilization. Reprinting a letter from a British officer in South Russia, in which the atrocities allegedly committed by the 'Bolshevik devils' were described in great detail, *The Times* characteristically commented:

> The man who has seen what Bolshevism really means cannot rest without enlisting his wife and all his family into a crusade against it and a campaign for the enlightenment of the British public.[13]

The general contempt for the revolutionaries was accurately reflected in a newspaper article by W. S. Churchill, published in June 1919, in which he warned of the dangers of an international 'league of the failures, the criminals, the unfit, the mutinous, the morbid, the deranged, and the distraught in every land'. Firmly convinced of the moral superiority of the political and economic systems of the Western world, he pointed out that 'between them and such order of civilization as we have been able to build up since the dawn of history there can, as Lenin rightly proclaims, be neither truce nor pact'.[14] Churchill's argument was fully supported in a popular pamphlet by G. Pitt-Rivers, *The World Significance of the Russian Revolution*, in which the Bolsheviks' ruthless struggle for world domination was discussed. Their first step, Pitt-Rivers argued, was to overthrow all existing states and institutions, which would set free all disintegrating forces and overturn occidental civilization:

> In this first phase of wrecking and destruction all those who have nothing at all to lose, all criminals, anarchists and homicidal maniacs will naturally rally to the call with the prospect of satisfying their lusts for licence, power, plunder, and rape.[15]

As a proof for the Bolsheviks' 'mad desire for a return to the primitive'[16] it was frequently adduced that they communalized women. Although it was recognized that this allegation was, in fact, untrue,[17] the theme was fully exploited in a special pamphlet addressed to female British voters, in which they were encouraged to use their newly acquired democratic rights in the support of civilization against barbarism, which appeared in the disguise of Bolshevism, 'a foul far-spreading poison which is trying hard (through enemy activity) to fasten its fangs upon England, Scotland, Ireland and the Empire as a whole'.[18] Bolsheviks allowed no proper education, it was asserted, they banished religion and forced all women between the age of seventeen and thirty-two to register with local authorities to be at the disposal of any citizen who applied for them.

The strong emotional conviction with which the anti-Bolshevik agitation was pursued, together with the fact that many Russian-Jewish radicals played a prominent part in the revolution, brought Jews to the limelight and entertained old prejudices. In January 1919 Lord Milner, then Secretary of State for War, circulated to his Cabinet colleagues a letter from a business man who had recently returned from Russia. The correspondent pressed for British intervention in Russia arguing that Bolshevism was a grave menace to European liberty and civilization:

We must not lose sight of the fact that this movement is engineered and managed by astute Jews, many of them criminals, and nearly every commissary in Russia is a Jew, and I have noticed, since I came to this country, that meetings of protest against intervention are largely composed of alien Jews, and that in constituencies where there is a large Jewish vote, it has invariably gone to the extreme Socialist candidate. . . . For the sake of humanity it is imperative that something should be done to put a speedy end to this criminal, bloodthirsty and horrible combination misnamed a 'Peasants' and Workmen's Republic'.[19]

Most reports from Russia invariably contained some reference to Jews, who were pictured as the only group gaining from the events. In 1919, the Foreign Office published a number of documents describing the conditions in the worst light. Many of the correspondents pointedly referred to the 'Jewish factor' in the revolution: a message from Brigadier-General Knox implied that the assassination of the Imperial family was due to Jewish influence.[20] 'All business became paralysed, shops were closed, Jews became possessors of most of the business houses and horrible scenes of starvation became common in the country districts',[21] another witness reported. A further correspondent maintained 'an arrest is the prelude to every kind of corruption; the rich have to pay huge exactions to intermediaries, who are usually Jews, before they can obtain their release'.[22]

Although it was a fact that many Bolsheviks were Jews, one could not justly deduce that Jewry as such was the instigator of the downfall of the Russian Empire and responsible for all atrocities committed in that country. In fact Russian Jewry – as Jewish communities elsewhere – was politically split from left to right and many Jews suffered greatly during the years of turmoil and tyranny.[23]

Given the general condemnation of Bolshevism, objective criticism of revolutionaries (a large number of whom were Jews) and passionate criticism of Jews as such (a large number of whom were radicals) quickly amalgamated. No attempt was being made to analyse why so many Jews were attracted by radical ideas. Intuitively, this was attributed not to their long-lasting oppression in Russia, but to inherent inclinations rooted in Jewish character and religion. This popular attitude was expressed in one of Churchill's contributions to the debate. While he pointed out that 'there is no need to exaggerate the part played in the creation of Bolshevism and in the actual bringing about of the Russian revolution by these international and for the most part atheistical Jews', he simultaneously stressed what he considered its intrinsically Jewish elements:

> This movement among the Jews is not new. From the days of Spartacus–Weishaupt to those of Karl Marx, and down to Trotsky (Russia), Bela Kun (Hungary), Rosa Luxemburg (Germany), and Emma Goldman (United States), this world-wide conspiracy for the overthrow of civilization and for the reconstitution of society on the basis of arrested development, of envious malevolence, and impossible equality, has been steadily growing.[24]

The proposition that wars and revolutions were instigated by 'international Jews', who undermined Christian societies in order to prepare their universal seizure of power, fitted in with the prevalent way of thinking in categories of friends and enemies. Many who previously had not been prejudiced against Jews on racial or religious grounds suddenly perceived a 'Jewish question' under the impact of the contemporary events, and came to believe in a world-wide Jewish plot against Western civilization. Leo Maxse, the editor of the *National Review*, seems to exemplify the change of attitude: in 1898 he had spoken out for Dreyfus, whom he considered a victim of 'the anti-Semitic pack', 'degraded through the diabolical machinations of the most atrocious conspiracy to be found in human history'.[25] After the Russian revolution he came to believe himself in the evil machinations of 'international Jewry', whom he denounced as wirepullers behind the scenes, responsible for pre-war pacifism as well as for the conciliatory policy towards the Bolsheviks. The 'hidden hand' of Jewry, Maxse argued, inevitably dominated the country: 'Whoever is in power in Downing Street, whether Conservatives, Liberals, Radicals, Coalitionists, or pseudo-Bolsheviks – the International Jew rules the roost.'[26]

The scare of an international Jewish conspiracy stimulated the fantasy and suspicion of numerous journalists, politicians and administrators. Jewish financiers were accused of manipulating the revolutionaries, Jewish servicemen were suspected of transmitting communist propaganda and the presence of Jews at 'extremist meetings' was noticed with apprehension.[27] The fact that any Jew was seen as a potential ally of anti-British intrigues became particularly apparent with regard to India, which Bolshevik propaganda had singled out as a target for revolutionary propaganda, appealing to the people to overthrow British rule and exploitation. The coincidence that two Jews, E. Montagu as Secretary of State for India, and Lord Reading as Viceroy, were in charge of Indian policy provoked many to blame the course of events on a 'Jewish conspiracy'. Arnold White, for example, openly complained that 'as an Englishman I feel deeply that my own race is underdog'[28] and argued that Jews were completely unqualified for the prominent positions they held:

The British Empire rests on the retention of India. To hold India it is necessary that the English race should hold all the prominent appointments. The proportion of posts now held by Jews is somewhat excessive, and the redundancy of semitic officials constitutes a possible danger to British prestige, because the Jews, being pure Asiatics, are regarded by our Indian fellow subjects without awe and frequently without respect.[29]

Many radical Tories firmly believed that there existed an

organized conspiracy to break up the British Empire, which had to be fought at all costs.[30] Frequently anti-Jewish sentiments can be detected at the core of their arguments. Frustration with Britain's decline in power and disapproval of the government's policy were directed against the Jewish scapegoat which was blamed for political developments that did not suit the postulate of a strong and united British Empire.

It is not surprising that when the *Protocols of the Elders of Zion* were published, coinciding with a widespread anti-Jewish hysteria, they received much attention. They circulated among British officers in the Middle East,[31] among delegates at the peace congress in Versailles and among leading politicians in Western countries. The English and German translations, which were the first non-Russian editions to come out, appeared early in 1920. The short preface which preceded the English edition, published anonymously as *The Jewish Peril. Protocols of the Learned Elders of Zion*, alluded to the contemporary relevance of the publication:

> It is impossible to read any of the parts of this volume to-day without being struck by the strong prophetic note which runs through them all, not only as regards the once Holy Russia, but also as regards certain sinister developments, which may be observed at the present moment throughout the whole world. Gentiles – Beware![32]

The fact that the English edition was published by the reputable company Eyre and Spottiswoode, His Majesty's Printing Office, lent the *Protocols* additional weight. In fact the brochure was printed on private order by the translator, and the printing company held no rights on the publication.[33] The actual translator, who remained in the background and never became associated with the *Protocols* in public, was George Shanks.[34] According to the art historian Robert H. Cust, Shanks made an exact transcript of Nilus's book, which was deposited in the British Museum, and translated it with the help of one Major Edward G. Burdon. Cust himself then assisted in what he described as the difficult task of finding a publisher for the manuscript.[35]

When the Eyre and Spottiswoode edition, which was said to have numbered 30,000 copies,[36] was nearly exhausted, Shanks met two representatives of 'The Britons', a society dedicated to disseminate anti-Semitic propaganda. Eager to keep the publication on the market, they proposed to launch a second edition. Shanks consented on condition that he be guaranteed a royalty of 3d per copy sold. The Britons approached Eyre and Spottiswoode to have a further 2000 copies reprinted under the name of the Britons, but the company refused, claiming that they could only print to the order of Mr Shanks. They suggested that he, as the owner of the copyright, should authorize them to prepare and deliver stereotyped plates from which any number of copies could be produced. This proposal was agreed upon and the plates were purchased by the Britons at £30.–.–.[37]

A second edition of the *Protocols* was published in August 1920, a third one followed in September. The Britons had sold about 5000 copies of the work when they published a new translation by Victor Marsden, the late correspondent of the *Morning Post* and author of the brochure *Jews in Russia*. Marsden's version was published in November 1923 as the sixth English edition of the *Protocols*. He had actually translated the brochure for the *Morning Post* as early as 1919, that is before the first publication of the text in England.

The editor of the *Morning Post*, H. A. Gwynne, firmly believed that there was some truth in the story of a world-wide Jewish conspiracy. He had a series of articles prepared covering the 'Jewish question', but did not publish them without first enquiring about the authenticity of the *Protocols* and circulated typescript copies to his confidants sounding their opinions on the 'documents'. On 27 January 1920 he urged Lady Bathurst, then proprietress of the *Morning Post*, to have the articles published and cited Rudyard Kipling, Leo Maxse and Basil Thomson as authorities who supported his view.[38]

Sir Basil Thomson, then Director of Intelligence, had been familiar with the *Protocols* when Gwynne came to ask his advice and knew they were taken from Nilus's book. Although he was not sure of their genuineness he supported the publication, arguing that 'so many people seem to be convinced that they are genuine that I do not see why they should not be published'.[39] Gwynne himself considered the *Protocols* 'a most masterly exposition – very highfalutin' of course, as would be natural in an oriental race – a distinct programme intended to achieve the aim of the political Jews, which is the domination of the world'.[40]

The question whether it was expedient to join in with anti-Semitic propaganda was, however, by no means undisputed, and some of Gwynne's advisers strongly recommended him to hold back. W. Tyrrell, then Assistant Under-Secretary of State at the Foreign Office, described the *Protocols* as 'very fantastic productions and a rapid glance at them confirms my impression that they almost verge on lunacy'.[41] C. W. C. Oman, Chichele Professor of Modern History and MP for Oxford University 1919–35, argued that he 'should *not* feel justified in passing it, though it is a most interesting document'.[42] A further correspondent considered them 'an apocryphal work by some anti-Semitic Russian or Polish journalist',[43] while another thought 'the allusion to English Freemasonry ludicrously inaccurate'.[44]

A detailed commentary by E. Saunders, former correspondent of the *Morning Post* and *The Times*, reflected a balanced judgement. In his memorandum 'An Indictment of the Jews – Or a Reactionary Extravaganza?' he closely examined the train of thought in the *Protocols*. Saunders concluded that they did not reflect any kind of 'authentic Jewish thought', but were framed by reactionaries who tried to denounce the Jews as the moving force behind attempts to overthrow the old order. He attributed the fact that many Jews appeared prominently in progressive movements to their continuous suppression, which would have had the same effect on other groups. As a people, he argued, the Jews were far from united and their methods appeared open and aggressive, not secretive, insinuating and conspirative. Saunders recognized the *Protocols* as the work of 'a believer in autocracy of the Russian variety and in the authoritative type of religion embodied in the more unenlightened strata of the orthodox Russian Church' and dismissed them as spurious documents which could only influence ill-educated minds who cherished them as apocalyptic visions.[45]

Peacock, Gwynne's colleague on the *Morning Post*, also considered the articles ill-founded and depicted them as 'mere midsummer moonshine'. Opposing Gwynne in a letter to Lord Bathurst, he expressed his fundamental disagreement with Gwynne not only with regard to the authenticity of the *Protocols*, but in particular on the impact of an anti-Semitic editorial policy on the future of their paper:

The Jews as a race possess enormous power, they have tremendous influence in finance and commerce – and it is on the goodwill of financial and commercial undertakings that we depend for our advertisements and revenue. They are good haters – a revengeful and vindictive people when attacked. . . . At a time when it is vital to us to keep up a big revenue what effect is the bitter hostility to the Jews going to have on the fortunes of the paper?[46]

Peacock's warning was indeed fully justified. Whether or not the withdrawal of financial support and the subsequent decline of the *Morning Post* were due to its anti-Semitic policy, the unrestrained backing of the *Protocols* did damage its reputation considerably. Gwynne carried his point despite all cautionary advice, and the disputed articles were eventually published in July 1920, first as a series of articles in the *Morning Post*, then in book form as *The Cause of the World Unrest*. Like the *Protocols* this publication enjoyed only an ephemeral success. The authors preferred to remain anonymous except for Gwynne, who signed the introduction, and Nesta Webster, who contributed two letters to the editor.[47] In the articles they proclaimed the existence of a world-wide anti-Christian movement, a 'formidable sect' said to be chiefly Jewish, which hoped to establish an absolute hegemony through revolution, communism and anarchism. A diabolical élite was suspected of undermining British authority at home and abroad by stirring the discontent of the masses:

Men's thoughts are continually being concentrated on things material, on the inequalities of wealth, on mean and trivial pleasures, and are being told that the cure of all their ills lies not in themselves but in a peculiar form of government.[48]

The *Morning Post* was not the only newspaper which considered the *Protocols* strikingly accurate in their description of the ambitions and machinations of at least part of world Jewry. *The Times* also appeared alarmed and intrigued with their 'revelation':

It is far too interesting, the hypothesis it presents is far too ingenious, attractive and sensational not to attract the attention of our none too happy and none too contented public. . . . What are these 'Protocols?' Are they authentic? If so, what malevolent assembly concocted these plans and gloated over their exposition? Are they a forgery? If so, whence comes the uncanny note of prophecy, prophecy in parts fulfilled, in parts far gone in the way of fulfilment?[49]

However, *The Times* did not go beyond giving the *Protocols* the benefit of the doubt and was later instrumental in discrediting the publication. Lucien Wolf, who had represented the Anglo-Jewish community at the peace conference in Versailles, immediately questioned the authenticity of the *Protocols* when they appeared, but he could not quote conclusive proof that they were a hoax and many considered his contributions to be a Jewish apology.[50] Evidence that the *Protocols* were indeed a forgery was produced in three consecutive articles in *The Times*, 'The Truth about the Protocols', published in August 1921.[51]

Philip Graves, *The Times*' correspondent in Constantinople, informed the editor on 13 July 1921 of what he considered an exciting discovery: a Russian monarchist, Mikhail Raslovleff, who was then working for the American Red Cross in Constantinople, had pointed out to him that the *Protocols* actually were a plagiarism of a political treatise published in French at Geneva in 1864.[52] Graves described the book in question, of which the title page was missing, as a series of dialogues between Montesquieu and Machiavelli, which closely – in some parts word for word – corresponded to the *Protocols*. A Russian ex-colonel of the *Okhrana* had given it to Raslovleff, who recognized it as a model for the *Protocols*, but kept his discovery secret. He only approached *The Times* when he was in urgent need of money, and proposed to exchange the book for a loan of £300.–.–, indicating that, if he could not come to terms with *The Times*, he would offer his document to *Agence Havas*.

Graves sensed a big scoop for *The Times* and encouraged Steed to seize the opportunity, stressing that the *Protocols* should be exposed by non-Jews. Eventually an agreement was signed by P. Graves on behalf of *The Times* and M. Raslovleff to the effect that the *Dialogues* were given on loan to *The Times* for five years. The paper thereby acquired exclusive rights to publish the book and its contents, and in turn agreed to advance Raslovleff £337.–.–. as a loan free of interest for the period of five years.[53]

Graves subsequently wrote three articles in which he revealed that the celebrated *Protocols* were straightforward plagiarisms. The 'Geneva Dialogues' were soon discovered to be a political satire by Maurice Joly, *Dialogue aux Enfers entre Machiavel et Montesquieu, ou la Politique de Machiavel au XIXe siècle*, a copy of which was traced in the British Museum. Graves and *The Times* persistently and successfully refused to reveal the name of their informant, and Graves was soon attacked for pro-Jewish leanings, for which a previous visit to

Palestine was considered further evidence. However, his detached and precise *exposé* demanded respect even from those who cons tinued to believe in the myth of a Jewish world-conspiracy.

Even Gwynne was moved to admit that 'internal evidence make-it quite clear that a large part of the *Protocols* was taken from M. Joly's book'.[54] Others were less deterred by the revelation: Baron Sydenham, whose preoccupation with an international Jewish plot was not shaken by the articles, argued that, even if they were compiled from a secondary source, the *Protocols* were still accurate forecasts. The identity of Judaism and Bolshevism appeared, after all, to be proven by historical facts.[55] Lord Alfred Douglas, the editor of an obscure weekly, *Plain English*, continued to promulgate the message of the *Protocols*. In 1924 he composed what he considered his finest poem, 'In Excelsis':

> The leprous spawn of scattered Israel
> Spreads its contagion in your English blood;
> Teeming corruption rises like a flood
> Whose fountain swelters in the womb of hell.
> Your Jew-kept politicians buy and sell
> In markets redolent of Jewish mud,
> And while the 'Learned Elders' chew the cud
> Of liquidation's fruits, they weave their spell.
> They weave the spell that binds the heart's desire
> To gold and gluttony and sweating lust:
> In hidden holds they stew the mandrake mess
> That kills the soul and turns the blood to fire,
> They weave the spell that turns desire to dust
> And postulates the abyss of nothingness.[56]

The *Protocols* themselves, although they continued to be published, had lost their propagandistic effect. They had been given a formidable reception, because they appeared at a time when the idea of a world-wide Jewish plot was already in vogue. But, after they had been discredited as forgeries, those who had initially given them publicity hurriedly dissociated themselves from the booklet. In themselves a most tedious reading, the *Protocols* no longer served to stir up hostility against the Jews and they only remained a reference book for anti-Semites who persistently refused to consider the matter pragmatically.

The myth of a world-wide Jewish conspiracy, however, was not discredited simultaneously. In J. Buchan's novel *The Thirty-Nine Steps* the *motif* had entered fiction, and it was revived in a popular almanac, which predicted that 1980 would be a turning point in history, when 'the Jews, or, as they will again be called, Israelites, will have made enormous strides in wealth, world position and power'.[57] Politically the conspiracy-theory remained a convenient subject for the conservative right which was confronted with political developments that did not suit its views – in particular the consolidation of the Bolshevik regime in Russia, and the progress of the Labour Party in Britain. The most prominent defender of the old order was the *Morning Post* which continued to point to the immense influence of international Jewry not only in post-war diplomacy, but equally in the British Labour movement. How widely its agitation was absorbed can be observed from the reaction of the 'exposure' of the Zinovieff letter. Speaking on the issue at a public meeting in Leicester, Lord Curzon, for example, did not fail to draw attention to the Jewish influence in Russia:

> Don't imagine that the Russian Government is a body of Russians who represent, at any rate, some section of their country. That is not the case. They are a small gang, only a few hundreds in number, few of them Russian by birth, and most of them Jews in origin, who are preying like vultures on the bodies of that unhappy people.[58]

Although widespread, the anti-Jewish sentiment of the post-war period did not generate mass anti-Semitism. It lacked the organizational transmission necessary to stimulate a popular movement and was never exploited by any relevant political force in a deliberate attempt to stimulate anti-Jewish feelings. Due to the relatively smooth assimilation of Anglo-Jewry during the 19th century, and the absence of a historical tradition of anti-Semitism, the 'Jewish question' carried little propaganda value in England. Although the Jewish scapegoat was readily blamed by some of those who were particularly affected by the social and economic problems of the post-war period, it did not figure as a national issue. Unlike Germany, Britain did not suffer from a collapse of the political order and the humiliation of a military and political defeat and there was no need to seek a new identity by uniting against a fictitious foe.

In England, anti-Semitism only crystallized in scattered publishing activities, which were all short-lived. By the end of 1926 the Board of Deputies, which had been alarmed by the diatribes and innuendoes, was satisfied that it was 'now rare to find anything to which exception can be taken'.[59] The revival of anti-Semitism, its systematic cultivation and instrumentalization during the 1930s was just not a resumption of the immediate post-war campaign: it was conducted by Fascist agitators who set out to organize and manipulate the politicization of the masses. Their anti-Semitism was the integrative element in an aggressive crusade in the name of an allegedly progressive totalitarian ideology. Although there was a continuity in anti-Jewish arguments, there was no momentuous coalition between those of the aristocracy who considered a Jewish world-conspiracy responsible for their own *déclassement*, and the 'masses' who responded to the propaganda appeal of anti-Semitism in an activist political campaign.

2 Social Discrimination and Militant Hooliganism

The manifestation of anti-Semitism in the context of post-war anti-Bolshevism, apparent in the publishing activities of a few groups and individuals, ceased during the early 1920s. As Britain's self-confidence grew in correspondence to increasing economic stability, symbolized in the return to the gold standard and the successful settlement of labour troubles, the bogy of 'international conspirators' lost publicity value. In the following decade, however, the latent prejudice against Jews surfaced again and became the main asset of extreme right-wing groups which prospered in the aftermath of a steep increase in unemployment and a prolonged economic crisis, and remained evident throughout the 1930s.

The impressive victory of the Labour Party in the parliamentary elections of 1929, in which it became the strongest party in the House, indicated a significant change of the political climate from the immediate post-war period. The economic crisis of 1929–31 prompted Britain to withdraw to a self-centred, isolationist policy guarding first and foremost British interests, which were still defined in Imperial terms, but with the emphasis on conciliation. Empire free trade and a protectionist system of 'Imperial Preference' were suggested as solutions to British economic problems. While attempts to reach international agreements on currency and disarmament questions failed, appeasement became the formula for avoiding political and military entanglements and international commitments.

The radical right responded to the challenge of the time by attacking the 'international Jew' as a scapegoat for the crisis. International Jewish speculators were blamed for the financial depression which forced Britain to abandon the gold standard, and the League of Nations was discredited as the central political institution of world Jewry, within which the fates of other countries were decided. Once again, a fundamental antagonism between

Britons and Jewry was projected and, wherever Britain's national pride was at stake and her interests were violated, it was attributed to 'the Jew'.

Traditional assumptions and beliefs were called into question under the impact of mass unemployment and poverty, loss of national prestige and influence. New groups and parties emerged, trying to capture the mood of those who no longer trusted the established political system and feared for their present and future social security. They focused on a nostalgic recollection of a seemingly more stable past, and the wholesale condemnation of the modern era *per se*, which had generated so many disconcerting reassessments. Jews, who indeed had contributed outstandingly to the rapid developments in the social and natural sciences as well as in the arts and mass-culture, were frequently identified with the 'modern menace'. Symptomatic for the tendency to trace the contemporary crisis back to Jewish roots was the following letter, published in September 1930 in the *Daily Express*:

How anyone can prize the downward trend of our national life by the infiltration of a semi-negroid, parasitic scum is beyond comprehension unless you regard the debasement of the country as a result to be desired. All thinking people are aware that the present world depression is a direct result of the Jewish intrigue, as they are also aware that the wave of moral laxity, the debasement of the decencies of life, and the general undermining of the body politic originate from, and are directly attributable to, the same source.[1]

The general dissatisfaction and aimlessness fertilized a vague hostility against Jews and a more acute 'Jew–consciousness' which manifested itself in sporadic incidents: a coroner, who discovered five Jews among a jury of eight summoned to an inquest of a man who had been killed by a motor car driven by a Jew, barred three of the Jewish jurymen, insinuating that they were biased because of their ethnic identity.[2] The same theme of alleged Jewish solidarity and the placing of Jewish group-interests over national interests was exploited by a prospective Labour candidate, Richard Davies, in an election address in 1933. When asked by J. S. Middleton, Assistant Secretary of the Labour Party, to clarify his sweeping anti-Jewish statements which had caused much resentment, Davies repeated his indictment of the Jewish race:

My experience of them [i.e. the Jews] has taught me that their support is limited to the interest of Jews and that their dominant idea is to despoil the Gentiles. . . . I stated that Plymouth was largely run by money-lenders, rackrenters and bookmakers and this is true. I said that in every essential department of human activity the Jews secured representation with the object of safeguarding their racial interests. . . . In my personal opinion the policy and methods associated with Jews will be among the primary objects for destruction before socialism will be realized. I have never had any business relations with Jews without being swindled in the end; and when they are pursued by the law their marvellous ingenuity in dodging legal processes makes honest folk stand aghast.[3]

Davies, who boasted of having spent forty-seven years as an active fighter in the Labour movement, was severely rebuked by Middleton, who pointed out that his anti-Jewish outburst was not only grossly unjust, but also damaging to the party interests, since it alienated its Jewish supporters. After this incident, Davies was dropped as the prospective Labour candidate for the Tavistock division, although previously he had been announced as such and had contested the constituency before. Similarly E. Doran, Conservative MP for North Tottenham, was dismissed by his constituency after he had publicly attacked the Jews and declared that English liberties had to be defended against Jewish invasion.[4]

Occasionally, churchmen joined in with cautionary remarks about Jews, holding them responsible for the declining significance of religion. This argument resumed the ideas of the anti-Bolshevik campaign. It was prominently expressed by the Rev. Dr Black in an address to the General Assembly of the Church of Scotland in 1932, when he complained that the Jews were paganizing the Christian world and remained an unassimilated lump in the body politic until they were converted to Christianity or 'wiped out'.[5]

The *Jewish Chronicle*, the official organ of Anglo-Jewry, recognized the increase in manifestations of prejudice. Always sensitive regarding anti-Semitic incidents, but careful not to generalize from indidivual cases, it drew attention to various examples of discrimination against Jews and thus confirmed the judgement of one paper, which in October 1932 stated that 'at least nine-tenths of the inhabitants of the British Isles think the worse of a man if they are told he is a Jew'.[6] Instances of anti-Semitic discrimination had appeared before, but during the early 1930s they seemed to assume greater proportions. In September 1932, a leading article of the *Jewish Chronicle* discussed the issue and concluded that a certain amount of racial discrimination against Jews existed, but did not think it was practised on a considerable scale. In January 1933 the same paper had to admit 'scarcely a week passes without one or more manifestations of the Jew-obsession in more or less acute form'.[7]

Discriminatory advertisements appearing in respectable newspapers reflected existing prejudice. The cases reported included the advertisement of a typist's job in the *Daily Telegraph* which specified 'No Jewesses', and one in the *British Medical Journal* which said 'No Jews or men of colour'.[8] Jewish teachers, it was said, had greatest difficulties in finding posts in better-known schools. Reports from people who had personally encountered differential treatment corroborated the impression that discrimination against Jews was not so unusual. The official town guide of Shanklin, Isle of Wight, accepted an advertisement which stated 'No Jews Catered For', while an entry in the *Hackney Gazette* offered rooms to let with the addition 'No children or Jews'.[9] Typical for the refusal to sell or let estates was the case of an English-born Jew who was told by a firm of builders in Ilford that 'under no circumstances would they sell to a Hebrew'.[10] This policy was vindicated by another firm which explained that 'people before buying or renting a house asked to be assured that the estate would be free from Jews'.[11]

A recurrent source of complaint from Jews was the alleged difficulty of placing Jewish insurances. When investigating the issue in 1922, the Law and Parliamentary Committee of the Board of Deputies found that some companies were biased against certain trades which involved special risks, and against certain districts which were regarded as particularly insecure, but that there was no discrimination against Jews as such.[12] In the 1930s, the subject was repeatedly brought up by Jews who were refused policies against certain risks, such as motor-car accidents, on the grounds that Jews had proved to involve higher risks than average clients.[13] Although RAF officers, actors, undergraduates and foreigners fell under the same category of 'bad risks' and were also excluded, the singling out of Jews was unique in that it stigmatized the whole community irrespective of its sociological stratification. Thus a diversified group was attributed collective characteristics and identified as a distinct homogeneous unit.

Anti-Jewish feeling was also noted in trades where Jews were prominently involved. The *Drapers Record*, for example, carried an advertisement which announced the sale of a millinery business with the addition 'No Jews entertained'.[14] Like corresponding organizations in Manchester and Harrogate, the Cardiff Credit Traders' Association adopted a resolution that the membership of 'folk of alien origin, such as Jews, should not be encouraged'[15] – a policy which was expressly regretted by the Bristol branch of the Association. A report on behalf of the Boot Manufacturers' Federation and the National Union of Boot and Shoe Operatives on conditions of employment on the boot industry in the East End of London suggested that Jews were largely responsible for the abuses in the trade, and that factory inspectors were bribed to favour Jewish as against British employers. When commenting upon the report, the Home Secretary pointed out that it was 'based not on facts ascertained by personal observation of the conditions at the works concerned but almost entirely on impressions derived from unverified *ex parte* statements'.[16] As in the case of alleged Jewish cut-price tactics in the grocery trade,[17] reproaches against individual malpractices were levelled at the Jewish community as such and Jews were indiscriminately considered the principal offenders.

Such examples of unconcealed discrimination were a significant deviation from informal or furtive biases against Jews which existed on a minor scale in various social spheres but rarely assumed political significance. The latter became apparent in bans imposed on Jews by local clubs, which represented the hierarchical structure of society and bourgeois class-consciousness. Typical of such social intolerance were the cases of a Table Tennis Club, a Motor Club and a Country Club which refused to admit Jewish members.[18] Usually there was no rationale behind such a policy except for an intuitive dislike of people who might have achieved wealth and social status but still carried the stigma of being different. 'As an Englishman,' one contemporary confessed, 'I have not yet descended, or ascended, if some think that way, to consider it a desirable distinction to be employed by a Jew, nor a valuable privilege to be allowed to mix socially with them on their terms.'[19]

When publicly exposed, such social discrimination was freely admitted and justified. As late as 1954, the Council of Christians and Jews appealed to the English Golf Club Union to exert its influence to stop racial discrimination, which apparently was the policy of a Blackpool Club. The Union replied that it was neither competent nor would it desire to intervene in the affairs of its members, who were free to set their own rules. 'The Union does not assume any moral obligation of the sort you propose,' it explained, 'as this would involve its intrusion into the domestic concerns of the private Clubs many of which are largely social institutions which conduct their affairs much along the lines of other social Clubs.'[20]

While such manifestations of sometimes passionate, but generally unobtrusive, aversion to Jews were silently tolerated, the open display of anti-Jewish prejudice which was likely to incite racial hatred was rejected by the overwhelming majority of the population. Such inhibitions, however, were not prescribed by the nature of English anti-Semitism, which in principle contained all potentials inherent in a total anthropo-ideology, differentiating between superior and inferior, constructive and destructive, worthy and unworthy people. Nor was the lack of support for political anti-Semitism due to a rejection of the anti-Semitic message as such, given that three-quarters of the total population were considered to maintain hostile, deprecatory, or at least unfavourable attitudes towards the Jews in Britain.[21] Instead, the failure of attempts to turn the latent social anti-Semitism into a nation-wide political force seems to have depended on the identification of anti-Semitism with political violence, and on its localization in East End politics.

Upper-class anti-Semitism not only manifested itself in the context of the reaction against the Bolshevik revolution, but in numerous passing remarks indicating a sweeping indictment of the Jewish race. Harold Nicolson, for example, at one point confessed: 'The Jewish capacity for destruction is really illimitable. Although I loathe anti-Semitism, I do dislike Jews.' On another occasion he recorded Lady Astor's reply to a political opponent: 'Only a Jew like you would *dare* to be rude to me.'[22] Sir Horace Rumbold pointedly stated: 'I hate Jews.'[23] Recalling her encounter with a French anti-Semite, Lady Angela Forbes, A. Sinclair's mother-in-law, agreed that 'the Jewish pest is a microbe that is multiplying in strength more rapidly than any known bacilli,' and warned of the danger 'to allow Semitic individuals to burrow indiscriminately, until they emerge triumphantly into every important post which should be a Christian heritage'.[24]

During the 1930s, this section of the population was strongly supportive of a conciliation with Nazi Germany, deploring the anti-Semitic 'excesses' but not the ideology which was the central purpose of the Nazi regime. The upper-class did not, however, prominently identify with the British anti-Semitic organizations, and only Sir Oswald Mosley's British Union of Fascists to a very small extent succeeded in enlisting its support. Mosley's campaign concentrated primarily on the East End of London, and was addressed mainly to lower middle class audiences. In England, where a hierarchical class-structure was still firmly established, the *Volksgemeinschaft* ideology, purporting the necessity of a united front against the common enemy, the Jew, did not receive much sympathy.

Physical violence, the concomitant of Fascist anti-Semitism, had no tradition in mainstream English politics. While authority appeared to be less imposed than voluntarily accepted, political pressure against the establishment tended to be exerted through moral rather than physical force.[25] The particular political culture, governed by the concepts of legality and compromise, restrained aggressive, violent anti-Semitism. English Jews recognized and relied on this safeguard. When the first instances of undaunted anti-Semitism were reported, the *Jewish Chronicle* considered them evidence for an outdated bigoted narrowmindedness, a relic from the past, rather than an indicator of a significant change of attitude among the host society. Jewish self-confidence and trust in British institutions and traditions were hardly affected by sporadic exhibitions of hostility. Although Anglo-Jewry was indignant about insults to the community as a whole, it did not fear that its established rights could be effectively threatened. It was considered sufficient, therefore, to expose discriminations, which in turn would discredit the prejudiced.

The feeling of absolute certainty that anti-Semitism would not thrive in England only began to wane under the cumulative experience of anti-Semitic incidents. The accession of the Nazis to power in Germany demonstrated that the irrational hatred of a few could well become the official policy of a modern state, condoned by a large part of the population. This increased the nervousness amongst British Jews, whose fears were enhanced by press comments such as 'that which has happened in Germany should serve as a warning to the Jewish people here in our midst'.[26] A memorandum submitted in 1938 to the Defence Committee of the Board of Deputies of British Jews maintained 'within three years we may be faced with anti-Jewish legislation in this country'.[27]

The change of perception was caused by the militant actions of a political fringe: Fascist organizations, which had emerged during the crisis 1929–32. Mirroring the flare-up of latent anti-Semitism, they adopted Jew-baiting as an instrument of propaganda. Their basic outlook was first and foremost anti-democratic and anti-modern, not anti-Jewish, but they identified Jews as the authors of the developments they despised and branded them as a national enemy. Their anti-Semitic campaign started with publishing activities intended to enlighten the public on the 'Jewish menace', complemented by public meetings at which the detrimental 'Jewish machinations' were exposed, and culminated in physical attacks on Jewish people and property.

The incitement of racial hatred was unconcealed in many instances, and anti-Jewish diatribes were frequently couched in offensive rhetoric such as 'dirty Jews', 'you damned Jews', 'long-nosed mongrel bastards', 'venereal-ridden vagrants', 'poxy bastards', or 'vermin from the gutters of Whitechapel'.[28] A Jewish evening-school teacher was approached by a stranger in the street who addressed him 'you filthy bloody f . . . . . . Jew', 'you dirty Russian Jew, I'd have you all castrated if I could'.[29] A speaker at a Fascist meeting held in September 1935 at Edgware was reported to have repeatedly referred to 'Jews, Communists and other scum', followed by 'You'll squeal when the day of reckoning comes. . . . I am a disciple of Julius Streicher. . . . Yes, you'll have reason to squeal.' He also abused Lord Melchett, calling him a 'hooked-nosed, yellow-skinned dirty Jewish swine'.[30]

The standard accusations against Jews were summarized in a letter to the editor which appeared in the *Middlesex County Times*. 'Jews are orientals who in every country have corrupted business by introducing the methods and morals of the oriental bazaar',[31] the correspondent wrote. He accused the Jews of controlling international finance, dominating the white slave traffic, controlling the media, introducing dishonest business methods, debasing the national culture and propagating communism. All these themes were extensively discussed by Fascist speakers and figured prominently in their campaign for popular support.

Many of the orators left little doubt about their ultimate intention of solving the 'Jewish problem'. An auctioneer, aged 45, addressing some 250 people in Finsbury Square, stated:

I would turn all the Jews out of England, headed by Belisha with a beacon on his head and one in each hand. On either side of him there would be Sir Philip Sassoon and Rothschild. Jimmy Thomas would take up the rear to write a biography on the Jews' exit from England. Epstein would be there with his grotesque monstrosities to keep the birds away from the Wailing Wall. No state can thrive where Jesus and Judas have equal rights.[32]

Another speaker, a tobacco worker, also advocated the expulsion of Jews and stated: 'If you want war, if you want a scrap, if you want a smack have a smack at the Jews in this country. Fight them here and clear them out.'[33] Another propagandist argued in the same vein: 'We have got to build up a healthy Britain. The Jew is ruining our country and we must get rid of him.'[34]

Other speakers were more precise and suggested a definitive approach. 'The Jews among us are the cancer and every foul disease', one was reported saying. 'The situation calls for surgical operation, and we Fascists intend making that operation. We will extirpate them thoroughly from our life.'[35] 'Mick' Clarke, a 24-year-old propagandist of the British Union of Fascists, notorious for his anti-Semitic speeches, was reported as saying that the Jews were 'the lice of the earth and must be exterminated'.[36] A 17-year-old clerk, addressing a meeting on 'Jewish finance', was alleged to have said: 'What are you going to do with them – are you going to kill them? I passed a nice cemetery as I came here.'[37]

The verbal anti-Semitic attacks were soon followed by acts of unwarranted vandalism. In May 1932, a synagogue in Leeds was desecrated – an incident attributed to children of the neighbourhood. A few months later, Manchester Jewry suffered from a wave of hooliganism. A brick was thrown through the window of a Talmud Torah. Labels were attached to it attacking the League of Nations as an instrument of world Jewry, accusing Jews of purveying sensual films, tampering with white girls and stirring unrest in Ireland, India and Egypt. In December 1933 a Liverpool synagogue was desecrated, its furnishings severely damaged and the walls defaced with swastika symbols. Similar incidents of sacrilege became a common feature during the following years. They included four cases where a pig's head was nailed to the door of a synagogue or left on its premises, and others where rashers of bacon were affixed to the portal.[38]

At first such outbreaks were relatively rare, but by 1934 the political organizations of the radical right had adopted violence as a major propaganda technique. Ostensibly this was in response to provocative behaviour from their opponents – an explanation which was endorsed in R. Skidelsky's biography of Oswald Mosley with reference to a numerical comparison between the number of arrests of Fascists and that of anti-Fascists at political meetings.[39] Quite apart from the fact that these figures are ambiguous, since most complaints on Jew-baiting from the victims remained untraced, the fact that a large number of Jews were embroiled in violent disturbances does not sufficiently support the thesis that they were also to be blamed for the events. The Fascists' whole framework of propaganda, their totalitarian concept of power and professed intolerance were designed to stir up emotions and set the stage for the transformation of verbal attacks into physical assaults, particularly after one group had been singled out for recurring criticism.

As a political movement whose solidarity was impressively exhibited in the wearing of uniforms, Fascism was bound to encounter opposition and the Fascist speakers always expected and induced 'provocations' – heckling, shouting and hissing – so as to react against it with utmost vigour. They hoped to benefit from the interaction of propaganda and violence, and were aware that opposition secured them the much desired publicity. As soon as local interest in them began to wane, they transferred their meetings to new areas where they aroused fresh opposition. Anti-Fascists, on the other hand, made all efforts to disturb or break up their opponents' rallies and consequently appeared as aggressors in the confrontation with a disciplined movement which claimed to preserve 'good order' by excluding all opposition.

The Fascists' strategy to agitate mostly in districts with a large Jewish population, where they hoped to mobilize the latent jealousy and dislike of Jews, and their indulgence in abusive language, naturally provoked protest from the targets of their campaign and reinforced Jewish group-consciousness. Despite the urgent appeals of their authorities, in particular the *Jewish Chronicle* and the Board of Deputies of British Jews, who recommended staying away from Fascist crowds, many Jews flocked to their meetings and formed a hostile group within the audience, ready to respond to any challenging remarks. When a speaker referred to Jewish and alien influence as controlling the City of London, they interrupted him by booing and cheering. On the other hand, tensions were certainly increased by retaliations such as the following:

> I thought they would squeal at this part of the argument. I'll tell them who their masters are. Who wrecked Lancashire and Yorkshire? Who attacks the Tory Party and the Socialist Party? International Jewry. They are the people who put their razor gangs on the streets. The big Jew puts you in the unemployment queue by the million and the little Jew sweats you.[40]

Organized opposition against Facism from the Left added to the political strain, particularly after many Jews living in the troubled areas joined its ranks. To them the Left was the ally they sought, because it offered an active resistance against a movement which challenged the right of Jews to preserve their identity while enjoying all rights as British citizens. The bitter confrontation led to frequent clashes between the factions, and complaints of insults, damage and assaults were raised from both sides. As a result of these scuffles, which mostly arose out of political meetings, the Jewish communities, particularly in London but also in provincial centres, felt terrorized and intimidated.

A wave of hooliganism overran the East End of London in 1936. It culminated in October 1936 with particularly numerous window-smashings, lootings and assaults. On 4 October 1936 a procession of the British Union of Fascists was effectively stopped by an anti-Fascist front of about 100,000 people. Disorder broke out, missiles were thrown and much damage caused to private property in what became known as the 'Battle of Cable Street'. A week later the Fascists staged a retaliatory attack. The windows of twenty-nine Jewish shops were smashed in Mile End Road, some sixteen shop windows were wrecked in a row in Green Street and, while the crowds shouted 'down with the Yids', a man and a little girl were thrown through the glass window of a Jewish shop.[41]

Jewish property was systematically damaged by gangs of mostly young men who hurled stones and bricks through shop windows. On one occasion some 1000 eggs displayed in front of a Jewish shop were smashed by Fascists.[42] Other Jewish shops were picketed and potential customers intimidated. 'Buy from people who celebrate Christmas', 'Boycott the Jews' and 'Why buy goods from stinking Jews?', the Fascist sentries mocked. Small bills were posted on Jewish shops saying 'Keep away. These Jews are here to rob you',

'Boycott Jewish shops' or 'Come in and be robbed. These Jews want your money'. A newspaper report of October 1938 pointed out that the Fascist campaign severely hampered local trade:

> Bethnal Green Borough Council is losing thousands of pounds in rates, because large numbers of Jews, owning shops and houses in the borough, have been forced to leave the district owing to the Fascist terror. Jew baiting and terror is so frequent and widespread, that it has come to be part of the recognized, everyday life of the East End.[43]

After the declaration of the poll of the borough elections late at night on 4 March 1937, a crowd of Blackshirts and their supporters marched through Bethnal Green. Again, the windows of fourteen shops were broken while the crowd shouted 'There goes another one'. When investigating the incident, at which only one arrest was made, the police found that the noise of the band accompanying the Fascists, as well as the shouting of the marchers, had largely muffled the noise of the deliberate window-smashing. No evidence was obtained of looting, and the report refuted the charge that the disturbances intimidated customers or hampered business, since they had occurred long after normal business hours.[44] There can be no doubt, however, that the repeated attacks on their property affected business and provided a major irritant to East End Jews.

Part of the Fascists' agitation was a continuous smear-campaign which depicted the Jews *en bloc* and was likely to stir up racial hatred. Offensive sticky-back labels were plastered on Jewish premises, cars, lamp-posts and pillar-boxes, bearing inscriptions such as 'Down with the stinking Jews', 'Every Jew is a parasite on the backs of white workers', 'The Jews are stealing your country', 'Labour and Communism is Jewish', 'Clear them out', 'Perish Judah', or simply 'Jew'. In a complaint to the Secretary of State for Foreign Affairs it was pointed out that similar 'Bolshevism is Jewish' labels were affixed to the British pavilion at the Paris exhibition in 1937, and attached to visitors' bags and attache cases.[45]

Swastikas, 'Perish Judah' and slogans like 'Englishmen guard your womenfolk against pollution by Jews and Blacks' were painted on walls and fences. The 'Star of David', two interlaced triangles, was scrawled upon an Epstein sculpture outside London Transport headquarters with a mixture of tar, carbolic acid and petrol. The

words 'Kill the Jews' were cut into a bowling green in Tottenham.
In Hampstead, the house where Karl Marx had lived was defaced
with anti-Jewish slogans, and the gates of Philip Sassoon's home
were painted with swastikas. In a public library the *Jewish
Chronicle* was so frequently defaced that it was removed from public
tables and only available on application.[46]

All these incidents were not just elements of rowdy street-corner
agitation in which unhappily Jews were involved, but amounted to
a systematic attack on the Jews as such, designed to pillory them as
outcasts of society. The totality underlying this Jew-baiting becomes apparent in the lines chanted by Fascist groups parading up
and down the street in Jewish quarters: 'We gotta get rid of the
Yids', 'We want Jewry's Blood' or 'Roll on the Pogrom'. It also
transpired in the following rhyme, printed in a Fascist weekly
publication:

> The old reg flag is turning pink,
> It's not as red as people think.
> We'll raise the golden fasces high,
> Beneath their shade all Jews shall die.[47]

Physical assaults on individual Jews matched the verbal attacks
on the community. The first documented cases occurred in 1935.
On Good Friday, a Jew was assailed while walking through a street
in Hackney. He was incapacitated for a week, but did not notify the
police for fear of reprisals. Instead, he sent a confirmed statement to
the National Council for Civil Liberties. On a Sunday night in
August 1935 a Jew, about 50 years old, was attacked by a group of
Blackshirts in Clapton. He was seriously injured and detained in
hospital for ten days. The police were informed, but could not trace
the culprits. In September another victim was struck on the head
with an iron bar by a 19-year-old member of the Imperial Fascist
League who was arrested and bound over. All three cases apparently were completely unprovoked assaults by gangs of Fascists who
indulged in a frenzied anti-Semitic campaign.[48]

The use of violence spread markedly during the following year.
Between January and June 1936 the Metropolitan Police recorded
fifty-one complaints of 'Jew-baiting', most of them in the boroughs
of Stoke Newington, Bethnal Green, Shoreditch and Hackney. The
majority of reports referred to damage of property, insulting
behaviour, distribution of offensive literature and the use of

obscene language, but there were also six reports of physical attacks on Jews. Another five cases of assaults were recorded by the National Council for Civil Liberties during the same period.[49] The accounts reveal a standard pattern of attack: shouting anti-Jewish epithets, several Fascists closed in on single Jews, beat them up by kicking them, hitting them and striking them, and usually disappeared before the arrival of the police.

Although these reports do not reflect a successful incitement of the masses, they indicate the militancy of the organized fanatical anti-Semites, which created an atmosphere of dismay and paranoia among the Jewish population in the areas concerned. In the parliamentary debate of 10 July 1936 G. Lansbury referred to this development as 'real terror among the Jewish population'. Undoubtedly both camps tended to magnify minor incidents, hoping to capitalize on the propaganda value. Yet, although sometimes exaggerated, the events caused considerable alarm not only among the Jewish population, but also on the part of the Government. Jew-baiting was considered to challenge the democratic system as much as threatening the safety of one minority. This was stressed by the liberal and left-wing press which advocated the enforcement of existing and the passing of new laws to keep these developments under control. The Home Secretary, Sir John Simon, also recognized a menace to democratic freedom and called for special police attention in the troubled areas, pointing out that 'the purpose is the protection of *citizens* not the special protection of Jews.'[50] In the autumn of 1936, the Government introduced a Public Order Bill, which came into force on 1 January 1937. It expressed the authorities' firm intention to re-establish law and order.

Complaints about Jew-baiting continued throughout 1937 when thirty-seven cases of damage of property and thirty-three assaults on Jews were reported to the police. Public opinion naturally focused on the latter. In Bow, a 15-year-old Jewish boy was knocked to the ground, kicked, and left unconscious on the pavement. A 54-year-old Jewish tailor was struck in the face with the buckle of a belt and had to be detained in Bethnal Green hospital with serious eye injuries. A Jewish motorist was assaulted by a 19-year-old member of the British Union of Fascists, while another Jew was punched whilst boarding a tram.[51] The *Daily Telegraph* of 17 September 1937 reported the unprovoked attack on a Jewish medical student who was threatened by a 32-year-old man who attacked him with a knife, shouting 'I will kill every Jew alive'. In November, five brothers attacked and wounded two of their Jewish competitors with pincers, knives and a razor in an attempt to settle a long-standing family feud. One was alleged to have shouted: 'Let me slash him; he is only a Jew. Kill him.'[52]

With war becoming more imminent the recurring theme of Fascist propaganda saw the characterization of Jews as international war-mongers, plotting yet again against Britain's interests. The belief that Jews dragged Britian into war was not, however, confined to Fascist agitators. On 9 December 1938 Beaverbrook commented on the prominent influence Jews allegedly held in the British press and their influence on public opinion. He argued:

I have been, for years, a prophet of no war. But at last I am shaken. The Jews may drive us into war. I do not mean with any conscious purpose of doing so. They do not mean to do it. But unconsciously they are drawing us into war. Their political influence is moving us in that direction.[53]

The problem of Jewish refugees provided another issue likely to rouse emotions. While public criticism over an apparent lack of concern by the British Government mounted after the *Kristallnacht* of November 1938, anti-alien and anti-Semitic feeling was also increasing. Popular papers, notably the *Daily Express* and the *Daily Mail*, frequently expressed anti-alien sentiment and stressed the limited capacity of Britain to absorb foreign Jews. The danger of growing hostility, particularly in view of continual high unemployment, was repeatedly stressed by those responsible for the admission of refugees and relief work.[54] Groups whose particular interests were affected, such as the medical profession, opposed a sympathetic policy even towards 'desirable' immigrants' 'Most of the alien doctors and dentists are Jews who are fleeing from the terror in Germany and Austria', one paper commented. 'And the methods those aliens are bringing into England are not always in accordance with the professional etiquette of this country.'[55]

The organized anti-Semitic campaign remained alive during the years immediately preceding World War II. Between January 1938 and September 1939 the Metropolitan Police recorded 122 cases of damage to Jewish property and 38 assaults on Jews. It was noted that some of these incidents were not politically motivated and either originated from personal animosities or could be attributed to hooligans attracted to both factions. They were, nevertheless, related to the Fascist campaign, since the unrestrained and monotonous attacks on the Jewish community set free latent hostilities and allowed people to give vent to their hatred, which was otherwise restrained by conventional inhibitions. This effect of Fascist propaganda was well recognized by the police. In a report on window-smashing in Bethnal Green it was pointed out:

> Bethnal Green is a working class neighbourhood with a large young hooligan element, who undoubtedly are attracted by the band and propaganda of the Fascist Party, who apparently have made Bethnal Green their stronghold. The attacks made on Jews inflame these hooligans, as the majority of Jews are successful in business in these districts, and trouble results. . . . The hooliganism described has not suddenly appeared. On the contrary it appears to have gradually grown since the two extremist parties, Fascist and Communist, established themselves in Bethnal Green.[56]

The anti-Semitic agitation of the Fascists channelled undirected discontent against an identifiable scapegoat, in particular among those who were exposed to daily contacts with Jews as neighbours, employers or competitors, and held stereotyped opinions of 'the Jew'. Youths, generally prone to discard established values in the search for their own identity, could most easily be mobilized to active Jew-baiting. But the political campaign evolved around the hypostatized 'Jewish question' seems to have appealed to all sections of East End Gentiles – small shopkeepers, artisans and labourers.[57]

Apart from attracting a fair cross-section of the population where they focused their campaign, the anti-Semitic groups appear to have also drawn a considerable number of fanatics who cultivated a pathological Jew-hatred. They provided an unabating source of energy to carry on a politically futile campaign by acts of petty molestations which presented a further vexation to the Jewish community. A favourite way of expressing their passionate Jew-hatred was to address scurrilous letters to individual Jews abusing and threatening them. Thus, one Jew received a postcard with 'Death to the Jews, perish Zion' inscribed upon it announcing that one day he would be publicly flogged to death.[58] Another received the following message:

Three years ago you had a warning from us as to your ultimate fate. We are determined to exterminate every Jew from our country. . . . You would be wise to get back to your sewer before you are too late. A sewer is infinitely preferable to six feet of rope (perhaps worse). We look forward with pleasure to your ultimate end. . . . . A Group of Aryan Patriots'.[59]

Some contemporaries mistook the wave of anti-Semitism in England as a straightforward imitation of Nazism. A closer investigation shows that anti-Semitism had its separate roots in England. As the organizations of the radical right became more aware of German Fascism, they naturally borrowed heavily from its 'advanced' anti-Semitic ideology, amplified their own political thought and adopted storm-trooper techniques in their campaign. In an embryonic state, however, anti-Semitism was part and parcel of their profound anti-modern, anti-materialistic and anti-democratic thought, and only needed expatiation.

The peak of the anti-Semitic agitation in England 1934–7, which briefly succeeded in terrorizing the Jewish minority in East London, coincided with a period of increasing domestic stability and national consensus. The movement as such, however, was a product of the crisis at the beginning of the decade, which had generated the emergence of anti-Semitic organizations in the first place. While the fringe groups who focused solely on anti-Semitism never achieved any political significance, Mosley's British Union of Fascists succeeded in attracting popular support. By the time this party effectively instrumentalized anti-Semitism as an escape-valve for socio-economic tensions and deliberately engineered Jew-hatred to appeal to the masses, the economic tide had turned. While the prospects for political success declined for a movement that advertised itself as the alternative to 'old gang' politicians as the latter managed to steer the country through its crisis, the sharp protest of mass media and the public against the persecution of Jews in Germany further handicapped and discredited the campaign for agitators who manipulated anti-Semitism for political purposes.

The significance of anti-Semitism in England as elsewhere is that it is a symptom of crisis, liable to surface in times of extreme stress, when xenophobia emerges as a form of sublimation of pervasive fear arising from unemployment, inflation, demoralization.[60] This was borne out by the fact that it recurred during the war, when Jews were bedevilled as war-mongers and profiteers, and leaflets appeared saying:

JEWS
they plan it
make it
finance it
and you fight it
WAR

'Perish Judah', 'Kill the Jews', 'End the War' notices were again posted in railway carriages, public lavatories and on pillar-boxes, and a persistent whispering propaganda circulated stories of Jewish rackets. The Crystal Palace, it was alleged, was set on fire by Jews, and advertisements excluding Jews reappeared.[61] At a private session at the Labour Party Conference of 1940 one delegate exclaimed to another: 'Sit down you bloody Jew', 'Sit down you bloody Yid – get back to Palestine'.[62] The new version of the old theme was also expressed in chain-letters sent to Jewish institutions and households blaming Jews for the outbreak of war, exacting:

Unless this WAR IS ABRUPTLY TERMINATED we pledge ourselves to deprive the Jew of all political and legal power in all the countries within the bounds of our world-wide societies, in the name of the youths whose lives have been so ruthlessly sacrificed in the name of Jewish revenge and Jewish capitalist world power. . . . It was this race which crucified Christ, martyred the Christian apostles, and will not therefore be deterred in its mad lust for world power and world gold by the Christian nobody of our day.[63]

This renewed wave of anti-Semitism is outside the scope of this study. By the time it occurred, the main agitators of the inter-war period were interned, their organizations abandoned. In an exemplary rather than exhaustive review of the particular ideologies of the promoters of political anti-Semitism, the theoretical concepts and factual propaganda of three anti-Semitic organizations will be discussed in the following chapters.[64]

Part Two
Promoters of Political Anti-Semitism

3　The Britons

The first organization in England set up for the expressed purpose of disseminating anti-Semitic propaganda was 'The Britons'. Henry Hamilton Beamish, who had originated the idea of forming a 'society to protect the birthright of Britons and to eradicate alien influences from our politics and industries', was unanimously elected president at the foundation meeting held on 18 July 1919. The fourteen people present agreed that

> in view of the fact that there was no Society in Britain which was actively fighting the Alien Menace, the time had arrived to form a Society which would specialize in fighting the Alien Menace and seeing that our Country was governed by our own people.[1]

The Britons' constitution was modelled after the Memorandum of Association of the Remembrance League. Membership was confined 'solely to Britons, men and women over eighteen who can prove that their parents and grandparents were of British blood'.[2] This provision was modified in December 1920, when it was announced that the Britons were also prepared to admit 'pure nationals of other branches of the Aryan family' as associate members, provided they were 'Whites who can show that their ancestry is free from Jewish taint, and who are themselves unallied with Jewry either by marriage, business association or control'.[3] The objects of the society were formulated in twelve points, which included the demand for an amendment of the immigration and naturalization laws which were considered far too lax, the exclusion of all citizens born of non-British parents from public office and voting rights, and the introduction of tariffs protecting native industry. With regard to Jews in Britain, the society asked to encourage their 'return' to Palestine.

Henry H. Beamish was born in Ireland in 1874. He was the son of a former ADC to Queen Victoria, a Rear-Admiral who, as he recalled, had focused his attention at an early age on the 'Jewish question', when he enlightened him about the 'intrigues of international Jewry'.[4] At the age of eighteen Beamish went to Canada, thereafter to Ceylon, and he participated in the Boer War as an officer of the Ceylon Planters' Regiment. He then settled in South Africa, where he saw his anti-Jewish prejudice confirmed and became convinced of the existence of a world-wide Jewish conspiracy. During World War I Beamish served with the Natal Regiment of South African Infantry. In June 1918 he contested the Clapham by-election as an Independent on a platform of extreme patriotism – 'pledged to support the Premier in ousting the Hun and making Germany pay for the War'.[5] He lost the contest against a government candidate by 1181 votes. In December 1918 he stood again as a parliamentary candidate for the same constituency, this time for the National Federation of Discharged Sailors and Soldiers. He came out second, defeated by a margin of 6706 votes.[6]

After these unsuccessful attempts to enter respectable politics, Beamish founded the Britons. He became associated with Lieutenant-Commander Harry M. Fraser, the founder of the Silver-Badge Party for Ex-Servicemen. Both Beamish and Fraser attracted considerable publicity in 1919 when they were sued for libel by Sir Alfred Moritz Mond, then First Commissioner of Works. They had placed a poster in the windows of the office of the Silver-Badge Party which read 'Sir Alfred Mond is a traitor, he allotted shares to the Huns during the war'.[7] For Beamish, this was a deliberate provocation to attract public attention. He voluntarily presented himself to court and claimed authorship of the poster after having appointed Dr J. H. Clarke, vice-president of the Britons, to look after his affairs. In a letter to Clarke, Beamish expressed the driving force motivating his political engagement:

> I have tried every avenue to escape the machinations of the International Jew financial gang who have and are selling our dear old England – the head of which is in my opinion Mond – but without success owing to the press and the trading politicians, including Lloyd George, being controlled by this Jew Gang, that I feel that the time has arrived to expose what is going on and if necessary go to jail in an endeavour to expose this appalling menace.[8]

In court, Beamish constantly tried to turn the proceedings into a forum where he could publicize his view that a Jew cannot be a loyal Englishman, and he provoked some applause from the back of the court when he stated that 'a person can't be by race both English and Jew'.[9] The judge had to reiterate throughout the hearings that the status of Jews was not the issue in the case, and finally Fraser and Beamish were sentenced to pay the plaintiff £5000 damages. An appeal against the judgement was dismissed, but Beamish embarked for South Africa without ever paying his share of the damages.

While Beamish was away, the Britons for a time cherished the myth of an exiled leader who, because of his crusade against Jewry, had had to leave a country 'unfit for heroes to live in'.[10] Apart from two spectacular reappearances in the spring of 1923 and again in 1932, he henceforth participated little in the society's activities, although nominally he remained president of the organization until his death on 27 March 1948.

In 1923, Beamish appears to have visited Mussolini in Rome and Hitler in Munich. He addressed one of Hitler's meetings at the Krone Circus on 18 January 1923, where his speech, delivered in English and translated by Dietrich Eckart, was said to have been received enthusiastically. He stated his attitude concerning the Jews in plain language, pointing to the mutuality of experience and understanding between himself and the leader of the new aspiring German movement:

> I also was in the war as a private in the infantry, but it did not take me long to realize that instead of the Christian nations fighting each other, we ought all to turn our guns against the Jew, who brings about all these wars. . . . The magnificent way in which you Bavarians have tackled this Jew problem has filled me with courage, and I hope it may be possible for all the Aryan races to join forces against the common enemy to our civilization and Christianity.[11]

During the 1930s Beamish participated with great enthusiasm in the pursuit of a world-wide anti-Jewish crusade. He corresponded with political friends in many countries, and visited the United States and Japan in 1936. When Beamish returned to Germany in December 1936, he attracted the attention of the British Embassy, who had received information that his visit caused some controversy among German politicians in the Ministry of Foreign Affairs and the *Auslandsorganisation der NSDAP*, the office responsible for NS propaganda abroad. The general opinion apparently was that Beamish's 'anti-Semitic views would be unpopular in England and that he would be an undesirable instrument'.[12] It was evidently felt that Beamish's support would carry little weight in winning over British public opinion, and could even damage the German propaganda efforts, since he was known as an eccentric, referred to by British diplomatic staff as an 'unbalanced and ill-educated propagandist with a bee in his bonnet'.[13] Ribbentrop, however, finally endorsed his visit and Beamish arrived in Germany as a guest of honour. He gave numerous lectures and was shown around being apparently even allowed to interview Thälmann, the imprisoned leader of the German Communist Party. Beamish seemed to have been duly impressed by the 'NEW and rejuvenated Germany', but felt that the 'Jewish question', the root of all problems, remained yet to be solved. In January 1937 he wrote to a friend:

> The Jew menace has NOT been dealt with in Germany and is very much to the fore and nothing but segregation will deal with the matter.[14]

Beamish, who on one occasion was publicly greeted by J. Streicher as a long-standing fellow-traveller of National Socialism, focused in his public talks on the alleged destructive influence of Jewry, suggesting that the Jews should be deported wholesale since it would be 'unkind' to sterilize or massacre them.[15] In September 1937 he attended an international congress of anti-Semites, organized by Colonel Fleischhauer, the editor of the newsletter *World Service*. Eventually, Beamish returned to Southern Rhodesia where he became an MP in August 1938, but lost his seat in the election of April 1939.

As the antagonism between Fascist and democratic countries increased, Beamish turned more anti-British in his campaign against the 'Kosher War' which he was convinced was imminent. From June 1940 until July 1943 he was interned for his Fascist leanings. After his release, he moved to a farm outside Salisbury. By then he had dissociated himself completely from the Britons, whom he accused of having betrayed the idea for which he had originally founded the society, namely for 'the sole purpose of exposing the Jewish Menace'.[16] Although the Britons had continued to publish anti-Semitic literature, most notably the *Protocols of the Elders of Zion*, Beamish did not consider them deserved successors and bequeathed a legacy not to them, but to Arnold Spencer Leese, founder of the Imperial Fascist League, whom he considered more reliable in his fight against Jewry. In his last letter to the Britons, written two months before his death, Beamish expressed his contempt for the remnants of his movement:

> Being a REALIST, I have to face FACTS and the latter are that the BRITONS after being established for over 25 years for the ONE purpose of exposing the Jewish Menace, and which long ere should have been the rallying centre of all Jew wise people throughout the world, is today practically a derelict concern. To myself it is a complete tragedy and as you are unable to rebut what I have stated the moribund verdict must stand. En passant, the CID not only searched my house, but took away many sack loads of literature, little of which has been returned, while you state that the BRITONS office was not even searched and seem proud of it. Comment is unnecessary.[17]

During Beamish's absence, the Britons were presided over by Dr John Henry Clarke, a doctor and champion of homeopathics, who had published a book in 1917, *The Call of the Sword*, in which he described the war as an Armaggedon for the liberation of mankind from mental and moral slavery. In this treatise, Clarke demanded Britain's emancipation from false ideas, the restoration of a Christian civilization and the expulsion of 'men of alien blood and alien instincts' detrimental to the British character.[18] In 1918 he edited another work, *England Under the Heel of the Jew*, in which it was argued that Prussia and its German successor-state were Judaic nations, and that the war was a war of Jewish finance aimed at an overthrow of the Christian civilization of England.[19]

Clarke, an associate of Beamish in the Vigilantes Society in 1918, had taken the chair at the foundation meeting of the Britons and was one of their most prominent members. He was chief consulting physician to the London Homeopathic Hospital, an experienced lecturer and author of many books. Clarke remained vice-chairman of the Britons until his death in 1931, and usually chaired their meetings, the perennial subject of which was the alleged fundamental antagonism between the British and the Jewish nation.

In conjunction with the Britons, Beamish founded the Judaic Publishing Company, renamed Britons Publishing Company in August 1922. Apart from numerous pamphlets and brochures they began to publish a monthly journal in February 1920, at first under the title *Jewry Ueber Alles*, referring to the presumed Judeo-Germanic conspiracy. The periodical was later published under the heading *The Hidden Hand*, and was finally called *The British Guardian*. In July 1925 it was discontinued for lack of funds.

From the beginning, anti-Semitism was the focal point in the Britons' propaganda. It was the key element in their ideology and functioned as an all-embracing framework for the articulation of diffuse criticism and discontent. True to their constitution, which conceived an 'entirely non-party and non-sectarian' society, the Britons presented themselves as sincere patriots above parties and social cleavages. Their over-riding aim was to have Britain governed by Britons only, a policy that was to be inaugurated with the restoration of the Act of Settlement of 1700, which circum-scribed the rights of aliens. As opposed to the 'good old days', the contemporary political system was described as a drudge for the élite of Jewry, in whose hands the leaders of the English nation were mere puppets. Under these circumstances, the Britons considered it futile to compete for political power. Instead, they recommended their readers to vote for the Conservative Party as the least sub-verted one of all, just as they drew attention to the *Morning Post* as the suitable daily paper for patriots.[20]

The lack of a political programme addressing itself to various aspects of complex modern societies reflects the Britons' narrow sphere of interest. In their periodical they commented only briefly on current political issues and used all topics exclusively to demon-strate the alleged evil influences of Jewry. Thus, when referring to the Imperial Conference of 1921, they restricted themselves to the following observation: 'With Lloyd George, General Smuts and the Israelites of India at the Council table, the interests of England and Britain's Empire won't have a look in.'[21] With regard to the Irish question, the Britons were also short of a clear-cut policy. Like the villains of the Russian revolution, they maintained, so was de Valera of Jewish descent, fully protected by the 'hidden hand' and therefore able to carry on his work of destruction. Both Eire and Ulster were encouraged to turn anti-Jew, and the latter was asked to 'refuse to accept any order from England's be-Jewed

Parliament until every Jew and every Jew's tool has been eliminated therefrom'.[22]

Their obsession with the idea of a world-wide Jewish conspiracy and the menace of British Bolshevism became evident in every issue of the Britons' periodical. Their view of a universal Jewish infiltration of all important institutions and enterprises was impressively conveyed in the title-page illustration of the *Hidden Hand* by their caricaturist 'Goy'[23] in the first numbers of the journal. The cartoon showed world Jewry, represented as an octopus reaching out for all continents with innumerable tentacles symbolizing Jewish interests in railway and shipping, white slave traffic, cotton industries, base metals, chemicals, mass-media, finance, government, raw materials and consumer goods.

Regarding history not as the outcome of long-term developments and cycles, but as entirely dependent on the men at the top, the Britons considered the first step towards national recovery to be the revealing of the Jewish 'hidden hand'. Outside the ghetto, they argued, Jews were 'parasites, carrying corruption, revolution, Bolshevism everywhere',[24] their ultimate goal being a Judaization of the world.

Jews were denounced as suspicious, alien intruders whether they tried to assimilate or to retain their identity. On the one hand considered guilty of keeping to themselves, separatists 'who have always declined and always will decline to be absorbed into any nation',[25] they were by the same token accused of disavowing their origin, adopting English names and passing themselves off for English. It was argued that the Jews tried to obliterate their racial identity by pretending not merely to be Englishmen, but super-Englishmen. Jews who were most successfully assimilated were regarded as the most deceptive ones who had to be unmasked:

> Against Jews as Jews we have no quarrel, but against Jews as Englishmen, Russians or Germans, we protest with all our power. Jews camouflaged as nationals *are* the Hidden Hand.[26]

In 1920, Beamish published what was to become an important reference book for the Britons, *The Jews' Who's Who*, in which the alleged Jewish financial and political interests were exposed. Compiled in order to enlighten the reader about 'the source of the sinister influences now so prevalent',[27] it contained a list of Jews prominent in public life, and some theoretical expositions as to the utter incompatibility of Jewish and English cultures, races and religions, which indicated the scope of the Britons' anti-Jewish argument:

> By his blood, by the shape of his mind, by his Pharisaic, Talmudic religion the Jew must be a foreigner in all countries except his own, and this no amount of 'naturalising' can ever alter.[28]

Stressing the notions of blood and race, the Britons assimilated a crude racial ideology which reflected the current concepts of white supremacy.[29] Although they were not systematically developed into a coherent theoretical framework, racist ideas constituted an ever-present theme in the Britons' publications. George P. Mudge, a lecturer at the London Medical School, one of their founding members and an early member of the Eugenics Society, appeared as the Britons' authority on racial questions. In a series of articles in the *Hidden Hand*, entitled 'The Pride of Race', he discussed the historical significance of the natural differences between nations.

Europe, Mudge explained, was inhabited by three different races – the Nordic or Teutonic, the Mediterranean, also referred to as Celtic or Iberian, and the Alpine race – of which the first two largely constituted the population of the British Isles.[30] He attributed particular value to the Nordic race, which had evolved under extremely harsh conditions in the forests and plains of Eastern Germany, Poland and Russia. Given the environmental circumstances, only the physically fittest of this race had survived, while 'weaklings, disloyal cranks, or long-haired communists' had perished. The Nordics distinguished themselves by tall stature, flaxen, light brown or reddish hair, blue, green or grey eyes and a high, narrow face. The outstanding physical characteristics of the members of this virile Nordic race, Mudge argued, were matched by their superb intellectual and moral qualities, which appointed them as the natural ruling class – courage, reliability, loyalty, trustworthiness, honesty, truthfulness, punctuality and efficiency.

Mudge observed, however, a disconcerting danger of a drainage of valuable English blood, which could only be met by race-conscious pairing and breeding. He considered it for every Briton 'a debt of honour to England, to his race and to the dead, to replenish that race', and an 'act of treachery' to marry a Jewess or any other Oriental woman.[31] Anticipating Hitler's outbursts against

Rassenschande, the Britons condemned 'cross-breeding' as 'a deep degradation and defilement of our stock'.[32] Similarly, any form of birth control was rejected as 'racial betrayal', a crime against race and country, and it was argued that every Nordic man unmarried and childless after the age of thirty deserved social disapprobation.

Contrasting the superior racial qualities of the English with the despicable characteristics of Jewry, the Britons repeatedly stressed the urgent need for developing an acute race-consciousness among all Britons:

> In every anthropological trait the Jewish race is inferior to the English. It is lower and more generalized in type; it does not possess our refinement, or our sense of justice, or our quality of altruism, or our capacity of playing the game, or our sportsmanship. When put to the supreme test, the Jew is shown to be vindictive, cruel, remorseless, and savage, delighting in torture, as is demonstrated in Bolshevic (Jewish) Russia and in many pages of the world's history. . . . Any English woman or English man who so far betrays the purity of his white blood as to marry into this Asiatic Jewish race, deserves life-long ostracism at the hands of his or her English fellows.[33]

From the alleged racial and moral superiority of the English people the Britons deduced a 'world responsibility' for the British race to uplift inferior people to a 'higher moral plane of dignity', a task that had been successfully accomplished in the case of India. The Jewish counter-race in their opinion not only obstructed and undermined these efforts, but also corrupted and paralysed British affairs at home. The 'penetration into our great English people of a vast Asiatic horde – the Jewish race' was compared to a fatal virus. Jews were described as 'poison in the national body', as 'cancer of humanity', as a tribe being a 'hot-bed for breeding tubercle *bacillus*', and were denounced as 'the most prolific spreaders of disease on this planet', immune carriers who were able to spread disease without being affected themselves.[34]

Closely related to the belief that Jews constituted a threat to the physical health of the nation was the frequent accusation that they controlled the white slave traffic. There was considerable concern about Jewish male aggressiveness, conveyed not only in articles but also in obscene caricatures, in which the noses of Jews were turned into phallic-symbols.[35] Jews, described as 'unclean, unclean-minded, unprincipled hostile foreigners' were accused of 'sexual filthiness' and considered a dangerous threat to Gentile women who might fall an easy prey to them, particularly since the war had diminished the number of marriageable young men. Pointing to the 'enormities, assassinations, dishonouring of women and destruction of religion that have marked the path and operations of the Jewish camarilla in Russia' an appeal was made to English parents to prevent their 'clean, frank English youths' from associating with Jewish children in schools and colleges.[36]

To support their doctrine of a racial inferiority of Jews, the Britons referred to a series of 8000 blood tests conducted by 'two medical men of the highest attainments' in Mesopotamia. They were said to have established that 'there is an essential difference between the blood of an Englishman and other European whites and that of the Jew', and so to have proved that 'the Jew is not the White Man's brother'.[37] Based on the assumption that fundamental biological differences existed between Gentiles and Jews, the Britons attached collective characteristics to racial identities. Jews became linked with all that was considered evil, and it was deduced that there was an unrelenting antagonism between them and all other people. Preconceived value judgements were thus sanctified as natural, innate facts, and fitted into a dualistic concept of the world common to all anti-Semites.

With the appeal to racial unity, which by its definition excluded the Jews, the Britons tried to exalt the nation as a whole, embracing the entirety of the people. Individuals were meant to become aware of what they had in common transcending their different backgrounds, education, income and status. 'It is not so much social standing that we should think of,' it was argued, 'but rather hereditary character in every stratum of our people.'[38] To emphasize the significance of race-consciousness not only for the English, but for all Nordic nations, the Britons did not fail to draw attention to congenial movements in other countries. They quoted in particular *Ostara*, published since 1905 by Lanz von Liebenfels, a periodical devoted to the propagation of Aryan superiority.[39]

The racial anti-Semitism of the Britons was complemented by religious aspects. Although it was firmly stated that 'the "differentia" of the Jew is his blood, not what he believes',[40] and maintained that 'the Jewish problem is primarily one of race, not religion',[41] the question of priority was not always clear. It was also stated that 'the struggle which we are engaged in is not wholly, or chiefly, one of race and blood.'[42] Instead, it was described as a moral and spiritual contest against the power of darkness, incarnated in the alien Jew. Many of their executive members being professed Catholics, the Britons adopted the view that the 'Jewish problem' could not 'be adequately presented or appreciated except from a definitely Christian standpoint'.[43] They reminded their readers that the New Testament had replaced the Old Covenant, appealed to the Christian churches to emancipate themselves from their father religion, and above all urged them to unite in the struggle against the universal foe:

> We appeal to the Clergy and Ministers of Religion, both Catholic and Protestant, to purge our common Christianity from the corruption of the Jew and Judaism. . . . Nothing is more calculated to heal our divisions, and promote the unity for which we long, than the recognition and removal of the common Peril which is hindering the acceptance of the true Faith, and the progress of Christianity in our land.[44]

As opposed to Judaism, which was identified with selfishness and materialism, the Christian religion was praised for representing sacrifice, restriction and the conquest of the lower, animal self. Ignoring the common traditions and the continuity of Old Testamentarian thought in the principles set forth in the New Testament, the teachings of Christ were interpreted as a revolutionary event, from which the former Lord had emerged as evil. The religion of the Jews, it was concluded, was the religion of anti-Christ, ultimately geared towards the enslavement of the world, body and soul, to the material, which would reverse mankind's liberation from bondage to material things achieved by Christ's self-sacrifice.

The *Protocols of the Elders of Zion* were cited as proof for Jewry's aggressive anti-Christianism, revealing its secret aspirations to subjugate the rest of the world. Because Judaism was considered a 'moral poison', and all Jewish influence supposed to represent a Satanic element, benevolent toleration of the Jewish minority was ruled out as being self-destructive. 'Every true Christian must be an anti-Satanite',[45] the *Hidden Hand* enlightened its readers, and encouraged all sincere Britons to oppose the Jews, the palpable personification of Satan. Appealing to their compatriots to preserve the English character, founded on English blood and the spirit of the New Testament, the Britons became increasingly proud of their ideology. While at first they vehemently denied being anti-Semitic, they gradually adopted anti-Semitism as their characteristic trademark:

> Anti-Semitism . . . is not a mere destructive reactionary force, the outcome of petty spite, but the force of the spiritual sword which Christ declared he came to bring. . . . No man can be a patriotic Briton and not be anti-Semitic, and above all things no man can possibly be a Christian and not be anti-Judaic, for the Jews constitute the one definitely anti-Christian force in the world.[46]

As with their request for race-consciousness, so with their appeal for Christian unanimity, the Britons fostered the image of a united people, in which common ideals surpassed social cleavages. Against the mounting threat of Jewry, the Britons argued, the Nordic race had to stand together in defence of their Christian civilization. There was no place for them in England, they maintained, nor anywhere else in Europe, and it was concluded that 'out of Europe, as out of Egypt, Jews must go'.[47]

Based on the assumption that Jews led a parasitical existence, corrupted industry, banking and trade, undermined the traditional cultural values, and deprived native Britons of their jobs, women and homes, the Britons discussed various schemes to circumscribe their influence. Since the Jews had internationalized all money of the world, it was argued, it was only just to return to the nation what should never have been taken away from it. Thus, the Britons wanted to see all Jews ousted from their jobs, and demanded the nationalization of Jewish property.[48] The key to get rid of the 'Jew-menace' was seen in segregation in the form of compulsory Zionism. This scheme, modelled after the example set by South Africa with regard to her natives, was advocated by Beamish in *The Jews' Who's Who* where he also stressed the need for all Western countries to unite in this crusade:

> There is only one cure for this world-evil, and that is for all the Christian white races to combine and to repatriate to Palestine and the neighbouring territories every Jew, male and female, and to take the most drastic steps to see that, once they have founded their Zionist state in their own Promised Land, they permanently remain there.[49]

Like Arnold White, who once argued that 'pogroms are futile, since they can never reach the point of total extermination; always arouse sympathy for the "persecuted" sons of Abraham',[50] Beamish disapproved of pogroms because 'history . . . proved that they have never produced the desired results'.[51] He did not deny the Jews a right to live, but reserved for the Nordic races the right to 'protect' themselves and to treat Jews as. inferior people, and thought it of vital importance to cut them off completely from the rest of the world. No Jew was ever to be allowed to leave the confined area, and no Christian was to enter the secluded territory. Beamish envisaged keeping all Jews collectively under solitary confinement, treating them like criminals or lepers with whom one had to avoid contact at any cost. 'All Jews', he argued, 'should be forced to live in Palestine in the same way that snakes and other vermin should be forced to live in the jungle and not in people's houses.'[52] When Beamish advocated Zionism, it was in order to establish a Jewish national home as the ghetto of the world, when he mentioned repatriation he thought of deportation as the means of eradicating all Jewish influence. Half-Jews, he reckoned, would be eliminated naturally within a few generations, since racially pure marriages would re-establish the original stock.

Beamish's ideas were taken up and expounded by his disciples. They all agreed that one way or another one had to eliminate Jewry, the most deadly enemy of all other nations, that one had 'to cut it out from the body politic, body economic, body social of every other nation', so that the white nations would have 'a chance for achieving, each for itself, its own destiny'.[53] For some time the Britons favoured Palestine as the most suitable repository for Jews, arguing that Britain had already accepted the mandate over that territory and therefore had interests and obligations there. It was also noted that this seemed to appeal to Jews themselves more than other settlement schemes such as East Africa, the Valley of the Amazon or Alaska. In April 1923, however, the Britons adopted a different policy and for the first time suggested Madagascar as a convenient Jewish homeland,[54] a proposal that had already been advocated by Paul de Lagarde in 1885, and was later pursued by various administrations.[55]

Madagascar, the Britons claimed, could accommodate 100 million people and was therefore large enough to receive the entire world Jewry, which was estimated at 50 million. It was proposed that it could be bought from France with money expropriated from

Jews. Beamish, who claimed to have been the pioneer of the Madagascar scheme, firmly believed that segregation was the only way to solve the 'Jewish question' permanently and the Britons fully endorsed his proposal, adding that Zionism was a political movement but not related to the mystic Zion. Madagascar, they argued, 'being an island, would make the problem of complete segregation a simple one'[56] and would serve much better as a Jewish national home than Palestine which, because of its crucial geographical position and the fact that it was already occupied, was now considered 'quite unsuitable for a race of people who for countless ages have consistently stirred up trouble, revolution and anarchy amongst every nation with which they have come in contact'.[57]

The most systematic outline regarding the Britons' policy of how to approach the 'Jewish question' was given in a series of articles entitled 'The Jew Conquest of England', published in 1924 in the *Hidden Hand*. After having described how the Jews rule the world by corruption, blackmail and subversion, the author proposed two alternative policies of solving the 'Jewish problem', namely extermination and expulsion. Extermination, what he called the 'Jewish Scriptural Method', struck him as obviously the most satisfactory solution, but not a practicable one, since it would not appeal to the 'kind-hearted English nation'. The alternative he recommended was expulsion, a method which had proved applicable in the past and seemed adequate enough provided it was strictly enforced and irreversible:

Male and female, children and adults, bag and baggage, this Asiatic tribe must be returned to its native Asia, without the option of return. Any attempt to evade this essential stipulation must be met with the death penalty on landing on our shores.[58]

This proposition, suggesting extermination or expulsion as alternative policies directed towards one and the same goal, documents the easy transition between the two schemes. The anti-Semite who advocates the exclusion of all Jews from his own society as the key policy to stabilize the economy, guarantee peace and purify his culture, is above all concerned with the total application of a policy which he considers the ultimate solution to all evils. Once the Jews are attributed such fundamental importance in the destiny of the rest of the world, practical considerations about the means used to eliminate their influence are subordinate to the general objective. Extermination figures in this discussion as the most radical and permanent solution and, although it might not be considered a popular and expedient policy at a given time, it remains there as a theoretical possibility, indeed the most effective option.

Either extermination or expulsion for all practical purposes serve to bring about the same effect: the complete removal of all Jews and the prevention of any contacts with them, so that for the Gentiles subjectively the Jews cease to exist. Although for those subjected to the policy the two proposals have different implications, the difference is a matter of degree, with extermination as a conceivable climax implied in the concept of expulsion. As soon as the exile of all Jews is no longer considered an adequate policy against the threat caused by the very existence of Jews, more rigid measures are bound to emerge. Where it is believed that national prosperity, welfare and security are at stake, moral inhibitions are quickly overruled and in fact the death penalty was suggested as the only answer to those who tried to evade the rule.

The ideas developed in the publications of the Britons closely resemble the political beliefs propagated by the leadership of the German National Socialists. There existed some connections between the two groups while both of them were still obscure and regarded as exponents of the political fringe. But they were founded independently and with definitely national, not international, bias, both absorbing the remnants of previously existing groups: whereas the NSDAP in its formative years recruited its supporters from the ranks of other *völkisch* movements, many of the Britons' leading members were also affiliated with other patriotic societies such as the British Brothers League, Eugenics Society, Loyalty League, Middle Classes Union, Navy League or Vigilantes Society.[59] In their publications, the Britons frequently referred to these congenial organizations.

Rooted in the tradition of an extreme nationalism – personified in such sympathizers as Admiral Domvile, Lord Sydenham and Arnold White – the Britons inherited the Anglo-German antagonism which until the end of World War I was the focal point for the British radical right. After the defeat of Germany and the Communist revolution in Russia, 'international Bolshevism' began to be perceived as an equally threatening menace as 'the Hun'. The Britons were quick to blame Jewry for both evils, propagating that

'Germanism is a contagious disease like the plague, and the ubiquitous parasite which carries the germ of it is the wandering Jew'.[60] The Britons' growing sympathy for 'Jewmany' as 'the dupe and the tool of the Jews'[61] did not, however, indicate a spontaneous change of attitude towards the former enemy. They rejected Germany's renewed colonial aims and insisted on their rights as the victorious power in the Great War, even after they had discovered that the NSDAP was an ally in the fight against world Jewry.

In 1922, the Britons published a brochure entitled *Jewish Bolshevism*, which featured drawings of Russian leaders supplemented by brief comments on their Jewish descent and affiliations. This booklet, which was prefaced by Alfred Rosenberg, had previously been published in English by the *völkisch Deutscher Volksverlag*.[62] The advertisement of other translations, such as Theodor Fritsch's *The Riddle of the Jew's Success*, soon followed. The groups also exchanged speakers with H. H. Beamish addressing an NSDAP meeting in Munich and Kurt Kerlen, member of the Thule-society, addressing the Britons in London. Apart from such manifestations of sympathy, however, there is little evidence suggesting a close cooperation of the two movements. In the context of Beamish's visit to Germany in 1923 the *Wiener Morgenzeitung* imputed, with reference to National Socialist circles, that 'Hitler has given Beamish a large sum of money for the purpose of founding a Nationalist Party in England'.[63] Given the financial state of the NSDAP at that time, this allegation does not seem likely. Conversely, in 1924, Kurt Lüdecke, one of Hitler's early supporters, approached the Britons, Lord Sydenham and the Duke of Northumberland, all well known for their anti-Semitic attitudes, for financial assistance for the NSDAP – apparently without success.[64]

Information about 'Germany's Aryan Party' remained rather sparse in the Britons' publications and there was even some confusion about the correct spelling of the name Hitler. It seems that the Britons looked upon Hitler's movement with increasing detachment, irritated not by his anti-Semitism, from which they themselves never wavered, but by his fascist concept of reorganizing the state and by the pagan elements in his ideology. Hitler's Munich *putsch* of 9 November 1923 was covered only briefly in one article in the January 1924 issue of the *Hidden Hand*. Commenting on a report that had appeared in the *Jewish Chronicle* of 27 February 1925 on the formation of a Fascist International against Jewish capitalism

and freemasonry, the *British Guardian* even expressed contentment
with the omission of the Hitler movement:

> Adolf Hitler himself is, we believe, a Catholic, but his movement
> is certainly not a movement of Orthodox Christians. . . . It is
> satisfactory to note then that this new Fascist International
> appears to be confined to distinctly Catholic movements.[65]

Summing up their political pretensions, the Britons can be
characterized as an ultra-conservative, strictly monarchical and
élitist movement, devoted to the restoration and preservation of a
glorified past, the Imperial tradition. Significantly, many of its
members who are not lost in anonymity were either ex-servicemen
or people who had travelled and lived in overseas territories and
had thus experienced racial superiority as a political reality, not
just as myth: H. H. Beamish, after years of restless travelling,
settled permanently in Southern Rhodesia; J. D. Dell, after having
served as the Britons' secretary for twenty-six years, retired to
South Africa in 1949; Lieut.-Comm. H. M. Fraser operated in
India; Captain A. E. N. Howard was acclaimed for having carried
the Britons' work into China; Lt.-Col. A. H. Lane served with
Kitchener in Egypt, then with Milner in South Africa; V. E.
Marsden, correspondent of the *Morning Post*, accompanied the
Prince of Wales on his Empire tour in 1920; E. J. Montgomery was
appointed the Britons' agent in South Africa with the right to
translate their publications into Afrikaans; Mrs B. Pullen-Burry
was celebrated for being one of the most widely-travelled women of
her day, member of various geographical societies; Lord Sydenham
of Combe, the Britons' most prominent sympathizer, occupied
among other appointments the post of Governor of Bombay
1907–23.[66]

More resembling a club than a political party, the Britons never
succeeded in recruiting a mass membership which would have
enabled them to fulfil their promise that 'when we have a thousand
members more, we shall smash Jewry as we smashed the Hinden-
burg line'.[67] They started with twelve members in 1919, which
diminished to eight attendants at their second meeting on 31
January 1920. Various means of reaching a larger public were
suggested, such as writing to provincial papers explaining the
Britons' objects, the distribution of leaflets and personal prosely-
tizing, but none had the desired effect.

According to the diary of the society, their peak of activity was in 1923 when their appeals met some response and £70 14s. 4d. was raised in a 'Patriotic Fund to fight the Hidden Hand'.[68] At a meeting held on 5 March 1923, attended by sixty members, Beamish asked for an endowment fund of £1000. About thirty of those present either paid or guaranteed contributions amounting to a total of £400 – a sum which was felt to be sufficient to allow the society to remain in business for another year. Thereafter regular monthly meetings were held at which speakers lectured on topics such as 'The Jew Control of Our Industries', 'Jewish Methods', 'Jewish Control of Music' or 'Who is the Jew?'. They were attended by small, albeit regular, audiences who did not contribute significantly to the society's funds:[69]

7 May 1923	56 present, 5 new members registered
	Collection: £6 0s. 3d.
	Sale of Literature: £0 5s. 8d.
11 May 1923	152 present (Hammersmith Town Hall meeting)
4 June 1923	45 present, 2 new members registered
	Collection: £1 10s. 2d.
	Sale of Literature: £2 8s. 1d.
2 July 1923	53 present, 1 new member registered
	Collection: £5 8s. 0d.
	Sale of Literature: £2 0s. 6d.
12 July 1923	38 present, 1 new member registered
	Collection: £1 12s. 2d.
	Sale of Literature: £1 4s. 0d.

In addition to the general meetings, thirteen executive meetings, all concerned with the society's financial state, are recorded. Internal disagreements led to the exclusion of ten members in November 1923, and the following month three executive members, J. H. Clarke, R. T. Cooper and W. A. Peters, constituted themselves as the 'Britons Publishing Society'. In a final meeting held in February 1932 the society was formally divided into the 'Britons' and the 'Britons Publishing Company', of which the latter is still in business despite various schisms.

As a political movement the Britons ceased to exist in 1925, when the only medium that held them together, their monthly journal, discontinued. Asking for an annual subscription of 1s., they were constantly under financial pressure and could not afford large-scale propaganda. Despite odd large contributions from its devoted members and the support of a few manufacturers,[70] they did not manage to acquire a comfortable financial basis to cover the costs of maintaining London headquarters and publishing leaflets, brochures and periodicals. Lacking also the leadership of able politicians, the Britons never succeeded in developing their society of discontented individuals into an effective political organization.

Despite their limited impact throughout their existence, the Britons were significant in offering a niche for those who shared a fanatical hatred of the Jews. By keeping anti-Semitic literature, such as the *Protocols of the Elders of Zion*, in circulation they helped to preserve the myth of a world-wide Jewish conspiracy and sustained the continuity of anti-Semitism after World War I. Different from the conventional extreme conservatism which manifested itself in the *Morning Post*, the Duke of Northumberland's weekly *The Patriot* or Lord Alfred Douglas's periodical *Plain English*, papers which reflected the contemporary drawing-room anti-Semitism, the Britons consequently developed an anti-Semitic ideology which led them to anticipate much of future NS propaganda. For an understanding of the phenomenon of modern anti-Semitism, the Britons' one-dimensional Jew-hatred, although confined to the political fringe, is more illuminating than the presence of latent anti-Semitism among various sections of the population. It reveals the function of anti-Semitism in a Manichean *Weltanschauung*, and documents the dynamics unleashed as soon as the Jews are singled out as the exclusive antipodes of civilization. Similar patterns can be observed in the anti-Semitic movements active during the 1930s.

4 Imperial Fascist League

Like the Britons, the Imperial Fascist League was founded by a man with a colourful background. Arnold Spencer Leese was born in 1878 in Lancashire, grew up as a protected child in a middle-class environment and was trained as a veterinary surgeon.[1] After having received his diploma in 1903 he practised for three years in the East End of London. He then took a post with the Indian Government to study the diseases of camels. After six years in India he went to Kenya, then returned to England at the outbreak of World War I. He joined the Royal Army Veterinary Corps and served in France and Somaliland. Shortly after the war Leese opened a practice in Stamford, where he gradually established himself as one of the notables of the town. In 1928, after having published a study on camels, he abandoned his career as a vet in order to devote himself exclusively to political activities and founded the IFL, which he led as the unchallenged leader until his death in 1956.

While the Britons remained a patriotic society with strong anti-Semitic bias but no further political programme, the IFL emerged as a political party with definite ideas regarding the political and economic set-up of the ideal state. During the first years of its existence, the League's activities were limited to the publication of the occasional pamphlet and of a periodical, *The Fascist*, which appeared monthly with a circulation of 3000 copies.[2] 'Progress was painfully slow,' Lesse recollected in 1951, 'because although I myself could produce the means to prevent collapse, I could get no funds to splash about for publicity.'[3]

Leese achieved some national notoriety in 1936 when he was charged with seditious libel and public mischief for accusing the Jews of ritual murder. On the first charge he was acquitted, on the second he was sentenced and accepted six months' imprisonment rather than pay a fine. His printer was also found guilty and sentenced to pay £20.–.–.[4] At the outbreak of World War II the general headquarters of the IFL were closed down and its members quickly dispersed to avoid detention. Leese was arrested in November 1940 and detained until February 1944 under Defence Regulation 18B. After having been released because of poor health he circulated the newsletter *Gothic Ripples*, subtitled 'An Occasional Report on the Jewish Question for the Jew-Wise by Arnold Leese's Anti-Jewish Information Bureau'. Leese continued his political work on his pre-war course, more than ever convinced of the existence of a world-wide Jewish conspiracy.

Like Beamish, Leese professed highly individualistic and unusual ideas. He despised Christianity, because in his opinion it did not meet the needs of an advanced culture for a refined religion. Revelling in a romantic adoration of ideals praised in medieval heroic legends, of a world which in retrospect appeared self-contained and vastly superior to the contemporary scene, he favoured a simple moral code teaching man 'to be straightforward, to be kind to animals, to be courageous, loyal and chivalrous'. Similarly, he recommended abstinence because he thought that 'England was at its best when it knew nothing of tobacco . . . and had no Jews'.[5]

Leese considered himself the model of a man who had gone his own way. His stay abroad seems to have increased the sense of isolation which he said he had already perceived as a child. Like many of his contemporaries he returned to England frustrated in his hopes for personal success and outstanding achievements, for which he compensated by scorn for those who allegedly under-estimated him. By nature impatient of discipline, he came to pursue his aims regardless of the opinion and response of others. Again, the prolonged residence in overseas territories seems to have induced a profound contempt for the masses and nurtured the feeling of superiority. It was there, according to Leese's own state-ment, that he realized that men were not equal and that an élite had to take lead over the rabble. Evaluating his change of attitude, he characterized his position after World War I as 'vaguely Con-servative, just as I had been vaguely Liberal before I went out to India and found that one man was not half as good as another'.[6]

Leese found a political home which suited his general outlook when he joined the British Fascists Ltd. which was founded in 1923 by Rotha Lintorn-Orman.[7] This organization was from the outset devoted to the campaign against Communism and attracted con-siderable support from retired military officers who endorsed its extreme patriotism. Not until the 1930s did the British Fascists advocate a Fascist programme, and it was then that they also became known for an anti-Semitic attitude. They published various periodicals at irregular intervals, held meetings in London and the provinces, but failed to recruit mass support. As their candidate, Leese was elected to the Stamford Borough Council in 1924, together with another Fascist, one H. Simpson. It is noteworthy that this was also the town of Arthur Kitson, factory owner and prominent champion of monetary reform schemes, who introduced Leese to the Britons. There he received the *Protocols of the Elders of Zion*, which turned out to be of decisive importance for Leese's future intellectual development. This reading channelled his hitherto undirected discontent and finally enabled him to identify what he came to consider the cause of the world's unrest.

When Leese founded his own movement in November 1928, he propagated a collection of reactionary planks with no coherent political framework. His political beliefs were those of a conservative middle-class citizen, betraying a general sense of dissatisfaction which manifested itself mainly in a negative criticism of the existent political affairs. When demanding a strong army and navy, Leese echoed the Conservatives' opposition to naval parity with the United States. When advocating a re-organization of the Empire, Leese voiced the die-hards' dream of coordinating the development of agriculture, industry and commerce so as to avoid competition among different regions. In the first issue of the *Fascist*, which appeared in March 1929, Leese described the aims of the IFL as follows:

1 Recognition of the failure of political democracy
2 Formation of a new governing caste of character and service
3 Organization of all industrial and economic interests into a Corporate State.

Fascism, Leese explained, was 'less a policy than a state of mind',[8] a new form of government which would stir people from their political apathy, a resuscitation comparable to the patriotic spirit which had possessed the nation and Empire in 1914. It would not transform the country into a people's republic, but would offer simply everyone his share according to his merits. The goal was not a social and political upheaval, but the awakening of historical thinking, the preservation of British character and British traditions, and a reversal of the unfortunate effects of democracy and liberalism in order to restore Britain's magnitude and glory.

Leese, who had observed Mussolini's advent to power with admiration, presented the state as a fictitious unit for identification, in which there was no room for opposition. Particularly the press, whose right to criticism he vehemently denied, should be totally subordinate to the state and 'give the Mob the news . . . it ought to read'.[9] 'All should be within the State, none must be against the State', Leese demanded, and admitted that 'Fascism itself is an expression of intolerance.'[10] Once it had been decided what the common good was to be, the individual was supposed to derive his own interests from those of the state, which was perceived as a given, permanent entity whose legitimacy was not questioned. Regarding heredity as the most decisive influence upon an individual, Leese advocated government by a political aristocracy, a strong executive of selected men, to replace the rule of ignorant majorities. This government would be appointed by and responsible to the Sovereign.

Leese cultivated the image of British society as that of an austere, conquering élite of Empire-builders, in which women were to play a subsidiary rôle. He deplored female suffrage and the increasing number of working women, both of which he thought were contravening the laws of nature. According to Leese, the male instinct was to secure the safety of his home and country, the female to care for her children, which naturally narrowed her scope of experience and political judgement. The nation required larger families of English stock, therefore women should be encouraged to marry early and devote their lives to domestic work. 'Unmarried men and unmarried women are not living the normal life; it is the married who are normal,' Leese observed in 1931, thereby anticipating almost *verbatim* Hitler's address to the NS *Frauenschaft* in Nuremberg on 8 September 1934.[11]

In imitation of continental Fascism the IFL considered the corporate state a commendable form of government, destined 'to replace the present one which is outworn and unworthy of the country, and the Empire'.[12] Its main characteristic was to be the division into three large federations of employers, employees and intellectual workers, each of them being subdivided into various categories of employment carrying different political weight according to their economic importance. These units would nominate delegates to represent their respective political interests in a 'Lower House', envisaged as the Industrial Parliament of practical experts, an advisory body to the Government with the right to pass or repeal proposed laws and to endorse the budget. The 'Upper House' was conceived as an assembly of distinguished life members who had conspicuously served the state and were to be appointed by the Sovereign on the advice of his Government.[13]

While Leese was vague in describing the constitutional framework of the future state, he laid down the hierarchical organization of the IFL more precisely. This, however, remained largely on paper, since the party never attracted enough support to implement a stratification of its membership. The highest authority with power to form, control and direct the League was the Director-General, a post held by Leese until 1939, when the general headquarters were closed down. Supervision of the local branches was assigned to county and district directors. The party was open to 'patriots desirous of giving active service to the cause of the League',[14] and the membership fee was fixed at a minimum of one shilling a month. Those who sympathized with the aims of the organization, but were not prepared to give active service, were encouraged to register as associates. The total membership was to be grouped into three divisions:

1 'Graduates Association', the future governing aristocracy.
2 'Fascist Legions', a force of disciplined loyalists for use in cases of 'national emergency'. These were to wear a standard uniform of khaki breeches, black shirts and black boots.
3 'Activist Confederations' of employers, employees and professional workers with the duty to spread Fascist thought.

In its publications the IFL appeared constantly preoccupied with two subjects – the Empire and the Jews. It valued the Empire, 'built by British pioneers, cemented by British blood', as a sacrosanct heirloom which had to be preserved intact, implying that the overseas territories could be exploited according to British interests. Emphasizing his strong belief in continuity, Leese referred to '*our* Empire, handed to us as an heritage to be guarded and passed on to those who follow us as a sacred birthright'.[15] Pressing for a confederation of the Empire states with London as the capital, Leese vigorously opposed those who appeared to surrender Britain's rights. In particular he appealed to all ex-servicemen to rally once more to the defence of the Empire by joining the IFL which opposed the Labour Party's lenient policy towards African natives.

The commitment to the Imperial tradition was firmly stated in terms of an assumed natural supremacy of Europeans:

> We are Imperialists to our Aryan backbone and believe that it was a short-sighted mistake for the government to further the Afrikaans language in a country which can only exist as a white man's land under the wing of a European power, which power is foolish indeed if it encourages the growth of the germs of separatism for the sake of a temporary sentiment.[16]

Leese retained an uncompromising view even when his Imperial aspirations clashed with the demands of his political friends abroad. Whereas the British Union of Fascists launched a pro-Italian campaign during the Abyssinian crisis, Leese opposed Mussolini's policy, alleging that the *Duce* allowed himself to be driven into war by 'Jewish gangsters' who hoped to stir black Africa into rebellion against the whites.[17] Unlike other British Nazi sympathizers who contemplated the return of former German colonies within the context of a proposed revision of the peace treaty, Leese categorically refused to return former German possessions. 'Some Hitlerites are still under the impression that the treaty of Versailles is to be torn up,' he wrote in 1931, 'this will not happen.'[18] Since a surrender of the ex-German colonies would be a betrayal of all those British soldiers and civilians who had risked their lives in the name of the Empire, Britain could only say 'these are mine; hands off; what I have I hold.'[19] As he acknowledged the validity of Germany's claim for living space, and considered it intolerable that 'a great and noble Aryan nation cannot find its place in the sun', Leese suggested that Germany should be given a free hand in Central and South America. Those countries, he argued, were at present inhabited by 'the most bastardised and degenerate race-mixture the world has ever seen',[20] and Aryan blood and civilization were badly needed.

Leese is attributed a degree of originality he does not actually deserve, when his anti-Semitism is contrasted against the Jew-hatred of his contemporaries as the only English version of racial anti-Semitism.[21] Initially, his paranoic anti-Semitism was not rooted in a theory of history which interpreted all historical developments as corollaries of racial differences, although he came to absorb the theory of racial anti-Semitism. There is no evidence for a preoccupation with racial concepts at the time when Leese founded his own organization, which significantly was called the Imperial Fascist League, indicating his attempt to launch Fascism in England within the framework of Imperial history. None of the eleven points proclaimed as the party's 'beliefs' touched upon the problem of race, Jews were not explicitly barred from membership, and the application form did not ask for the candidate's creed or descent.[22]

During the first year of its publication the *Fascist* did not concede the 'Jewish question' the prominence it was to achieve later on. If recent immigrants into Britain were said to be 'mostly of inferior races', this referred to various groups of immigrants and was not aimed at Jews in particular. The latter were opposed not in principle, but as aliens whose interests were said to be incompatible with British national interests. Since they could not be tolerated by true patriots as equals, the *Fascist* recommended that aliens should be treated as second-class citizens. They should not be employed as long as a Briton was available for a job, nor be entitled to vote, to serve on juries or in the army, but should compensate for such duties of citizenship by paying high taxes. Although one member demanded 'the drastic weeding out and expulsion' of aliens who had nothing to contribute to British life,[23] the prevalent attitude was to apply social ostracization and political repression as apt policies against all foreigners, including Jews.

A change of attitude regarding the 'Jewish problem' became apparent in the spring of 1930, when the IFL started to blame Jews for Bolshevism, freemasonry, democracy and international finance. This coincided with the first advertisement of the *Protocols* in the *Fascist* and seems to reflect Leese's sudden recognition of the existence of a world-wide Jewish conspiracy which came to him as a true revelation when he, by then already in his late forties, first read the *Protocols of the Elders of Zion*. This reading matched his bipartite concept of life which differentiated between traditional, preserving, stagnant positive forces and modern, changing, dynamic antipodes. 'Everything in this little book rang true,'[24] said Leese describing his first encounter with the *Protocols*, and quickly incorporated this new perception into his political work, which meant that henceforth Jews were regarded as the personification of an omnipotent universal foe.

Having recognized the Jew as the most dangerous threat to civilization, the myth of a Jewish world-conspiracy was fitted into the racist ideology of white supremacy, a linkage expressed in the demand for a 'clean Aryan British Empire', or a 'League of Aryan Nations', in which all Jewish influence was to be eliminated.[25] Considered worse than black, brown or yellow species, the Jews were regarded as the most dangerous threat to civilization. Depicted as a race fundamentally opposed to the character and ideals of the Nordic, all Jews were accused of composing one political organization, a secret Jewish brotherhood which united the 'nation without domicile'. They were accused of disintegrating Gentile religion, corrupting morals and ethics, fostering the cult of the decadent and degenerate in arts, fomenting class-war, breaking up the Empire, strangulating industry and finance, and aiming at universal political control.[26] Whatever was considered evil, disagreeable or deceitful was dubbed 'Jewish', a category which did not require further discussion. Whether it was the League of Nations, democratic parties, suffragettes, the gold standard, theosophy or psychoanalysis – all were considered an emanation of evil Jewish machinations.

The attribute 'Jewish' was also applied to discredit rival Fascists. Leese accused Mosley, the leader of the British Union of Fascists, of having defiled racial purity by his marriage to Cynthia Curzon, who was suspected to be of Jewish descent. Whereas Mosley quickly dropped his initial interest in the IFL and ignored the obscure movement, Leese tried to gain publicity by propagating a fictitious difference between the two groups, ridiculing his much more successful opponents as 'Kosher Fascists'. He launched a bitter campaign against the 'British Jewnion of Fascists', and even denounced the Mosleyites with the police for selling their publications in streets where the IFL had been turned away.[27]

Leese's expositions on racial questions were crude vulgarizations of concepts discussed at the time, which singled out racial criteria as the most important factors explaining the social, political and cultural identity of nations.[28] Although he did not usually acknowledge the influence of other writers, Leese's eclectic method is revealed in his personal notes, consisting of numerous excerpts of books, newspapers and pamphlets. In his own publications, he inevitably focused on the alleged conflict between Aryan civilization and Jewish barbarism, but Leese failed to outline a coherent racial ideology in a systematic fashion.

Leese proudly admitted a close relationship with the Britons, an intellectual affinity that was matched by the active participation of former members of the Britons in the campaign of the IFL. Apart from H. H. Beamish himself, others were known for having served both organizations, namely Miss Beaumont, Brig.-Gen. R. B. D. Blakeney, Capt. R. T. Cooper, A. Gittens, Capt. A. E. N. Howard, Arthur Kitson, Lt.-Col. A. H. Lane. The aggressive anti-Semitic cartoons which appeared in the *Fascist* were drawn by the same 'Goy' who had already contributed to the Britons' periodical, and some of the illustrations were merely reprints of caricatures which a decade earlier had adorned the *Hidden Hand.*[29]

To the range of ideas taken over from the Britons, Leese added some current Nazi thought. In the advertisement columns of the *Fascist*, attention was drawn to the most racist and anti-Semitic stock-in-trade published in NS Germany, such as H. K. Günther's *Racial Elements of European History* and the periodicals *Stürmer* and *Judenkenner*. In his trial on a seditious libel charge in 1936 Leese stated that he had no connexion with Germany and had started his movement before he had ever heard of Hitler.[30] His latter assertion seems credible, but there can be no doubt that National Socialist circles in London soon discovered the IFL as a congenial group ready to absorb their propaganda.

In April 1931, the *Fascist* acknowledged a donation from a 'German "National Socialist" in London', emphasizing that 'the White Races will eventually get together to fight the Asiatic peril of the present day, which is spelled J-E-W'.[31] The following month the periodical saw a contribution from Dr Thost, London correspondent of the *Völkischer Beobachter* from October 1930 until November 1935, in which he described 'Hitlerism' as a peaceful movement working for the unity of the Nordic race. Again, the *Fascist* responded quickly with an appraisal of the Hitler movement, in which one surmised 'something more far-reaching for the White Man than there is even in the Italian movement'.[32] 'Hitlerism at its base is the true Fascism of the Northern European, and true guide to our own politics in the years ahead',[33] the IFL declared in August 1932.

Hitler's advent to power was followed with keen interest, and the *Fascist* was always ready to publish articles from German correspondents, in which the need for cooperation of all Nordic races was stressed. In January 1933 the IFL adopted the swastika as its official emblem to distinguish itself from Mosley's blackshirts. The new symbol, Leese maintained, symbolized 'the White Man's Good Faith against the Jewish pollution of his civilization', and declared 'his determination finally to root out the Jewish pestilence from our midst'.[34] Simultaneously with the adoption of the swastika symbol the IFL drew attention to a new society, the Nordics, which stood for selective breeding, mental and physical fitness and the formation of character. Membership was open to 'Britons by birth and ancestry, and of Nordic blood and ideals'. The Nordics also advocated the friendship with foreign nations sharing a Nordic race-consciousness, and stressed the necessity of eliminating Jewish influence. 'If we don't do it constitutionally,' one of its speakers asserted, 'we'll do it with steel.'[35]

Leese's growing familiarity with the nature of National Socialism seems to account for the increasing rabidness of his anti-Semitic propaganda. A first, abbreviated translation of Hitler's *Mein Kampf* was published in England in October 1933.[36] Before it came out, *The Times* published extracts from the book in July 1933. Excerpts from chapter 11, section 6, entitled 'The Course of Judaism's Development' which were not identical with passages printed in *The Times*, appeared in the August edition of the *Fascist*.[37] Like other *völkisch* literature, which was regularly reviewed in the *Fascist*, *Mein Kampf* provided a fountain of inspiration for Leese, who was always ready to appropriate captivating ideas.

Leese gradually assimilated a theory of history centred on the concept of race. In 1932 he wrote:

The most precious possession of the nation is its blood, for upon the Nordic Race depend its character and its sound inherited instincts. Rome fell because of its neglect to keep pure its Nordic blood.[38]

Paraphrasing Hitler's differentiation between *Kulturschöpfer*, *Kulturträger* and *Kulturzerstörer*, Leese pointed out that civilization was established by Aryans and that only they could maintain it, while Jews had no culture of their own, led a parasitic, non-productive life and were intrinsically destructive. 'Civilization is Aryanization and Aryanization is Civilization', he argued and concluded:

The absolute subjection of the Jew to the Aryan is the first necessity for the preservation of civilization, and it is the first object of Racial Fascism to accomplish it, because all other reforms are useless until it is done.[39]

Parallels between the postulates put forward by Hitler and Leese include the belief in aristocracy and the leadership of élites as opposed to mass-participation; the appraisal of a healthy agriculture as a corner-stone for the well-being of the nation; the contrasting of 'Semitic democracy' advocating liberty, equality and fraternity with Aryan ideals of nobility, truth and justice; the distinction between 'citizens', 'subjects' and 'aliens' – *Staatsbürger, Staatsangehörige* and *Ausländer*; the cultivation of ancient pagan traditions and the image of a male-dominated society in which women would only count as potential mothers. In unison they drew attention to the 'pollution' of cultural values by the decadent, immoral and gross Jewish spirit exhibited in modern art and literature, the responsibility of Jews for prostitution and white slave traffic, and the display of 'Jewish filth' in cinemas. Both advocated a 'National Health Campaign' involving the prohibition of intermarriage with Jews and the sterilization of conveyors of hereditary diseases.

Whereas Hitler incorporated these issues into a not always unequivocal, but fundamentally coherent political framework, Leese plagiarized most of these ideas without developing them into a systematic theory, which accounts for a number of contradictions in his writings.[40] Hitler consistently treated the Jews as a race, not as a sect, and rejected the proposition that they should be regarded as a nomadic people. On the contrary, he pointed out, they established themselves wherever they considered it profitable and, protected by their religious dogma to maintain their racial purity, had retained their identity in a most remarkable way.[41] Hitler's differentiation between 'scientific', 'rational anti-Semitism' and 'emotional' or 'pogrom anti-Semitism' was echoed in the *Fascist* where the 'alien menace' was said to require an unsentimental policy inspired not by hate, but by national foresight. Similarly, Leese maintained in his autobiography that he had researched the 'Jewish question' 'in much the same scientific spirit as when I was investigating camel diseases in the world's deserts. I have been after truth, not propaganda.'[42]

In line with Hitler, Leese repeatedly urged that the 'Jew menace' be treated not as a religious issue, but as a racial problem, and pointed out that Jews converted to Christianity merely to camouflage their true identity. 'Race is the basis of all true politics', the IFL declared, and described the Jews as an inferior race-mixture, characterized by the destructive instincts the tribe had inherited from its Asian ancestors. On the other hand, it was observed that 'the Jewishness of the Jew begins to fade when he mixes with Gentiles',[43] and admitted that 'it is obvious that no hard and fast line can be scientifically drawn to make water-tight the division between Aryan and non-Aryan in cases where there has been a great mixture of blood'.[44] These statements clearly conflicted with the racist shibboleth that mixing with Jews irrevocably contaminated Gentile blood.

While such contradictions remained unsolved, Leese and his disciples appealed to patriotic sentiments to stir racial hatred. Resuming the slogan of the 'yellow peril', Jews were characterized as a 'pestiferous nomadic tribe', 'bereft of elementary humanity', 'yellow negroid horde', or 'mongrel conglomeration' of Asiatic, Negroid and Alpine strains and many articles ended with the traditional slogans of Jew-baiters: 'Perish Judah!', and 'Hep! Hep! Hooray!'. Claiming that there were three million Jews in England – 'roughly the same number as there are unemployed Englishmen'[45] – the *Fascist* urged upon its readers never to employ a Jewish doctor or dentist, never to buy from Jews and, above all, never to support any society which would not expose the Jew.

In August 1934 the IFL began to show concern about the possibility of war with Germany. 'We will not fight for the House of Rothschild', was its answer and it stated that its members would not join the British forces in the interests of Jews against men of their own Nordic race. While in principle the IFL approved of war as the legitimate means of an expanding, conquering élite, it denounced the conflicts that threatened peace in Europe as artificial machinations stirred up by Jewry. Instead of falling into this trap, it suggested that the 'Aryan nations' should combine against their real enemy, the Jew, resolving the eternal antagonism in a final Armageddon. The IFL envisaged itself as the 'rallying point for the new kind of conscientious objector, the true Patriot. But he will not be a Pacifist. He will declare war on the ENEMY – THE JEW in this country.'[46]

Like Hitler, Leese regarded the fight between the Aryan and the Jew as a matter of life and death, a 'duel with the Devil',[47] and he proposed three alternatives to master it: to kill, to sterilize or to segregate the Jews. Of these, the last seemed the most opportune policy and Leese returned to the plan that had already been advertised by H. Beamish: the Madagascar project. Only in a world free of Jews, he argued, would the Aryans be able to develop their civilization, and the Jew had to be confined to a territory of their own.

Leese completely rejected the idea of Palestine as a national home for Jews. Zionism he considered a scheme artificially created by the leaders of Jewry to maintain the group-consciousness among Jews, while actually only a few Zionists would want to go and live in Palestine.[48] The Middle East, he pointed out 'is ours by right of conquest'[49] and to give it away as a Jewish settlement area would be a betrayal of British soldiers as well as a betrayal of the Arab allies. As future Jewish territory, the IFL argued, a region should be selected which would have to be purchased by Jews. To ensure that the segregation would be complete and irreversible, an island would be the best choice. A League of Aryan Nations could then patrol the surrounding areas, and the death penalty would be imposed upon any Jew found outside the secluded territory after a given time.[50]

Frequently this rational approach to solving the 'Jewish question' was subordinated to an aggressive 'pogrom anti-Semitism'. 'To Hell or Madagascar', the *Fascist* answered the question of where the Jews would have to go when they were expelled from England, and proposed the toast 'Death to all Jews' touts and long life to racial Fascism'.[51] One IFL speaker told an enthusiastic audience of about 100 people that IFL members should greet each other by saying 'P.J.',[52] and the IFL welcomed acts of hooliganism in the East End of London as an 'orgy of Jewish window-smashing . . . a most valuable contribution to the cause of peace'.[53]

The IFL's ultimate conception of a 'final solution' was betrayed in its frequently expressed aims of wanting to rid the world of the 'Jewish plague', 'to deal ruthlessly with the two and a half million Jews', 'to remove the bestial influence of the Jew from every branch of our culture', or 'to root out the evil influence from our midst'. Although ostensibly they advocated peaceful methods, the result of their anti-Jewish crusade was to be 'the same as of whole-sale massacre'.[54]

Like some NS officials who carefully distinguished between a complacent private life and an infernal daily routine of mass-slaughter, Leese possessed a dual character. While he cared for his pets with an extreme sensibility and affection, he also brooded over the most inhuman schemes to do away with the Jews. Rather regrettably he noted that pogroms were now out of date, and out-lined the only efficient and satisfactory way of solving the problem in unambiguous terms:

It must be admitted that the most certain and permanent way of disposing of the Jews would be to exterminate them by some humane method such as the lethal chamber.[55]

Although Leese qualified his statement by saying that it was a practicable but at the time not expedient procedure, the concept of an ultimate solution was clearly spelt out.

Unlike the Britons, who firmly adhered to Christian beliefs and traditions, the IFL questioned the Church, which it considered to be a judaized institution, 'one of the principal agents for the spread of defeatism and internationalism . . . advancing the fatal Masonic and Jewish teaching of Universal Brotherhood'.[56] Leese wanted Christmas to be understood as the commemoration of 'Yule Tide. An Anti-Semitic Festival', the 'Celebration of a great Yid-sloshing'. He had special cards printed, decorated with a cartoon illustrating the attempted rape of a young girl, representing civilization, by Jewry, depicted as an aggressive, vile snake, with a patriotic knight in the background. The text of this 'Christmas card' read: 'Get a move on, St George! With Arnold Leese's best wishes for a Happy Yule Tide and a White Man's New Year!'[57]

The image of St George defeating the dragon was also conjured on the occasion of the coronation of King George VI. The IFL reiterated its belief in monarchical leadership and loyalty to the throne. Again trying to link up the present with a more happy past, it described the fight against Jewry as the Sovereign's most important duty:

The Jewish dragon, whose foetid consuming breath penetrates into almost every channel of national life, is there . . . to be slain! . . . Let but our King turn upon the foul dragon and pierce it to the heart, and the instinctive determination to uphold the Royal dignity which moved the loyal multitudes on Coronation Day will itself be eclipsed by the enthusiastic joy and love with which men, white and coloured, the world over, will greet the Emperor who followed the footsteps of King Edward I, saved their civilization and kept it clean.[58]

Leese never faltered in his anti-Jewish agitation, not even when the persecution and extermination of Jews under the NS regime became known in its entirety. He continued to support the Jew-baiters, particularly J. Streicher, and denounced the Nuremberg trials as an 'act of Revenge taken against those who were chiefly authoritative in the German attempt to free their country from the twin plagues, Jewry and Freemasonry'.[59] Leese, who had been honoured with an occasional report of his activities in the *Stürmer*, proved a loyal student of Nazism and offered the defendants of Nuremberg to give evidence on the 'Jewish question'. He supported their policy without reservations and strongly opposed the efforts of some neo-Fascists to whitewash Hitler's intentions and decisions. This becomes apparent in a letter he sent to Dell, secretary of the Britons, which also reveals Leese's impulsive, unrefined personal style:

> The theory makes Hitler & Co. out to be raving madmen who never understood their Jew; and fell like amateurs into their 'plot'. No, it's not for me, that story! and I am no hero-worshipper! That the Jews were working for war against Hitler we all know: but why make out that Hitler was blind and a tool of theirs? He walked into no trap: what evidence have you that he was in any way a dunderhead? All the evidence seems to me that he knew his Jew inside and out and would be the last man to fall into any trap. What else could he have done but what he did? We all know he wanted peace with this country not war, but he wasn't allowed to have it. No, Dell, I think it's all Bunk with a big B. Sorry Jewish Question coming to an end. It is in fair demand.[60]

A chronic lack of funds limited the IFL's scope of activity throughout its existence. Leese's bourgeois background was reflected in his repeated demand for sound financial methods as the precondition for all successful enterprises, which let him keep all his activities strictly within the means of the IFL.[61] The stock was provided by Leese's own savings, which he had accumulated during his time abroad. Small donations contributed by members seem to have been sufficient to cover the current expenditure. When need arose, as with Leese's trial, the IFL launched special fund-raising campaigns, like the 'Aryan Defence Fund', which yielded £107 8s. 4d. within four months.[62] After World War II Beamish appointed Leese as his heir to continue the anti-Jewish propaganda. When A. S. Leese died himself eight years later, his widow turned his legacy over to a neo-Fascist group under Colin Jordan.

In addition to its poor financial circumstances, the IFL failed to attract a large membership. It was estimated by the contemporary press at some 800 persons, but a more realistic figure was probably arrived at by the Home Office, which in 1934 put the IFL membership at 150 people.[63] Leese, who even ejected ineffective members, perceived the IFL as a virile élite organization whose members were to act as 'drummers' to awake their contemporaries and to open their eyes on the deficiencies of the democratic state, an evil machination of Jewry. In its lack of an ostentatious leader- and hero-cult the IFL differed markedly from other Fascist parties. While the rôle of a national father-figure was reserved for the monarch, Leese himself, who was no charismatic leader but a psychopathic eccentric, acted as Jack-of-all-trades in his movement, editing the periodical, addressing meetings and selling the *Fascist* in the streets.

In 1934 the IFL opened two branches in addition to their headquarters, in Hackney and Chalk Farm. The *Fascist* of December 1938 listed four branches in London, one country branch in Maidenhead, and seven 'centres for enquiry', presumably the addresses of some of its members, in Richmond, Kensington, Birmingham, Worthing, Belfast, Manchester and Southampton. These branches served as meeting places for regular assemblies of members, which were addressed by various speakers usually on some aspect of the 'Jewish problem', and as centres for the dissemination of their publications. In 1936, when the anti-Semitic campaign in the East End gained momentum, the IFL stepped up its campaign, advertising regular outdoor meetings at Victoria Park Square, Finsbury Square, Dalston, Mansfield Road and Hoxton. Benefitting from the BUF's turn to anti-Semitism, the mobilization of anti-Fascist forces, and an increasing militancy of Fascist and anti-Fascist groups, the IFL evidently contributed to the stirring up of racial hatred in areas with a large Jewish community.

Undoubtedly it was frequently members of the IFL who were responsible for acts of hooliganism commonly ascribed to 'the Fascists', which for most people were synonymous with Mosley's group. One can safely assume, for example, that IFL supporters were responsible for what became known as the 'swimming-pool outrage', a case which attracted public attention in May 1936. Oil and reddish dye were poured into the swimming-pool of a roadhouse, and a swastika sign was left with a placard 'Britons Awake. Your property is passing into Jewish hands. Bolshevism, Freemasonry and P.E.P. are Jewish. Wars are the Jews' harvest. We will not fight for the House of Rothschild.'[64]

The police were fully aware of the vicious character of IFL propaganda and considered its activities more provocative and likely to stir anti-Semitic feelings than those of any other political organization.[65] Small stickers posted in tube stations and on shop windows, each decorated with a swastika, clearly betrayed the standard diction of the IFL: 'Britons! The Jews are stealing everything – even your names!'; 'You Fools! To let the Jews control your politics'; 'When Edward I expelled the Jews, Britain found her soul'; 'Don't take your kiddies to see filthy Jewish films'; 'Britons! Do not allow Jews to tamper with white girls!'.[66]

Conscious of the fact that they did not receive much public attention, the IFL did try to publicize its name in sporadic campaigns. In February 1933, for example, prominent guests who had attended a Friends of Palestine dinner received a cryptic message from A. S. Leese on IFL stationery: 'Your name has been noted as that of a guest and supporter of the enemies in our country. Yrs Faithfully Sec-Gen.'. Lady Astor, one of the addressees, inquired as to who the 'enemies of the country' were. Instead of a reply, she received several copies of the *Fascist* and a mimeographed note recommending the purchase of further IFL publications.[67] On another occasion the IFL hoisted a swastika-flag on Westminster County Hall in an effort to attract public attention.[68]

A less conspicuous aspect of IFL propaganda was to distribute leaflets addressed to particular sections of the population who were likely to take in the anti-Jewish message because of Jewish competition in their occupational realm. British taxi-drivers, for example, were encouraged to take action against the issue of licences to Jews; tradesmen were incited against Jews who were said to import goods from abroad and to sell at cut-throat prices; 'Gentile Jesters' and musicians were asked to protest against Jew-controlled agencies and ostracize these 'people of pestilence'; finally, shoppers were asked to boycott Jewish shops, which were said to drive British traders out of business.[69]

Although the IFL constantly stressed that it had no links with Mosley's BUF, there was some fluctuation between the membership of the two groups. Mosley, receiving much more publicity than the IFL, had better opportunities, and Leese's fear of losing members to this competitor was not unreasonable. But the IFL also attracted Mosleyites who were dissatisfied with their leader's 'soft' attitude regarding the Jews. Thus in 1934, BUF officers of the Bristol and Wolverhampton branches joined the IFL because it promoted 'the Racial Fascism which the Empire requires'.[70] Leese's particular assessment of people and the criteria he considered important when admitting turncoats follow from a letter he wrote about a new recruit from the ranks of the BUF:

> I got to know this youngster well on Saturday. Left the Mosley Party in disgust; well grounded on the Jews; strongly wanting to be activist, with gas chambers complete. . . . He is not Nordic, a pleasant face with a hint of Dinaric. Hazel eyes. But likes our race pamphlets.[71]

Although the IFL failed to mobilize large crowds and to generate a charismatic leader, it was not without significance: in the first place, it presented itself as a devoted mouthpiece of NS ideology in England. Secondly, the movement provided a political home for those who shared a fanatical Jew-hatred and profound anti-modernism. After the Britons had dwindled away, the IFL maintained the continuity of an organized anti-Semitic fringe with largely the same actors. Thirdly the IFL was instrumental in creating a sense of insecurity among parts of the Jewish population, particularly in London, which in turn entailed political repercussions with the mobilization of a defence against organized anti-Semitism.

For the analysis of anti-Semitism, the most important aspect of IFL propaganda is the self-perpetuating nature of anti-Semitism, which has already been observed in the case of the Britons. Like the latter, the IFL started from a platform of extreme patriotism, prone to absorb any theory which could explain the national decline in terms of external causes, but devoid of positive anti-Semitism. Once it stumbled on the Jew and discovered in him the eternal conspirator against the welfare of non-Jews, the totality of anti-Semitism began to manifest itself. After the opponent had been identified, the only way to restore harmony was to remove the Jewish influence, an object that inspired various plans of implementation, ranging from the disfranchisement of Jews to their actual extermination.

5 British Union of Fascists

The British Union of Fascists (BUF), founded in October 1932 by Sir Oswald Mosley, was the only group among radical right organizations in Britain which succeeded in attracting wide public attention and some mass support. Mosley's formula at the time was 'action', whereby he sought to differentiate himself from his contemporaries who, in his opinion, were conventional, passive, mediocre politicians incapable or unwilling to rise to the challenge of the period.

Until 1931, Mosley's political career had been extremely successful.[1] He was born in 1896, went to Winchester and Sandhurst and served in the RFC until the spring of 1916 when he was invalided out of the army. In December 1918, Mosley was elected into Parliament as a Coalition-Unionist. In May 1920 he advanced into the highest ranks of the establishment when, in the presence of King George V and Queen Mary, he married Cynthia Curzon, a daughter of the Foreign Secretary.

Opposing the Government's Irish policy, Mosley crossed the floor in November 1920. He favoured a dominion solution, granting Ireland independence with restrictions in defence and foreign policy, and rapidly gained publicity when he took a lead in condemning the atrocities committed by British troops and challenged the Government on its policy of reprisals. Formulating an ethnocentric concept of foreign policy, which he retained throughout the 1920s and 1930s, he suggested a policy of non-intervention and withdrawal instead of ambitious attempts to police the world at Britain's expense.

As an independent Mosley was returned to Parliament in the general elections of 1922 and 1923. In 1924, after a brief flirtation with the Liberals, he joined the Labour Party and began to distinguish himself as an expert on economic policy. By a narrow margin he failed to win his contest against Neville Chamberlain in a Birmingham constituency in the general election of 1924, but he was returned to the House in the by-election of Smethwick in December 1926 and retained his seat in the following election. He rapidly advanced in the Labour Party, and was elected to its National Executive Committee in 1927. When Labour took office after the election of 1929, he was appointed Chancellor of the Duchy of Lancaster.

Mosley's political wanderings betrayed dissatisfaction and restlessness as well as a profound sense of self-importance. He developed a widely admired capacity to capture his audiences, and cultivated the image of an ambitious young man – gifted, self-assured, obstinate – who would rapidly aspire to the very top. Mosley obviously enjoyed the public attention he received and fancied himself in the rôle of a main actor on the contemporary stage. His rapturous, emotional style of public speech matched his perception of history as a continuous drama, an attitude already apparent in a speech delivered in 1925:

> We are faced with a desperate situation. We have reached a supreme crisis in the history of humanity. We stand, indeed, at the cross-roads of destiny. For good or ill we live in an epic age. Once again the lash of great ordeal stings an historic race to action. Once more the soul of man is on the march. A lead is the clamant demand of the hour. . . . We must awaken and mobilize our country to save itself by heroic measures before the sands of time and fate run out.[2]

It is difficult to assess to what degree Mosley really was concerned about the welfare of the nation and not just acting the part of the non-conformist. How little he was prepared to submit to party discipline and majority decisions revealed itself in the controversy over unemployment policy. Realizing that the departments concerned did not sympathize with the proposals he had evolved in close cooperation with Keynes and Strachey, Mosley in January 1930 submitted a memorandum directly to the Prime Minister in which he outlined a scheme of immediate state-intervention to solve the economic problems.

In what became known as the 'Mosley Memorandum' he analysed the economic depression, which he thought was characterized by a lack of consumption. As a remedy, he suggested a raise of purchasing power in order to create a market which could occupy the labour of the unemployed as well as of those who would become redundant by future rationalizations. Pressing for the development of the home market, Mosley dismissed the priority of export trade. He argued that Britain had lost many of her overseas markets for good, due to the rapid industrialization of former customers and to an increasing competition on the world market. As a short-term relief for unemployment he suggested comprehensive public work schemes, to be financed by loans, complemented by emergency retirement pensions and the raising of the school-leaving age.[3]

During the ensuing debate, Mosley expanded his proposals and added the dimension of 'inter-Imperial planning' based on mutual agreement rather than on one-sided exploitation and aggressiveness. Such imports as were necessary, namely raw-materials and foodstuffs, he suggested should be bought from countries within the British Empire, who in turn would buy from Britain. This, he argued, would lead to the 'largest and most economically self-contained area in the world, bound together as it is by a common loyalty to the Crown'.[4] With these proposals, Mosley pitted himself against the orthodox belief in free-market economy. The report on his memorandum by the Unemployment Committee, headed by Snowden, categorically rejected his proposals and maintained that in the long run the economic equilibrium would restore itself. Once the staple industries of cotton and wool, iron, steel and engineering, coal and shipbuilding had passed the temporary slump, it was argued, the competitive power of British industry would increase and the general prosperity would be restored.[5]

In view of the firm opposition against his proposals, Mosley resigned from office on 20 May 1930. When a week later he advocated his views in the parliamentary debate on unemployment, he scored an impressive personal triumph, receiving the warmest congratulations on his performance from many colleagues and the press. This recurred when he argued his case at the Labour Party Congress in October 1930, and many observers became convinced that he was the man to supersede MacDonald. A resolution to reconsider his memorandum was, however, narrowly defeated, and Mosley remained on the fringes of power. Impatient to see something done, and disillusioned with his previous experiences of crossing the floor, he decided to found a new party and to appeal to what seemed to be a large section of his generation – those who were equally bored and frustrated with the 'ostrich brigade of Old Gang politicians'.[6] This move again betrayed Mosley's relentless quest for personal success which increasingly distorted his assessment of British politics.

In February 1931, Mosley founded the New Party. With him, a few other MPs seceded from the Labour Party: his wife, O. Baldwin, W. J. Brown, R. Forgan and J. Strachey. Failing to win popular support in the general election of October 1931, Mosley finally turned to Fascism. Intrigued by the success of Mussolini, whom he visited in January 1932, he founded the British Union of Fascists in October 1932, a paramilitary organization modelled after similar continental movements.

Adopting the label 'Fascist' and advocating a totalitarian form of government lost Mosley the support of former associates – most notably that of John Strachey and Harold Nicolson. It also alienated potential followers who had agreed with his economic policies and his demand for a corporate state. Arguing that it was an anachronism that the power of the executive should be limited and that the government be subjected to parliamentary rules, Mosley went far beyond those of his contemporaries who favoured corporatism as a formula suitable to accommodate plural interests, thereby guaranteeing social harmony.[7] In *The Greater Britain*, Mosley's political platform of 1932, he proposed to invest the government with absolute power, enabling it to overrule paralysing opposition, which in his opinion had no constructive contribution to make. Here, he expressed in principle the political philosophy that guided him throughout his political career.

Since the BUF never attained power and never thus implemented its political platform, its ideology can only be ascertained with reference to its theoretical pretensions. The indiscriminate use of the term 'Fascism' has rightly been criticized, since the preoccupation with similarities neglects the more significant differences among totalitarian movements, rooted in their specific historical conditions. Despite these reservations, the classification of the BUF as a Fascist party seems valid, because it shared some principle assumptions with comparable movements in other countries: its policy was devoted to safeguard the 'national interest', which was hypostatized as the ultimate criterion transcending sectional interests; it opposed the parliamentary system in favour of the authoritarian state ruled by a leader; it defined itself as a dynamic movement rather than as a conventional party committed to its particular interests and planks; it attempted the mobilization and hierarchical organization of the masses.[8]

Mosley successfully copied the propaganda techniques of his continental fore-runners. Drummers, flags and the singing of the national anthem were prominent features in his campaign. He placed great emphasis on the notions of leadership and discipline, and marched his uniformed 'Blackshirts' in military fashion through London. In return, he was acclaimed by his followers, who believed in him as the man who 'has welded us, men and women from all ranks and all trades and all professions, into a Corporate movement that is to be the fore-runner of the Corporate State'.[9] Mosley's success at permeating the life of his followers, their total subjugation and identification with the movement, is best expressed in the following BUF poetry:

> Mosley! Leader of thousands!
> Hope of our manhood we proudly hail thee!
> Raise we this song of allegiance,
> For we are sworn and we shall not fail thee!
> Lead us! We fearlessly follow
> To conquest and freedom – or else to death![10]

Black House, the party's London headquarters, functioned as a community centre where members spent their time regimented by a rigid schedule. Youth sections were formed, camps set up, 'troops' inspected in order to drill the members for their ascent to power. With emphasis upon physical fitness and comradeship, Mosley was eager to present his movement as a symbol of British manhood, distinct from the parties of effeminacy and decay which he considered typical of democratic societies. Time and again he stressed that the BUF was the party of the young generation, destined to build a 'new Britain', to restore Britain's greatness:

> The story of our generation is an epic of the human race that has gone from victory to victory, from triumph to triumph. . . . We have fought and conquered while they muddled and destroyed. . . . Their system is decadent, rotten, reeking with the stench of corruption and decay.[11]

Loyal to traditional institutions such as the monarchy, and affirmative of traditional values like Christianity, at the beginning of its political campaign the BUF lacked the revolutionary element that was inherent in National Socialism. While it cultivated a dogmatic hostility against Communism, it initially also lacked the missionary claim of representing a bulwark versus world Jewry, again a particular trait of National Socialism. Instead, the 'Jewish question' was dismissed as totally irrelevant to Fascism *per se*. In the BUF's first official statement on 'Fascism and the Jews' it was pointed out that 'the early propaganda of the Nazis against the Jews has considerably complicated their accession to power and their ability to deal with the Socialist, Communist and financial enemies of the State'.[12] 'In Germany,' it was argued shortly afterwards, 'anti-Semitism is a symptom, not of Fascism but of Germany',[13] and the Italian Fascists, who had firmly established themselves by avoiding any conflict with sectional interests, were held up for emulation.

When launching Fascism in England, Mosley evidently contemplated introducing an anti-Jewish plank by referring to an alleged conspiracy of 'international Jewish bankers'. Harold Nicolson, who perceived 'a Nazi note, a yellow press note in these denunciations – which will cause many people to blink'[14] dissuaded him from the idea, arguing that it would be detrimental to pick on the Jews. The BUF press repeatedly pointed out that Jew-baiting in every shape and form was forbidden by order of the movement. It stressed that an 'alien menace' existed and argued that in view of more than two million unemployed Britons, foreigners should not be permitted to enter the country. Those who had already come to Britain, it was suggested, should be compelled to leave. This policy was to apply to all foreigners – Poles, Jews and Lascars alike. Jews were not to be treated as a separate nationality, but were to be judged according to their performance as citizens. Those who had fought for King and Country and had thus proved themselves were positively set off against the 'low type of foreign Jews', who were said to have come to Britain as parasites.

The general anti-alien attitude, an ultra-nationalist answer to contemporary problems, was soon superseded by a specifically anti-Jewish propaganda. This change in policy was signalized in a front-page article in *Blackshirt* in November 1933, in which the allegation that Jews constituted a state within the state was revived. Jewish interests were said to dominate the press, international finance and the established parties, and Jews were accused of using their influence for the benefit of their own race, which was considered diametrically opposed to British interests. One no longer differentiated between 'good' and 'bad', 'loyal' and 'disloyal', 'national-minded' and 'international-minded' Jews, and instead considered the Jews the symbol and source of all evil. The gist of the argument was that Anglo-Jewry, inflamed by the fate of their kin under the new German government, tried to embroil Britain in another war with Germany:

> The Jews have now organized as a racial minority within the State to conduct a furious agitation with all the force of their great money power, which can have no effect except to drag this country towards war with Germany.[15]

Although the BUF continuously denied attacking the Jews on racial or religious grounds, racial categories emerged in this article as implicit criteria for defining a Jew, whose innate instincts were said to determine his identity. 'International Jewry' and 'Jewish finance' were treated as autonomous political realities and declared to be anti-British. Jews were thus identified as the main counter-force against British interests, and said to sponsor all that was perceived as an indication of national decline – communism, socialism, conservatism, democracy, the press, cinema, broadcasting and, of course, the vigorous opposition against the only movement that put 'Britain first'.

The most important aspect of this article, which inaugurated the BUF's anti-Semitic campaign, was that it attributed to the Jews an extraordinary influence far exceeding their numerical strength. Thus the BUF began to exalt Jewry as a fictitious unit and succumbed to the myth that the world was placed under a Jewish yoke. Once it had come to define the interests of Jewry as fundamentally opposed to the welfare of Britain, it acknowledged the existence of a 'Jewish question', which it had previously denied. The logical conclusion was that it had to ally with like-minded patriotic movements who wanted to liberate themselves from the alien mastery.

After the *Blackshirt* had ventured a sweeping indictment against Jewry in November 1933, the anti-Jewish issue was toned down in the ensuing months. It was not resumed until Lord Rothermere, whose *Daily Mail* had come out with a 'Hurrah for the Blackshirts' in January 1934, publicly dissociated himself from the BUF in July 1934. In the meantime, attacks against Jews were conspicuously absent from the publications of the party. Even so, the BUF's hostility against Jews was the substantial matter of controversy raised in the open correspondence between Mosley and Rothermere over the latter's withdrawal. Whether or not Rothermere's position was, as Mosley maintains, caused by Jewish threats to stop advertising in Rothermere's papers[16] – the fact remains that the BUF's anti-Semitic alignment was noted and discussed. In his letter of 12 July 1934 Mosley repeated the arguments already articulated in the *Blackshirt*, and justified the exclusion of Jews from the BUF:

> We do not admit Jews to membership of our Movement because (a) they have bitterly attacked us; (b) they have organized as an international movement, setting their racial interests above the national interests, and are, therefore, unacceptable as members of a national movement which aims at national organization and revival.[17]

In his reply Rothermere expressed his disappointment that Mosley, whom he considered gifted with a unique personal appeal, had not taken the lead of a Conservative front against Socialism. He insisted that he could never support 'any movement with an anti-Semitic bias, any movement which had dictatorship as one of its objectives, or any movement which would substitute a "corporate state" for the Parliamentary institutions of this country'.[18] After this episode the BUF adopted an unrestrained anti-Semitic policy and began to employ the full range of themes instrumental to anti-Semitic propaganda. The *Blackshirt* of 2 November 1934 heralded 'The Leader's Great Clarion Call' which was to mark a new phase in British Facism,

> the commencement of a new battle in British history in which the forces are arrayed – on one hand the great cleansing spirit of Fascism, and on the other, organized Jewry, representing an unclean, alien influence in our national and imperial life.[19]

During the ensuing months, Jews were systematically juxtaposed against the British society at large and accused of anti-British behaviour. Opposition at Fascist meetings was no longer attributed to local Jews – which indeed would have been a justified case – but was blamed upon the anonymous entity of Jewish finance, which was said to inflame, support and finance anti-Fascism. The existence of a genuine left-wing front against Fascism was denied and said to be the wicked invention of Jewish masters who paid the mob to yell,[20] while in reality British workers were 'perfectly prepared to turn out and welcome us and to hear the British Union case'.[21]

The exculpatory argument that Mosley's outbursts against Jewry were a response to the bitter attacks from organized Jewry, those who 'went out of their way to be provoked' does not exonerate him from anti-Semitism. In November 1933, when the BUF first ventured anti-Jewish propaganda, it was hardly 'a Jewish malaise . . . to be obsessed with Fascism'.[22] Many Jews indeed expressed a firm disapproval of Nazi anti-Semitism and launched a campaign to boycott German goods as the most effective form of protest. Others, in Germany as well as in other countries, in fact appeared rather credulous when assessing their future under the National Socialist regime. As yet, Fascism *per se* was generally considered to be a political movement aimed at an authoritarian state which would weld the nation into a whole and exclude any form of opposition. It was not, however, synonymous with the developments that gradually emerged under National Socialism – legalized terror, racism and cultivation of violence.

The columns of the *Jewish Chronicle* convey beyond doubt that at first established Jewry opposed Fascism not on principle, but only when alarmed by anti-Jewish innuendoes. Thus, in January 1933 the paper firmly asserted 'Sir Oswald has definitely arrived at the safe haven of tolerance and common sense'.[23] At that time the *Blackshirt* even acknowledged Anglo-Jewry's political restraint and argued that 'any Jew attacking members of the BUF does so, not as a Jew, but as a Red'.[24] The replacement of 'Reds' by 'Jews' as a negative object of identification and the main target of attack was therefore not only objectively, but also in the self-understanding of the BUF an important revision of its attitude against Jews. To suggest that 'official Jewry – both through its publications and through the utterances and actions of many of its leading men – gave its warm approval to these outrageous attacks on the Mosley movement'[25] was a demagogical simplification. Both its contentions – that the anti-Fascist movement was exclusively Jewish, and that Jewry as an organized unit sponsored anti-Fascism – were manifestly false.

Apart from postulating a distinct, homogenous Jewish behaviour, the BUF earmarked Jews with derogatory physical characteristics stressing their alleged foreignness. This completed the image of a repulsive, totally un-English group, which was purported in public speeches, caricatures and in the following BUF poem:

His hair was sleek and full of oil,
And so his manner too,
His hands were far too soft for toil,
The Son, of a Son, of a Jew.

. . .

Wholesale trading is in his line,
Britons he'll often sue,
When they go broke for him it's fine,
The Son, of a Son, of a Jew.[26]

The BUF categorically denied that Jews could possibly add a valuable contribution to British life, that they could effectively assimilate, or that they could ever be completely absorbed. 'Jewish' was used as an epithet synonymous to unscrupulous, dishonest and unpatriotic. This issue was taken up by Lord Camrose in a libel suit against the BUF paper *Action* and its editor, John Beckett. On 2 April 1936 it published an article implying that Camrose was of Jewish extraction and that his paper, the *Daily Telegraph*, was subservient to international finance. The jury agreed that the allegations were not true and that the article was defamatory. Damages of £12,500 were awarded to Lord Camrose, £7500 to the *Daily Telegraph*.[27] The BUF's indiscriminate opposition against Jews as such became obvious in Beckett's defence. He apologized to Lord Camrose, regretting that he had relied on false information. He explained that to him 'two of the deadliest insults to address to a man were to tell him that he was a Jew and that his financial interests were far greater outside his country than inside it'.[28]

BUF propaganda provides an excellent documentation that 'half-hearted' and 'total', 'normal' and 'excessive' anti-Semitism cannot be divided. Because of its reluctance either to acknowledge the totality of the ideology it had adopted or to renounce it *in toto*, the BUF got entangled in logical inconsistencies and contradictions which became particularly apparent in its attitude on race. It was pointed out that the British Empire, embracing a multiplicity of races, could not afford the stigmatization of one nation as inferior or outcast. On the other hand, a hierarchy of races was assumed in which Jews ranked as 'a rabble race'.[29] Mosley himself argued that British social sense and justice had always prevented debasing race-mixtures and 'pollution', and had relieved Britain of the necessity to pass protective legislation to safeguard her racial purity. If, however, this innate race-consciousness would one day decline, such legislation would have to be introduced.[30]

Mosley maintained that Jews were mentally and physically different and 'more remote from British character than any German or Frenchman, for they are Westerners, and the Jews are Orientals',[31] yet he used the term 'British race' without properly defining it. Other BUF officers more pointedly considered the British a people of predominantly Nordic blood, a creative and expanding race of pioneers and empire builders, infinitely superior to its essentially destructive Jewish antagonist, which was said to seek fulfilment through the overthrow of western civilization. Evaluating the 'debasing' impact of 'Jewish culture' upon the host society, A. K. Chesterton compared it to a poisonous cancer producing decay: 'When parasites crawl in and out of art like woodlice, then culture is decadent and the people brought face to face with doom.'[32]

The BUF subscribed to the conception characteristic of modern anti-Semitism, the conjunction of the myths of blood and of a Jewish world conspiracy. Jews were not only seen as an eternally foreign, inferior element whose religion, ethics and instincts were anathema to Europeans, but an innate aggressiveness was attributed to them which allegedly distinguished them as a singular peril threatening the very existence of the nation.[33] While the various charges BUF speakers and writers levelled against Jews to denounce them as a political, economic, social and cultural evil have been enumerated elsewhere,[34] its schemes for solving the 'Jewish question' once in power deserve closer investigation.

Ostensibly, the BUF rejected Jew-baiting, persecution and pogroms as counter-productive and un-British. Instead, compulsory Zionism was advocated as a peaceful 'final solution' – a phrase repeatedly used by Mosley himself. The policy of segregation and deportation of Jews was advocated in the BUF press, and was popularized in the following BUF song:

> Abie, Abie, now that we've tumbled you
> You'll go crazy before we are done with you
> What with your cut-price tactics,
> Secret meetings in your attics,
> It'll be grand, when you leave our land
> On the barges we've made for you.[35]

Although the policy proposed as a solution to the 'Jewish question' was to be implemented without use of violence, it appeared to be of essential importance for the future of the nation, 'a matter of life and death for our people'.[36] Thus it assumed the same degree of qualitative importance for the BUF as for other anti-Semitic groups as a key for survival, rationalized as 'a natural reaction to the uncertainties of our age, especially on the part of a nation which has known and still feels the encircling menace of remorseless enemies'.[37] Since the recovery of the nation was considered to be pending upon segregation, its total application was of utmost importance. Again racial criteria were to be decisive in ascertaining who was a Jew, and race-consciousness was advocated as a most natural biological urge:

> Anti-Semitism is intrinsically a normal reaction to the anti-social activities habitually practised by the alien. . . . Exactly as the human blood stream, infected by a poisonous bacillus, responds by mustering germ devourers to attack and eliminate the invader, so does a race conscious community at once mobilize its forces to fight the alien influences which instinct teaches would imperil its very existence.[38]

The BUF never solved the question of where the Jews would have to go once they were expelled from Britain. Neither Palestine nor any other territory within the British Empire was considered suitable as future settlement areas, since these regions were already occupied. Some vast wasteland had to be found, it was argued, where the Jews could establish a life of their own and would cease to lead a parasitical existence. Again Madagascar was mentioned, but not promoted as the party's official solution. The BUF did not consider it Britain's duty to free the world from the 'Jewish pest' and was satisfied to have found an answer to her own 'Jewish problem': expulsion, which would 'restore the glorious idealism of our Imperial tradition'.[39]

Mosley's proposals for mass-deportation have been described as 'a complete *non sequitur*' in his political campaign.[40] Yet he himself referred to the 'Jewish problem' as 'a European question of first-class magnitude, in which Britain must offer leadership in accord with British tradition'.[41] While to him it remained only one aspect of British Fascism, other high-ranking BUF members evolved their entire propaganda around this issue. Like Mosley's explications, their anti-Jewish remarks took the form of theoretical statements of policy and cannot be excused as momentary responses to offensive Jewish behaviour. This became particularly apparent during the campaign for the London County Council elections in 1937, in which the BUF advertised itself as a champion against the parties of Jewry. Every vote cast, Raven Thomson, an executive member of the party, explained after the election, was a vote on the 'Jewish question'. Another speaker confirmed that this was the party's main concern when he argued: 'We have given the Jews notice to quit and next time we are going to see they are cleared out altogether.'[42]

The totalitarian dimension of BUF anti-Semitism is belittled when it is explained as a mere by-product of the jargon of street-corner meetings, arising out of the context of stormy campaigns. It can be observed from a number of speeches delivered by BUF officers, who elaborated the 'Jewish question' as their favourite theme. E. G. Clarke, who acquired a particular reputation for the incitement of racial hatred, confessed: 'For my part, I have no intention to mingle with them [i.e. the Jews] whatsoever. The only time when I would visit the land of the waving palm is when the gas masks are issued.' Rejecting any differentiation between 'good' and 'bad' Jews, Clarke suggested on another occasion 'perhaps the best thing to do when you meet a good Jew is to shoot him'.[43]

A number of BUF officers well-known for their rabid anti-Semitism left the BUF, disappointed with its lack of instantaneous action against Jews. John Beckett, A. K. Chesterton and William Joyce were the most prominent members who seceded. Beckett launched a 'National Socialist League', Chesterton a 'League of Empire Loyalists', and Joyce went to Germany to render his service to the National Socialist regime. Others joined the IFL, which devoted itself exclusively to the fight against the 'Jewish menace'. Although they did not remain with the movement, they contributed to the public image of the BUF advertising it as destined to free Britain from 'the tentacles of the Jew's tenacity' and arguing that the Jews 'must be totally eradicated if the blood of Christian life is to flow unrestrained.'[44]

This vulgar element in BUF propaganda cannot be isolated from the more respectable part of the movement. It dominated a substantial section of the BUF press and Mosley himself, as the supreme leader of the movement, cannot be released from responsibility for the entire campaign, including its anti-Semitism. Despite the fact that, given his other activities, he cannot possibly have supervised all that went into print, it is unlikely that he was unaware of the general bearing of the party press and that he left its editorial policy entirely to the members in charge.[45] When the police noted dissension within the BUF headquarters in 1936 the controversy focused on the question as to whether the BUF should modify its anti-Semitism. It is significant that this suggestion was equated with 'retreat' by those who pressed for an unabating anti-Jewish campaign.[46] As long as Mosley, who was known to claim an autocratic position within the movement, allowed them to indulge in an anti-Semitic campaign, he appeared to condone their efforts.

It has been argued that the BUF adopted anti-Semitism in an attempt to revive its flagging fortunes by exploiting the latent popular hostility against Jews.[47] This interpretation ignores the fact that the BUF began to propagate anti-Jewish slogans when the future of the movement was still undecided. A definite decline only set in after Rothermere and other prominent supporters dissociated themselves from the party, disconcerted precisely by its anti-Semitism, its totalitarian ideology, its increasing use of violence and display of Nazi propaganda techniques. The resumption of the anti-Semitic campaign in the autumn of 1934 appears not so much as a new policy intended to compensate for growing losses, but as the continuation of a theme which, probably due to Rothermere's influence, had been temporarily dropped.

As far as the mass appeal of anti-Semitism in Britain was concerned, Mosley seems to have been aware of the adverse effects of Jew-baiting on the party image, an understanding that is reflected in his directive not to indulge in anti-Jewish attacks liable to lead to arrests.[48] The doubtful propaganda value of anti-Semitism was repeatedly brought home when members resigned over the issue. Much publicity was given to G. Wegg-Prosser, a former Blackshirt candidate in East London, who left the BUF in May 1937. In his letter of resignation to Mosley he argued:

Anti-Jewish propaganda, as you and Hitler use it, is a gigantic side-tracking stunt, a smoke-screen to cloud thought and divert action with regard to our real problems. . . . You side-track the demand for social justice by attacking the Jew, you give the people a false answer and unloose the lowest mob passions.[49]

The conclusion that the BUF's turn to anti-Semitism suggested itself because its leaders were psychologically predisposed towards anti-Semitism[50] appears equally far-fetched. Mosley relished the idea of witnessing a dramatic period in history on which he wanted eagerly to leave his impact, but this is not to be equated with fear of imminent disaster. In view of his outstanding career until 1932, he cannot be justly summed up as a paranoid and insecure person, harbouring the traits typical of anti-Semites. The fact that he excelled in the sport of fencing hardly seems sufficient reason to characterize him as a solitary personality, and the image of a mourning widower sublimating his grief over the death of his first wife by devoting himself exclusively to politics appears defective given the fact that Mosley continued to enjoy the company of close friends and rapidly became attached to Diana Mitford, his future wife.[51]

In evaluating BUF anti-Semitism, two trends have to be considered: on the one hand the fact that from the outset the movement attracted convinced anti-Semites, on the other the progressive incorporation of anti-Semitism into the political programme of the BUF. The first observation suggests that by 1933 anti-Semitism was in the air, an issue that was present and only needed expatiation. Those susceptible to it flocked to the BUF, a movement which professed to stand for 'Britain first'. Their anti-Jewish prejudice was reinforced by the active involvement of many Jews in the anti-Fascist opposition: first their efforts to launch a boycott movement against NS Germany and, since the organization of Jewish defence activities in 1936, their determined campaign against the BUF itself. The elevation of anti-Semitism as the BUF's main political message, on the other hand, has to be seen in the context of its shift of emphasis from domestic to foreign policy.

The political and economic issues, which had originally prompted Mosley to start his own party, lost impetus after the formation of a National Government. Although his specific proposals for regulating the economy were not implemented, a general sense of collective effort to steer Britain through the crisis began to prevail over apathy. Measures such as the introduction of an emergency budget and abandoning the gold standard, as much as the very formation of a National Government, presented a response to the crisis, and the people expressed their trust in the political leadership in the general elections of 1931 and 1935. The overvhelming consensus which was thus established defeated the New

Party's and later the BUF's claim to transcend the party system and to rally the people to a common cause. With slow but steady economic recovery, the BUF's initial shibboleth, the disdain of 'old gang politicians', became ever less effective.[52]

To replace the obsolete party platform Mosley turned from domestic to foreign policy, which provided further issues over which he could continue his campaign against those in power. 'Britain first' to Mosley meant pursuing the preservation of the Empire, which would allow her to establish an isolated, self-sufficient economy. Appealing to national sentiments, and particularly to the pride of ex-servicemen, he vigorously attacked the government for surrender and betrayal of British traditions, especially over the Indian policy. In the Albert Hall rally of March 1935 Mosley appealed to his audience:

> Hold high the head of England; lift strong the voice of Empire. Let us to Europe and to the world proclaim that the heart of this great people is undaunted and invincible. This flag still challenges the winds of Destiny. This flame still burns. This glory shall not die. The soul of Empire is alive, and England again dares to be great.[53]

In order to allow Britain to pursue her Imperial policy unimpaired, Mosley was prepared to sacrifice Britain's influence in Europe and to leave Germany's position unchallenged. He argued strongly against a European commitment, pointing out that the concept of 'balance of power' was totally archaic, since it divided Europe into rival camps. Mosley wanted to see it replaced by a Union of Fascist Europe, maintaining collective security against the common menace of Communism.[54]

Ignoring the fact that the political geography had changed with World War I, Mosley analysed the future political development from a predominantly European perspective. Within Europe he perceived Germany as the most dynamic power, Britain's natural ally in establishing a long period of peace. He argued with verve for a conciliation with Germany which in his opinion enjoyed a triumphant national revival under its congenial leadership. This would not only give Britain the freedom she needed to safeguard her interests overseas, but would effectively balance 'oriental Communism', which in his opinion meant anarchy under the mastership of Jewry. Mosley was eager to stress the mutuality of understanding, experience and interests between Britain and Germany and the party press gave much publicity to Hitler's pledge of friendship to Britain in his *Reichstag* speech of May 1935, 'the most important European event for a decade':

> We welcome the rough, gauntletted handshake of the New Germany, glad to feel again the iron grip of a worthy foe now comrade in the struggle against the enemy of mankind [i.e. Communism]. . . . Let us be thankful to Heaven that she stands out as a stout bulwark against the perfidious advance of Communist World Revolution which would assuredly otherwise overrun Europe and bring about the collapse of Western Civilization.[55]

Mosley unhesitatingly conceded Germany the right to aggressive expansionism, based upon the desire to unite the Germanic people. He considered her aims to achieve a 'racial union' legitimate in their own right, but recognized their disparity from British objectives, which were derived from the duty of preserving the Empire, which he understood as the beneficial administration of a multi-racial unit. Pursuing different political aims, the two powers would not interfere, but complement each other in striving for peace, stability and civilization.

The turn to foreign policy, defined as the conservation of the *status quo*, mirrors the BUF's transformation from an intentionally progressive party, searching for concepts to solve the problems of advanced societies, into a fundamentally reactionary movement. It began to glorify the virtues of the past, and to identify modernity with decline. This process moved the BUF closer to the conventional Fascist movements in Europe, which had from the beginning adopted a retrospective policy aiming at a revival of an allegedly happier past.

Mosley's instrumentalization of anti-Semitism seems to correspond to this realignment. His shift of allegiance from Mussolini to Hitler manifested itself in the change of name to 'British Union of Fascists and National Socialists' in the summer of 1936. The party press now confessed that the BUF considered 'the principles of National Socialism . . . necessary to the salvation of Britain'.[56] BUF speakers reproduced its characteristic terminology of missionary pathos, and an increasing emphasis was placed on the notions 'blood and soil', the touchstone of National Socialist thought. The latter development entailed portraying the Fascist crusade as a perpetual struggle to which its pioneers had to devote their lives. This aspect was stressed in many BUF marching songs, but most persuasively in 'Britons Awake!':

> Comrades: the voices of the dead battalions
> Of those who fell that Britain might be great,
> Join in our song, for they still march in spirit with us
> And urge us on to gain the Fascist State.
>
> We're of their blood, and spirit of their spirit,
> Sprung from the soil for whose dear sake they bled,
> 'Gainst vested power, Red Front, and massed ranks of
> Reaction,
> We lead the fight for freedom and for bread.
>
> The streets are still; the final struggle's ended;
> Flushed with the fight, we proudly hail the dawn!
> See, over all the streets the Fascist banners waving –
> Triumphant standard of a race reborn![57]

Eager to corroborate the mutuality of their political aspirations, the BUF not only showed sympathy for the German regime by advertising sightseeing tours to the 'NEW Germany' and attending NSDAP events, but they assured the German authorities that they shared a deep concern for the 'Jewish menace'. BUF delegations visited Germany as enthusiastic admirers of the Hitler regime, impressed by the obvious national revival, the efficiency by which government schemes were implemented, and the apparent happiness of the citizens. Some were received by Streicher, who excelled in a particularly odious campaign against Jews, and greeted them as 'brothers and comrades in the fight. We have only one common enemy, and that is the Jew'.[58] Mosley himself, not the least embarrassed about such support, confirmed the unanimity of their political campaign. This was clearly expressed in a thank-you note to Streicher which, even if it has to be seen as a routine courtesy, reveals a remarkable zeal to please his political friends abroad:

> I value your advice greatly in the midst of our hard struggle. The power of Jewish corruption must be destroyed in all countries before peace and justice can be successfully achieved in all

Europe. Our struggle in this direction is hard, but our victory is certain.[59]

Mosley himself continuously rejected the contention that his 'quarrel with the Jews' over such a limited issue as their alleged war-mongering can be subsumed under the category of anti-Semitism. His Jew-hatred indeed seems to have been '100 per cent insincere'[60] in that he used it as a propaganda asset without the devotion of a frenzied fanatic. Already, when starting his own political movement, he toyed with the idea of introducing the Jewish scapegoat to rally emotional support,[61] a policy that was at that time not considered suitable but was endorsed later as an opportune move to serve a different purpose. Whether or not Mosley ever believed that his diatribes against Jews were justified is of no relevance. The important fact is that in the course of his campaign he succumbed to the dynamics of that ideology. He cannot escape the totality of the movement he chose to embrace, and no attempt to rationalize any particular aspect of his campaign can vindicate its general corollaries.

Mosley's initial success as Fascist leader was astonishing, to some observers perturbing. While his impressive mass-meetings proved his charismatic appeal to the people, he also appeared to be capable of evoking sympathetic response from the political establishment. Right-wing aristocrats such as Rothermere, Nuffield and Lady Houston were associated with his movement. The January Club, founded in January 1934, provided a platform for Fascist speakers, and Mosley addressed various meetings of industrialists and businessmen who favoured his political campaign. After Rothermere's withdrawal, however, these connections seemed to have cooled off.

In an analysis of the sociological composition of BUF membership it was shown that the movement attracted a distinct middle-class element, a disproportionate number of young, generally well-educated people, a large number of ex-servicemen, and in particular 'restless' individuals with a high employment variability.[62] They seem to have shared a profound dissatisfaction with the contemporary state of affairs, some because they were personally affected by the slump, others because they were deeply distressed by the poverty they witnessed. Mosley's rhetoric, promising action and generating enthusiasm, obviously proved appealing, particularly since it addressed itself specifically to middle-class audiences.

The support Mosley received on the basis of his platform of patriotism, national pride and a vague demand for 'action' was, however, largely deterred by the introduction of storm-trooper techniques which alienated many of his potential supporters who had remained indifferent towards BUF anti-Semitism. Organized Blackshirt violence was displayed for the first time at the Olympia rally of 7 June 1934, which had been conceived as a demonstration of the BUF's growing strength. The Left also mobilized its supporters to mount an impressive counter-demonstration that would convey the force of anti-Fascist opposition. The meeting thus received much publicity in advance and succeeded in attracting a large number of curious onlookers who did not want to miss what promised to become an exciting event. Some 12,000 people gathered inside the hall to attend the Fascist show which culminated in Mosley's solemn entry. His speech was frequently interrupted by people shouting 'down with Fascism', 'Fascism means hunger and war' and similar slogans. Any hecklers were promptly ejected by Fascist stewards who proceeded with utmost violence to silence the opposition. One police sergeant, a special branch officer stationed inside the hall, reported:

I saw about 50 persons ejected. They were handled in a most violent manner and in some cases were punched unconscious and their clothing torn. They were then roughly dragged or carried towards the nearest exit. Although many of the combatants were bleeding from the face and hands, I saw no weapon used. Women were maltreated in the same manner as the men. As the evening drew on, the blackshirts grew more vicious at the interruptions and as soon as a person shouted, he was pounced on by a number of fascists and felled to the ground.[63]

Another sergeant, who left the hall to observe the proceedings from outside, reported:

I saw at least 30 persons, of both sexes, ejected into the roadway through this entrance. Almost every person bore some mark of violence and was in a state of semi-collapse. Several men were bleeding profusely from wounds on the face and chin. . . . I saw through the open door that each person ejected was surrounded by at least twelve blackshirts, who were frog-marching, kicking and raining blows on him. I also saw three women being very roughly handled when being thrown out. One woman was bleeding freely from the mouth.[64]

Other reports from policemen and private eye-witnesses confirmed that the ejected persons were flung or pushed into the street, bruised and bleeding, their clothing badly torn. The extreme humiliation some had to endure was observed by another special branch officer, stationed at the entrance to Olympia:

> At 10.43 p.m. . . . a man was thrown through the entrance by three fascists into the street. One leg of his trousers had been torn off, and the other was round his ankle. His private parts were exposed, and he was bleeding freely from a head wound. . . . At 10.47 p.m. a pair of flannel trousers was thrown over the gates into Beaconsfield Terrace. Immediately after, the gates were opened, and a man with only a shirt on, was thrown by three fascists on his back in the streets, where he lay with his private parts exposed. This man was bleeding from a head wound.[65]

In his final report the police superintendent in charge of keeping order outside Olympia was satisfied that the 762 policemen on duty had prevented serious disturbances or damage of property without use of truncheons or batons, and had 'successfully carried out and upheld the law'. He confirmed that inside the meeting proceedings appeared to have been rough, that the people ejected showed signs of harsh treatment and that in several cases they had received first aid by the police. He stressed the reaction of the public outside, including casual passers-by, 'who were horrified to think Police could not go into the building and stop the whole thing'.[66]

The BUF's vindication that the harsh treatment of opponents was due to the anti-Fascist opposition could not efface the blemish Olympia had caused. The interruptions indeed seem to have been systematically organized, but this did not warrant the indiscriminate use of violence by a private uniformed guard usurping the function traditionally performed by an authorized executive. If the Fascists were unseemingly attacked and provoked by their opponents, the legal way of dealing with them would have been to hand them over to the police, who were in attendance outside the Hall. By the display of ruthless brutality, however, which was a gross infringement of accepted political behaviour, Mosley lost his chance of winning momentous mass-support just after having gained wide publicity and a reputation as a brilliant orator, sporting what many regarded as a policy of common-sense. As in his decision to push his memorandum on unemployment at all costs, he showed a profound lack of sensitivity and misapprehension of the situation which offset his charisma, rhetorical excellence and intellectual gifts that had distinguished him as a potential political leader of his country.

Amongst all the radical right movements active in Britain in the inter-war period, the BUF by far attracted the widest support. Although its funds were limited it was able to spend more than any other fringe group on propaganda and had sufficient means to publish numerous pamphlets and brochures in addition to various newspapers and periodicals. In February 1935, the Prime Minister received a report which estimated the BUF's total weekly expenditure at the height of its activities at £8225. The cost of rents for the offices of some 650 branches was stated at £1300, salaries for full-time organizers estimated at £4224, the maintenance of a defence guard of some 600 men at £450, and expenditure on literature at £500. The Home Office, however, thought these figures exaggerated. Based upon the data available, it calculated the annual expenditure for 1934 at something between £40,000 and £80,000.[67] After 1934, drastic expenditure cuts were effected. Black House, for example, was closed down, the publication of one weekly paper, *Fascist Week*, was discontinued, and the number of large indoor meetings was reduced.

Apart from Mosley's own contributions, which he said amounted to a total of £100,000,[68] the movement claimed that it was financed by donations and subscriptions of members and supporters. Mosley always denied having received funds from abroad, a charge frequently levelled against him. A Foreign Office memorandum of 14 December 1935 mentioned that he received £3000 a month from Mussolini in return for moral support over the Italian Abyssinian policy. This information was confirmed in the parliamentary debate of 6 June 1946 by the Home Secretary, who stated that correspondence between the former Italian ambassador in London, Count Grandi, and Mussolini had revealed that between 1933 and 1935 the BUF had received about £60,000 per annum from the Italian government. No similar assistance was claimed to have come from Berlin, and no factual documentation was ever produced to prove that the BUF had indeed received financial support from abroad.[69]

Corresponding to its political campaign, the membership of the BUF seems to have reached a peak during 1934. After the Olympia meeting, the break with Rothermere and growing government concern, which eventually produced the Public Order Act, popular support declined steadily. Estimates on the total membership, which was said to have fluctuated greatly, vary. In a Home Office memorandum on Fascist activities, considered to be based on optimistic reports, BUF membership in 1934 was estimated at between a quarter and half a million. It was pointed out that the BUF had succeeded in enlisting members of the 'British Fascists Ltd.', and had figured as the main rallying point for the extreme right.[70] John Beckett maintained in 1939, after having left the BUF, that its highest membership was achieved during 1934 with some 20,000 people. By 1940, at any rate, some 9000 paying members were left when the organization was disbanded.[71] Mosley and some 800 members of this movement were arrested in May 1940 and detained under Defence Regulation 18B, an emergency decree which allowed the Government to intern anyone suspected of being likely to injure public safety or the defence of the realm, anyone who had associations with enemy governments or who showed sympathy for the enemy powers.

The drop in membership the BUF experienced between 1935 and 1940 epitomizes its progression from a respectable group that had to be taken seriously to a movement of the radical fringe. As long as it presented itself as a patriotic organization advocating an authoritarian leadership principle, the neutralization of social conflicts by corporate decision-making in the pursuit of an absolute common good, and the elimination of disruptive opposition, it presented a controversial but viable alternative in a situation of general dissatisfaction and apathy. Mosley injected enthusiasm, action and vision into political life and briefly succeeded in stirring the political establishment. His sympathetic attitude towards Hitler and his henchmen and his turn to political violence, however, alienated an apprehensive public, who came to regard the BUF as the imitator of continental Fascism. The coincidence of the Olympia meeting and the Röhm purge in Germany suggested an obvious affinity of techniques which disproved Mosley's repeated assurance that his movement stood firmly in the tradition of British politics and was not to be identified with political methods alien to that tradition.

As a political movement aiming to achieve power within the

existing parliamentary framework, the BUF proved to be a failure even before the Government stepped in to curb its activities. While the abeyant anti-Semitism present in its early campaign proved no irritant to its supporters, anti-Semitism as a main feature of propaganda was not sufficient to attract mass-support. Even when it concentrated its campaign on the East End, an area with a large Jewish minority and considerable antagonism against the Jewish community, it failed to win sufficient electoral support to be represented in local councils. It succeeded, however, in stigmatizing the Jewish community and intensifying the dislike of Jews which culminated in assaults, riots and destruction of property. The agitation of the BUF like that of its contemporary, the IFL, thus became an increasing threat to the preservation of public order even when it had ceased to present a serious challenge to the political establishment. Against this background, the Government proceeded in 1936 with the passing of the Public Order Act.

Part Three
Reactions Against Anti-Semitism

6 The Forces of Law and Order

The reaction of the political authorities against anti-Semitic propaganda has to be seen in the context of their reaction against domestic Fascist organizations in general, and in particular against the political violence caused by Fascist agitation. While obscure movements like the Britons or the IFL received little notice despite their vigorous anti-Semitism, the BUF stirred enough support and commotion to focus attention. As early as October 1933 Lord Trenchard, Commissioner of the Metropolitan Police, warned the Home Secretary of the adverse effects of Fascist activities. He argued:

> The wearing of uniform by members of a political organization is looked upon as provocative, not only by members of the Communist Party of Great Britain and kindred organizations, but by more responsible members of the public. Moreover it is an incentive to their opponents to adopt similar measures; for example, the Communist Party is endeavouring to resuscitate its 'Defence Force'. . . . The Fascists, however, are more active in this respect, and numerically stronger, and there is reason to fear that these displays will cause further breaches of the peace before the end of the winter.[1]

This perception was not immediately shared by other politicians. Only when they realized that uniformed Blackshirts were not a negligible body of eccentrics, but able to mobilize support and to interfere effectively with customary politics, did some become alert. This was the case when on 8 January the *Daily Mail* announced its support for the Mosley movement. Shortly afterwards the Home Secretary approached the Prime Minister on the issue. Referring to Trenchard's apprehension of the Blackshirt-movement, he proposed to take action against the wearing of political uniforms. The number of disturbances resulting from the Fascists' activities was increasing, he said, and he anticipated that they would become more frequent in proportion to the growth of the movement. Pointing out that these disturbances imposed a severe strain on the police force and damaged the prestige of constitutional authority, the Home Secretary suggested that action be taken before the situation got out of hand. He maintained:

In my view . . . the wearing of political uniforms in this country is already a public mischief. The Fascist movement has begun to attract a better class of recruits and its membership is increasing. It will accordingly become much more difficult to take effective steps to deal with this mischief when the numbers are really considerable. Should the movement expand to the dimensions which it has already attained in certain continental countries (a contingency which cannot be ruled out of consideration) it would probably be too late to deal effectively with the mischief. [2]

The Home Secretary's fear that the Fascists could become a serious threat in British politics was shared by other politicians. The Prime Minister, who doubted that the prohibition of political uniforms would produce the desired results, agreed that the progress of the Fascists required careful observation:

This of course ought to be watched. It is not at all unlikely to grow and if anything could be done now to remove its dangers to public order it should be done. The question, however, is what can be done and what ought to be done? These questions cannot be answered wisely by police nor by anyone who knows the movement from the outside. I think that M[osley] is capable of any advertising and self advancing action and may prove to be awkward. [3]

John Simon, then Secretary of State for Foreign Affairs, also showed interest in the issue. His attention was increased when some fifty Blackshirts interfered in the Suffolk tithe dispute in February 1934. For two weeks they occupied a farm as self-appointed guardians to 'defend the farmer's rights' by erecting barricades to prevent animals impounded for tithe arrears from being claimed. Before they were arrested and bound over in court, the Foreign Secretary urged his colleague in the Home Office to take swift action against the agitators who imitated the continental dictators:

> Here are some 50 'blackshirts' with a 'leader' who must be supplied with funds from some central source, who are defying the law and making a nuisance of themselves and a mock of the most elementary civil rights. . . . I should have thought that the Attorney-General might think it well to move the case to the Old Bailey . . . and then a good criminal judge, if they are found guilty, could first give them and their like a proper dressing down and then send them to three months' imprisonment with hard labour. I am very deeply impressed with the danger of letting this silly business of 'playing at Mussolini' go on in this country. . . . Our young people are accustomed to fresh air and healthy exercise without the folly of coloured shirts and tin trumpets. But, of course, as long as people in this country imitate Germans or Italians without breaking the law one can only deplore their want of national spirit. When it comes to a flagrant breaking of the law, by digging trenches and cutting down trees on other people's land, I think such lunatics ought to be taught that in this country we have no use for such methods.[4]

The principle amplified in this letter is characteristic for the attitude the state authorities adopted towards Fascist organizations, namely their willingness to extend democratic rights to the opponents of democracy. As long as they did not break the law, Fascists were to be conceded the same scope of action as any other political movement. 'The propagation of Fascism as a political philosophy,' it was stated in a Home Office minute as late as June 1937, 'is as lawful as the propagation of any other creed.'[5]

The permissive attitude was not shared by the Commissioner of the Metropolitan Police, who continued to press for government action to curtail the Fascists' activities. After the notorious Olympia rally of 7 June 1934, he submitted a memorandum to the Home Secretary in which he argued that effective steps had to be taken to preserve public order and civil peace. He suggested either legislation modelled after a Swedish bill prohibiting the organization of defence corps for political movements, or at least the prohibition of the wearing of uniforms for political purposes. He also proposed to empower the police to enter meetings, which would alter the existing rule that they could only enter if requested to do so or if they had reason to believe that a breach of the peace was taking place. Trenchard argued that the presence of police would have a restraining effect on those who intended to create disorder as well as on those man-handling hecklers. Furthermore, he suggested that processions intended to break up political meetings should be disbanded. He recognized that both Communists as well as Fascists were involved in the disturbances, but pointed out that in his opinion they were undoubtedly caused by the Fascists' provocative display of military methods:

> I am fully convinced that the present difficulties arise primarily from the existence and methods of the Fascist party, and that the only really effective way of dealing with them is to put a stop to the present organization and to prevent similar organizations from being formed in future. The patient may feel better for a time if you relieve his symptoms, but he won't be cured till you tackle the disease itself.[6]

Despite Trenchard's pressure no action was taken after the Olympia meeting to curb the Fascists' activities. The failure to introduce a public order bill at this stage again reflects the reluctance to circumscribe civil liberties with regard to one particular group. The Government's sensitivity towards public opinion became apparent in the correspondence between Barrington-Ward and Dawson, editor of *The Times*:

> Trenchard is pressing for a law against the wearing of political uniforms. . . . Before they launch anything, the Government would like to know that it would have our support. They expect opposition from the *Mail*, of course, but nothing in the House. The case would be, of course, that there can be only one fighting uniform – the uniform of His Majesty.[7]

Rather than giving them additional publicity by suppressing the Fascists at a time when public support seemed to diminish, it was decided to watch the developments still further. Conceived as a neutral attitude however, the toleration of Fascist groups amounted in practice to favouring them. Anxious not to alienate the police and hoping for their protection, the BUF operated in close alignment with their instructions. They always notified the police of meetings and submitted proposals as to the routes of their marches, which seemed to give them an official sanction vis-à-vis their opponents in the streets.

A sandwich-board parade held on 6 October 1935 in the West End in order to draw attention to the Abyssinian crisis illuminates the *de facto* police acceptance of Fascist enterprises. The course of the march and the posters to be carried were known to the police well in advance. They included the following slogans: 'Britons! Fight for Britain Only!', 'It's a long way to Abyssinia but sanctions will send you there!', 'Jews and Reds want war. Britain wants peace'. While these headlines passed without objection, others were considered likely to embarrass the Foreign Office, namely 'Litvinoff needs you. Don't go!' and 'Line up with Litvinoff! No thank you!'. After having communicated the issue to the Home Office, the Commissioner decided to allow the parade. A total of 102 police officers were drafted to supervise the event.[8]

In view of the probability of militant opposition at Fascist meetings, particularly after the Olympia incident, the police had to give their processions and assemblies special protection. Large numbers of police were usually drawn upon to ensure orderly proceedings and to guarantee the Fascists the right of free speech. A BUF parade held on 3 March 1935, for example, which was attended by some 700 people, was policed by a total of 4 superintendents, 13 inspectors, 27 sergeants, 279 constables and 49 mounted officers. The meeting passed without incident and the police did not take action.[9]

Some 6937 policemen were on duty for the BUF Hyde Park rally held on 9 September 1934, which attracted some 3000 members. A hostile crowd numbering about 20,000 gathered, and the police had to cordon off the Fascists' platform to allow the speakers to get access. The meeting passed off in an orderly way and only eighteen people were arrested for insulting behaviour and obstructing police. In a letter to the officer in charge Mosley expressed his appreciation of the police arrangements. Conscious of the sensitive nature of his collaboration with the police, he added: 'I do not desire any acknowledgement of this letter, which might possibly embarrass you, and shall never refer in public to having written it'.[10]

At first sight the Fascists appeared to be the targets of attack, while the Communist and anti-Fascist factions seemed to be the aggressors. Proceeding against those who started the disturbances, police usually took action against the militant anti-Fascists, whereby in practice they assumed the function of stewarding Fascist meetings. Although they were repeatedly instructed to proceed against any offender irrespective of his political association, and to confine their actions to suppressing actual breaches of the peace and obtaining particulars of the mischief-makers, the proportion of anti-Fascists who were arrested by far exceeded that of Fascists. Given their declared intention of putting a halt to Fascism by disturbing the organized, disciplined meetings of a party that glorified the principle of law and order, this is hardly surprising. The dilemma of properly evaluating who threatened public order most was pointed out in a further letter from the Commissioner of the Metropolitan Police to the Home Secretary:

> The large number of police which it has been found necessary to employ to keep the peace at Fascist demonstrations is creating the impression among anti-Fascists that Sir Oswald Mosley's semi-military organization is being permitted to develop under police protection. The increased activities of the BUF in attending meetings in uniform and holding semi-military parades have already had the result of coordinating the anti-Fascist organizations, over which the Communist Party now exercises indirectly a controlling influence. . . . I would therefore again emphasize that it is the military nature of the Fascist organization, and particularly the wearing of uniform, which is provocative, and I am more than ever convinced that it is necessary, in the interest of good order in London, that legislation should be adopted, either on the lines of the Swedish Law or to prohibit the wearing of uniform for political purposes.[11]

As yet, the majority opinion in the Cabinet and the House appears to have been that in principle Britain would be able to cope with domestic Fascism without introducing special legislation. The Left, knowing that any action restricting free speech and political demonstrations would affect the anti-Fascist opposition as much as the Blackshirts, championed the right of free speech as much as the Liberals and Conservatives. While definite legislation was deferred to avoid the impression that the Government was being stampeded, the development of the Fascist movement was closely observed. As it turned out, after the rowdy Olympia meeting which had caused so much adverse publicity, the BUF's campaign appeared more restrained as far as display of violence was con-

Title-page of *Jewry Ueber Alles* (May 1920)

'The Cuckoo', *Hidden Hand* I, Nr 10 (Nov. 1920)

The Champion of Truth.

'The Champion of Truth', *British Guardian* VI, Nr 8 (27 Feb. 1925)

'Get a Move on, St George!', *Fascist* Nr 103 (Dec. 1937)

'The Bigamist', *Blackshirt* Nr 176 (5 Sep. 1936)

'How Dare They Say Britain for the British', *Action* Nr 79 (21 Aug. 1937)

'Oi oi vot a Game', *Action* Nr 79 (21 Aug. 1937)

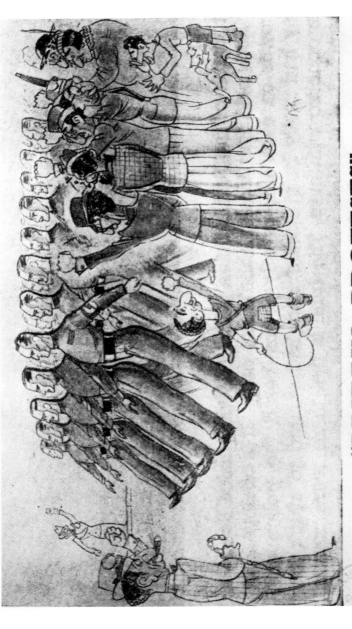

"BRITAIN PROTESTS"

'Britain Protests', *Action* Nr 86 (9 Oct. 1937)

cerned. It was not until it exalted anti-Semitism as its main propaganda asset that the question of legislative action against Fascist activities was raised again.

On 14 June 1934, in the full parliamentary debate on Fascism in Britain, only one speaker, C. Attlee, mentioned that Mosley's movement was not only anti-democratic but 'at times definitely anti-Semitic',[12] whereas the other speakers focused on the military character of the BUF. In the parliamentary debates of 5 March and 10 July 1936, by contrast, the Fascists' anti-Semitic campaign emerged as a particular concern. Jew-baiting began to be considered a novel threat to traditional political values that could not be tolerated like the propagation of political philosophies which merely tried to convince potential supporters. Regular attacks upon Jewry in the Fascist journals, appeals to boycott Jewish shops, anti-Jewish diatribes delivered by Fascist speakers and acts of physical violence were recognized to inflame racial hatred and to endanger the safety of Jewish citizens. It was observed that the anti-Semitic propaganda appealed in particular to the discontented, those suffering from poverty and concerned about unemployment, who were taken in by the argument that they were being robbed and exploited by Jewish shopkeepers and Jews taking their jobs. Although it was noted that the Fascist movement was in fact declining in membership, the perception of the danger of Fascism in Britain changed with the cognition that anti-Semitism was an inherent part of its ideology. This prompted the Home Secretary, Sir John Simon, to implement a rigid surveillance of the anti-Semitic agitation.[13]

On 16 July 1936 the Home Secretary issued an *aide mémoire* in which he asked the Commissioner of the Metropolitan Police to take decisive action to suppress the anti-Jewish activities of Fascist groups. He asked him to concentrate police in Jewish areas, to observe all Fascist meetings, and to have shorthand minutes taken of all speeches. Simon stressed that the police should be instructed to intervene promptly if they witnessed provocative language or behaviour, particularly by stewards at Fascist meetings. Aware of the frequent allegations that the police remained apathetic towards Jew-baiting, he asked them to report all Fascist publications likely to constitute defamatory or seditious libel.[14] The Home Secretary further pointed out that everything possible should be done to clear up all complaints about assaults and public mischief reported to the police, and left no doubts about the importance he attached to the problem which, he feared, could develop into 'unmanageable proportions':

> I should like to feel assured that not only the senior officials at Scotland Yard and the higher ranks in the police divisions but each individual police officer who may be called on to deal with anti-Jewish incidents is made fully aware that grossly abusive language of the Jews, either individually or as a race, is a serious offence and that there can be no question in this matter of good-humoured toleration of language which in other circumstances might not call for intervention on the part of the police.[15]

On 3 August 1936 the Commissioner, Sir Philip Game, issued a confidential memorandum entitled 'Anti-Jewish Activities', in which the policies outlined by the Home Secretary were conveyed to all ranks of the Metropolitan Police. Great care was taken to avoid giving the impression that Jews were to be granted special pro-tection.[16] It was pointed out that racial denunciation of the Jewish community was the main concern, since it constituted the immediate mischief, but that the principle involved was not the exclusive protection of Jewish citizens and that it applied to all groups irrespective of their political opinions. Paraphrasing the Home Secretary's memorandum, the Commissioner emphasized that the organized promotion of racial hatred through insults and abuse must not be tolerated under the cloak of free speech, and had to be treated as a serious offence. Speakers or members of the public indulging in provocative language and behaviour were to be arrested. In cases of assault, immediate action was to be taken if the event was observed by police. Otherwise detailed inquiries were called for to obtain information from eye-witnesses, and the injured party was to be persuaded to apply for proceedings to be taken against the assailants. The Commissioner insisted that the police should react firmly and instructed the officers to err on the side of action rather than inaction in doubtful cases. Conviction, he argued, was not of primary importance. What mattered most was to demonstrate that violence and provocative abuse would not be tolerated.[17]

Despite the clear-cut instructions to adopt a stern attitude in dealing with Fascist and anti-Fascist activities in general, and anti-Jewish agitation in particular, the police were continuously accused of pro-Fascist leanings. When the issue was raised in

Parliament, several members indicated that there was a strong feeling in the East End that police were remarkably lenient in dealing with Fascists. Mr Pritt (Labour, Hammersmith) criticized the laxity and inefficiency of the police, who 'stood by as if they were paying amusement tax', while Sir Percy Harris (Liberal, Bethnal Green) described the bitter feelings amongst East End residents:

> If the police do not arrive, there is a fear of riot, but if they do arrive the general impression is that they are there to give special protection to these organized semi-military bands. . . . There is a feeling going right through the East End that somehow or other the police are acting in collusion with the Fascists.[18]

One obvious case of police inaction occurred at the Hornsey Town Hall meeting in January 1937. The meeting was attended by some 1300 people, and the police were not called into the hall. Fascist stewards were, however, accused of having ejected opposition members with unnecessary violence. When three men complained about maltreatment to police officers outside the hall, the latter refused to accompany them back to identify their assailants although it was plain that the men had been treated very roughly: one had a cut on the upper lip, another a discoloured eye and his spectacles broken, the third suffered from swollen lips. Pointing out that the complainants had presumably been thrust out because of disorderly conduct, one inspector argued that no useful purpose could have been served by entering the meeting, particularly since the victims were not able to name or describe their assailants. Instead, he recommended them to consult a legal adviser as to the possibility of proceeding against Mosley, who had given orders to eject the hecklers. In his report the superintendent in charge of the meeting admitted that the assaulted had not received proper assistance from the police and expressed his dissatisfaction about the way the inspectors had handled the incident.[19]

The National Council for Civil Liberties alleged that it was 'a settled policy at Scotland Yard that insulting words and behaviour shall be overlooked by the police when uttered by Blackshirts and that orderly and legitimate heckling shall be prevented by the police'. This was, in fact, as unwarranted a statement as the accusation that 'the Home Office has actively discouraged the police from stamping-out terrorism and racial incitement which have been such ugly features of political life in East London in recent years'.[20] At no point was it official policy to gloss over provocative language and behaviour, and the Commissioner, urged by the Home Office, repeatedly stressed that impartiality was imperative in dealing with the disturbances.

Irrespective of these orders, however, the lower ranks of the police indeed frequently displayed a lenient attitude towards the Fascists, which vindicates the judgement that there was some partiality amongst certain officers. The Commissioner, in fact, repeatedly expressed his dissatisfaction at the way his policies were implemented, and criticized police inertness with regard to Jew-baiting. In particular he specified that 'at a meeting of any size or where disorder is considered likely an officer not below the rank of Inspector should be in charge'.[21]

Examples of obvious police inaction were plentiful. The *News Chronicle* published a letter to the editor in which the correspondent quoted a case where a speaker had referred to Jews as 'venereal ridden vagrants, who spread disease to every corner of the earth'. When the audience protested loudly, he heard an inspector ordering people to be quiet, threatening to arrest them for insulting behaviour.[22] An observer who attended a small BUF meeting at Victoria Park Square reported that the police constable on duty laughed with the audience when the speaker referred to British people as 'to all intents and purposes lying in a ditch and lousy with Jews. The Jew can no more help being a parasite than a louse can being a louse.'[23] On another occasion, police officers proceeding against anti-Fascists were reported to have used abusive language such as 'You Jew bastards' and 'Go back to Whitechapel, you Jewish whores'.[24] A woman reported to the National Council of Civil Liberties that she had heard an inspector using the most abusive anti-Semitic language. She maintained that he had said all London prostitutes were Jewesses, Jewish masters habitually chased their servant girls, and that he had referred to Jews as a 'cancer which should be cut out'.[25] Some policemen without doubt treated Jews as a class apart rather than as individuals. This becomes manifest in the report of one inspector, who mentioned that 'Joseph Jacobson, a Jew' had been arrested. In the corresponding report to the Home Office, this reference was replaced by 'Joseph Jacobson, a shoe dealer'.[26]

At a BUF meeting held on 23 June 1937 the speaker, E. G. Clarke, referred to 'Jewish scum and ghetto boys' and 'filthy licene Jews'.

He also commented 'the Jews are the lice of the earth and must be exterminated', and alluded to Sir Philip Game as 'darned old fool who hasn't the guts of a louse'. Despite his insulting language, which was recorded in shorthand notes, Clarke was not even cautioned by any one of the police officers who patrolled the meeting. When questioned why he did not take action against Clarke, the inspector in charge of the meeting argued that on the outskirts of the crowd he could not hear distinctly what was said on the platform. Ignoring the possibility of incitement by the speaker, he maintained that breaches of the peace were likely to occur from the audience, which therefore had to be watched more carefully than the speaker. Even when challenged in retrospect he defended his decision and clearly stated that his criteria for interference was not the cause of unrest, but its event. He also admitted a remarkable degree of intimidation among the police force:

> By reason of the fact that the crowd was definitely of Fascist sympathies, and was quiet and orderly throughout, neither being inflamed or provoked and no Jews being present, there was not the slightest sign of a breach of the peace taking place at the time. I am of the opinion that had an arrest been made at this meeting, the crowd would have undoubtedly become disorderly and the Police present would not have been sufficiently strong to have maintained order with the result that the crowd would have resorted to window smashing in the vicinity, as they have done in the past.[27]

This incident exemplifies that, contrary to the instructions from the Commissioner, in practice police evaluated Jew-baiting not as an abstract issue, but in relation to the actual disturbances specific incidents entailed. In consequence, offenders seem to have been treated rather arbitrarily, since police tended not to interfere when the audience appeared sympathetic to anti-Jewish remarks. 'Somewhat strong anti-Semitic language of a general nature was used by William Joyce, a member of the National Socialist League,' the Special Branch report for December 1937 reported. 'No exception was taken to his remarks,' it pointed out, which evidently stopped the police from taking action.[28] For referring to Jewish premises in East London as 'foul stinking sweatshops' one speaker was cautioned. An arrest was made when someone accused the

Jews of fomenting war and referred to 'the blood bath they are preparing'. The following remark, noted down at a public meeting, was not considered strong enough to warrant police action:

> The Jew is the greatest Fascist in the world; he stands for his own: he trades for his own: he lies for his own, robs for his own, and what he does not do for his own is not worth naming.[29]

Reports drawn up by the National Council for Civil Liberties quoted cases when the police had confiscated anti-Fascist leaflets, but had allowed the Fascists to sell their publications. It was observed that hecklers who challenged Fascist speakers in an orderly manner were frequently cautioned and arrested, while the police turned a blind eye to Fascist provocations and did not interfere with those who interrupted anti-Fascist meetings. The latter, it was alleged, were frequently closed down as soon as opposition became apparent. In one instance, an orderly anti-Fascist meeting was dispersed and a Fascist meeting installed at the very spot from which anti-Fascists had been turned away. When questioned in Parliament, the Home Secretary explained that this case had been 'an error of judgement' on the part of the police.[30] An East End Borough Councillor complained:

> Police interference with public anti-Fascist meetings is becoming intolerable. . . . At the last two meetings Fascists have created disturbances whereupon the Inspector has forced me under pain of arrest to close the meeting. In vain I have pointed out the people causing the trouble, and have told the Inspector to deal with the Fascists, but I have always been instructed to close the meeting. At the Fascist meetings nearly the complete reverse is the case. The first person to begin interrupting is either warned or arrested.[31]

The uncompromising attitude the police maintained against anti-Fascists can partly be explained by the fact that they were the aggressive element stirring political scuffles. From the police officer's point of view, the undisciplined, agitated crowds seemed to be the constant trouble-makers, not the organized body of Fascists who provoked passionate opposition. Such latent biases against the anti-Fascist front cannot, however, suffice to explain the fact that the police tolerated anti-Semitic propaganda despite the explicit instructions to proceed against insult and abuse even where an immediate breach of the peace was not likely to occur. Nor can they vouch for the unrestrained use of violence on some occasions.

The most notorious case of ruthless police action against anti-Fascists occurred at the Thurloe Square meeting on 22 March 1936. It was arranged to coincide with a BUF rally in the Albert Hall, and was held just within a half-mile circle laid down as a prohibited area by the Commissioner of the Police. The meeting was quiet and orderly but, since it was staged within the proscribed area, the police took offence and dispersed the crowd. Allegedly without warning to the speaker or chairman, a large number of mounted and foot police charged and batoned the crowd, for which they were heavily criticized.

The National Council for Civil Liberties appointed an unofficial committee under Norman Bentwich to investigate the events. The Commissioner of the Metropolitan Police was invited to submit written or oral evidence on behalf of the police force, but refused to do so. The Committee collected over a hundred statements and heard thirty-one eye-witnesses in its investigation. They all pointed out that the police reaction was completely unprovoked and that they had behaved with unnecessary brutality. 'Men and women were struck on the head and back of the neck without provocation in a manner which we doctors consider might easily have proved fatal,' one witness reported. 'It was a disgusting sight when a man on foot was held by the wrists by two mounted policemen and as the horses parted so his arms were stretched out,' another related.[32] In the evaluation of the report a cleavage between the Home Office and the Metropolitan Police became visible. Sir F. Griffith, who analysed the report for the Commissioner, thought that it rested on 'extravagant' and spurious evidence and dismissed it as a 'singular example of special pleading'. A Home Office counsellor, on the other hand, commented:

In spite of the one-sidedness of the inquiry, the report seems to me to give evidence of careful preparation and to merit careful consideration. It is a pity that it is not possible to test more fully some of the allegations of unnecessary use of force against individual constables.[33]

The attitude of the police has to be seen in relation to the severe pressure put on them by the escalation of violent political confrontations. They received a constant stream of complaints about annoyances, assaults and damages from Fascists, anti-Fascists and the molested or simply disconcerted public. Since most assaults occurred at night and the victims could rarely identify or describe their assailants, the police were hardly ever successful in tracing the offenders: during 1937, thirty-three complaints of alleged assaults on Jews were recorded; in four cases arrests were made, twenty-nine cases remained untraced. During 1938, twenty cases of alleged assaults were reported, all of which remained unclarified.

Disturbances that did not happen in connection with meetings were extremely difficult to control and, although the police patrols were augmented, it proved impossible to watch all areas constantly. Given the heavy duties the police had to cope with, which by far exceeded their routine work, impatience with individual complaints is hardly surprising. What to a Jewish family, constantly oppressed by a collective persecution syndrome, appeared a vital issue, was considered trivial racial strife by the police. Symptomatic of this attitude was the comment of a police officer who investigated one case of assault and noted that the family of the complainant were all 'highly excitable and nervous individuals, who appear to be obsessed with the idea that they will be seriously injured by fascists'.[34]

While the police retained what seems a forcibly detached view, the Home Office, constantly under political pressure from the House and the public, was more sensitive about allegations of partiality on the part of the authorities. The difference between the two departments was epitomized in their discussion relating to the alleged assault of three Jewish youths in February 1936. The case was communicated to the Home Office by Captain Hudson MP, who drew attention to the frequent cases of intimidation and persecution of Jews after Fascist meetings. The Home Office considered such events disquieting and asked for special protection of the much molested Jewish minority. A police official, in return, minuted the file casually 'Home Office are inclined to be panicky but I think we must take a reasonable time before we reply and make certain that we have the truth'.[35]

Some evidence suggests that the extent and significance of anti-Semitic agitation was deliberately minimized in the monthly reports submitted to the Home Office. In his report for February 1937, the Commissioner suggested that the routine reports on

Jew-baiting which had been introduced in August 1936 could be discontinued. He pointed out that:

> criticism and heckling kept within the bounds usually considered permissible at election times and were directed more at Governments – classes, the organization of finance and commerce and, as regards the Jews, race than against individuals.[36]

Compared to the wording of the draft and the Special Branch report for the same month, it appears that the degree of anti-Semitic agitation was definitely played down in the final report to the Home Office. The corresponding passage in the Special Branch report read:

> A good deal of strong anti-Jewish language of a general nature has been made use of by Fascist speakers; in fact, the whole theme of the election speeches has been to attack Semitism. International financiers (alleged to be Jews), Jewish landlords in the East End, shopkeepers, employers of labour and Jewish members of the London County Council have all been strongly criticized.[37]

Opposition groups not only criticized the police for irresponsible laxity in pursuing Fascist offences, but also accused police courts of extremely forebearing treatment of Fascist defendants, which was considered 'a direct encouragement to this kind of lawlessness and . . . a very definite deterrent to the Police in doing their duty'.[38] Cases were quoted where the magistrate had merely admonished Fascists charged with causing grievous bodily harm, or bound over agitators who had addressed Jews by abusive or insulting language. Such lenient sentences were contrasted with the heavy penalties inflicted upon anti-Fascist offenders. Herbert Morrison raised this point in Parliament. He quoted the case of a Blackshirt Jew-baiter with a criminal record who had been bound over, and maintained 'that if a man with that record had come before a good many London police court magistrates and had happened to be a Communist, he would not have been bound over, but would probably have been given "time".'[39]

Again, it seems that the treatment of Fascist offenders varied. While the cases quoted by anti-Fascist observers indeed reflected a certain partiality of the judges concerned, there were others who adopted a firm attitude against Jew-baiting. One magistrate, for example, told a defendant:

> You know language of this kind is utterly intolerable and insulting, and calculated to cause unrest, possibly to create disturbance. I have said before and I repeat that this sort of thing cannot be allowed. There is no reason why people who hold strong political views should not express them but there is every reason why people should not be grossly insulted. You used words about the Jews which were intolerable. If I had been at the meeting and I were a Hebrew, I might possibly, with others, have been minded to take some steps.[40]

Police were by no means only accused of *pro*-Fascist leanings. There were occasions when they could not arrest Fascist offenders because they were given shelter and covered up by local residents. Also they received letters from 'patriotic Britons' who complained:

> It is bad enough to be ruled in the House by a large majority of Jewish people, but we are not going to be crushed altogether. . . . It is quite bad enough when an Englishman is barred to walk through his own country without having the privilege of a meeting at any corner. Communism has grown enough and has been allowed to do so by our Jewish Government.[41]

Others encouraged Scotland Yard to bring 'the dogs . . . to heel' and to 'give the Jews in the East End to understand . . . that Britain is *quite* as free to Britons . . . who are out for "King and Country" as it is to Britons who are traitors and intimidators'. More specifically, one correspondent actually suggested that Communist 'wretches' and 'vermin' 'should be expelled from the country or soaked in mustard gas and hung up at the cross roads to rot away'.[42]

The degree to which particularly the anti-Semitic message in Fascist propaganda was sympathetically received by contemporaries is documented in a letter by a member of a first-aid organization, who had been on duty at one BUF rally. He congratulated the Commissioner on the 'quiet way tipical (*sic*) of one of our Race' with which he had handled the situation. At the same time he expressed his regrets that the 'alien opposition' was not dealt with more effectively:

One finds many persons whose names usually end in 'vitch', 'stein' or 'berg' were arrested for brutal assaults and indecencies. I wish specimens of this type were not allowed to permiate (*sic*) this fair country of ours as they cause a lot of worry of ordinary citizens and keep the police busy when they have enough to do as it is.[43]

Harassed by fanatics from both sides and indignant about obstruction and physical attacks on its officers, the police force in the troubled areas was strained to its limits. A daily average of some 300 officers were drafted into the East End throughout October 1936 for relief duties. 5132 policemen were on duty on 4 October 1936, when the 'Battle of Cable Street' took place; 2870 were on duty on 11 October, when the anti-Fascists held a 'victory march'. 'Obviously the drafting of all these men to the East End has imposed a serious burden on the police generally,' the Commissioner explained, 'and has reacted to some extent on the ordinary Police work over the whole of the Metropolitan Police District.'[44] He recognized that the police inevitably had to neglect other duties while defending public order against political violence, and registered an increase of house- and shop-breaking and simple larceny as a corollary of the general unrest. This development had, in fact, been predicted by Lord Trenchard in July 1934 when he proposed 'to increase the numbers of police in London, in view of the serious depletion which takes place in beats and patrols due to these [i.e. Fascist] meetings'.[45]

The battle scenes which disrupted life in the East End in 1936, the obvious strain on police resources owing to political disturbances, and the awareness of the dangerous impact of the anti-Semitic campaign strengthened the position of those who called for special legislation to stop the militarization of politics. In contrast to the MacDonald Government, the succeeding Baldwin Cabinet took the view that, however displeasing, some action was necessary to resist the possibility of a permanent encroachment of civil liberties. As before, the discussion focused on the question of political uniforms. It was recognized that the Fascists' wearing of uniforms underlined the unity, strength and potential militancy of their movement. Individual members submerged into a collective body, which ostentatiously transformed them into parts of a whole, releasing personal inhibitions and exempting from personal responsibilities. Fascist uniforms moreover challenged the authority of those privileged to wear uniform in the service of the sovereign and the state – a fact that might have contributed to the opposition towards political uniforms from the higher ranks of police, whereas the lower ranks seem to have been favourably disposed toward the movement akin to their own organization.[46]

The Public Order Act became effective from 1 January 1937, and prohibited the wearing of uniform in public places, the formation of paramilitary forces substituting police functions and promoting political objectives by physical force, and the possession of offensive weapons at public meetings and processions. It also entitled the chiefs of police to alter or ban processions likely to cause serious public disorder, and allowed the authorities, on application of the borough or district councils, to ban all processions in a certain area for a period not exceeding three months, if there were good reasons to believe that they might lead to breaches of the peace.

It has been argued that the Public Order Act of 1936 was directed specifically against Fascists, designed to cripple Fascism and thus supporting the case of the anti-Fascists.[47] The decision to introduce a bill prohibiting the wearing of political uniforms and empowering the police to ban marches likely to cause a breach of the peace was indeed a political decision and thus a value judgement against Fascism. Yet it was not conceived as an emergency regulation, but as a 'strengthening of the ordinary law of the land'.[48] The combination of the impact of continental Fascism on British public opinion, and the disconcerting effects of Fascist activities at home, inspired the decision to pass legislation which would enable the government to take action not only against political violence *per se*, which could be dealt with under the existing law, but against political movements whose agitation trespassed upon the traditional right of free speech and exceeded the 'threshold of violence' that the state authorities were prepared to tolerate.[49] Confronted with political violence that threatened in particular the safety of a minority, the Government finally was prepared to restrict civil liberties. The underlying object was to defend the conventional liberal order against those who abused their rights as citizens and disturbed civil peace by organized rowdyism.

The parliamentary debates related to Fascism in Britain reveal clearly that both Fascism as well as Communism were considered fatal threats to freedom and liberty, and that whoever adopted totalitarian methods should fall under the provisions of the bill.

Any political movement actively menacing the established order not by persuasive propaganda but by violent agitation was meant to fall under the ban. The preoccupation was, however, with political methods rather than philosophies. Just as plans were quickly dropped which contemplated legislation prohibiting the political activities of bodies in receipt of financial assistance from abroad, a specific clause dealing with racial incitement did not pass the committee stage. An amendment to the Public Order Act, proposed by various Labour and ILP members, which intended to outlaw propaganda 'calculated to incite racial or religious prejudice whereby a breach of the peace is likely to be occasioned', was defeated. Summing up the argument of those who opposed the amendment as an attempt to stifle free speech, Lord Winterton insisted that freedom of thought included the right to be prejudiced:

> It would be an intolerable abuse of public liberty if people were not permitted to make speeches which showed either racial or religious prejudice. If a speaker uses threatening or abusive language he can be summoned under the present law, but to say that no one shall make a speech showing racial or religious prejudice is preposterous. It has existed in this country for hundreds of years, and will always exist.[50]

If the Public Order Act was worded so as to meet Fascist activities in particular, it was related to the fact that the existing law provided ample ground for proceedings against anti-Fascists who overstepped the legal norms of opposition and indulged in violent attacks on their enemies, while it did not restrict the activities of Fascists operating within the framework of the law. It was well recognized by police and civil servants that neither party was solely to be blamed for the events, and that offence bred reprisals on both sides. All the time it was the determined policy of the police not to take action if complaints were based on political biases rather than serious molestations and anti-Fascist activities were given as much, if not more, attention than those of the Fascists.[51] The transition to the principle of 'pugnacious democracy' was, therefore, conceived as a neutral policy and not as a deliberate endorsement of anti-Fascist attitudes.

The event which finally gave the impetus to limit the general permissiveness regarding the political disturbances was the 'Battle of Cable Street' of 4 October 1936, when some 100,000 anti-

Fascists assembled to stop a BUF march through the East End. The following day the Labour Party Conference passed an emergency resolution to the Prime Minister and the Home Secretary demanding effective action, and the London Diocesan Conference unanimously carried a motion calling upon all Christians to stand firm against all attempts to arouse anti-Semitic feeling.[52]

Although worried at the developments, the Home Secretary at first appeared hesitant to rush through a bill which would restrict freedom of speech and political propaganda. He was aware, however, of growing pressure for government action among the public and in the House and agreed that some legislation was needed to meet the new situation of monster demonstrations and counter-demonstrations calculated to lead to disorder. While he insisted that new legislation should not be directed against a particular organization as such, he accepted that 'customary decencies' had to be restored.[53] The Prime Minister sympathized with the view that the banning of uniforms would eliminate a major source of provocation and clear the government of the charge of inactivity, and declared the bill a matter of great importance.[54] The issue was raised in the King's speech of 3 November 1936, and a Public Order Bill was introduced to the House the following week. It was passed quickly with a large majority and became effective as from 1 January 1937.

The Act was met with general approval except by the parties concerned. Anti-Fascists, most audibly the Communist Party and the National Council for Civil Liberties, recognized that some of the provisions might be used against themselves, and criticized the loose wording allowing the police too much scope for interpretation. They also deplored the lack of measures dealing explicitly with racial incitement. Mosley and the BUF accused the Government of rendering the Fascists defenceless by prohibiting them to train and equip defence units to steward Fascist meetings. In a letter to the Home Secretary, Mosley suggested that, since his movement had been divested of its security force, it was now the responsibility of police to preserve order at their meetings – an argument which underlines the fact that the BUF troops had actually been intended to perform police duties – and argued that in the event of a fatality occurring the Government would be morally guilty of murder.[55] The Home Office again firmly rejected the contention that there was any partiality on behalf of the police. It also denied that it was the duty of the police to silence opposition at outdoor meetings, where 'any member of the public has right of access, no question of ejection can arise, and a person cannot be removed unless he is guilty of conduct in respect of which the law empowers his arrest without warrant'.[56]

During the debate on the Public Order Bill apprehensions were raised that section three, dealing with the ban of processions, left the control and regulation of marches largely to the arbitrary interpretation of the police. Great inconvenience to the police, or the mere threat of opposition, clearly could not be sufficient reason to infer serious public disorder and to impose the ban. As it turned out, the police used its powers conscientiously. In April 1937, the Deputy Area Commissioner for the East End submitted a balanced memorandum in which he reviewed the situation, concluding that a ban of public processions would greatly improve conditions in his district. Describing Fascist marches accompanied by bands at 10 p.m. or later, he argued:

The marchers are often carried away by their anti-Jewish feeling, and acts of damage occur. The unfortunate inhabitants are deprived of sleep, and some of them are more or less terror-stricken, for to the Jewish resident of the East End, the Fascist is a source of grave apprehension. The activity is not all on one side, as the Jewish and Communist elements too are active, and their meetings and processions need quite as much policing. . . . I am forced to the conclusion that there is now no immediate prospect of improvement, and that we cannot continue indefinitely sending large numbers of extra Police into the East End in order to encourage masses of young men to stage demonstrations which are not peaceful but provocative. . . . I therefore ask the Commissioner to consider seriously the question of taking steps under section 3(3) of the Act to prohibit for three months from 3rd May 1937, all public processions of a political nature in the Boroughs of Shoreditch, Poplar, Finsbury, Islington, Stoke Newington and Hackney. I realize that meetings will still go on, but what I want to do is to stop the practice of marching away in formation from political meetings, with bands playing, and men singing and shouting late at night. . . . The ban would apply to all parties, and I believe it would be welcomed in the Boroughs named.[57]

After consultation with the Home Office, the Commissioner

replied in this case that at present he was not prepared to ban all processions. This power was only to be used in wholly exceptional circumstances and, before it was to be applied, conditions of time and route could be imposed in cases likely to lead to a breach of the peace. It was essential, he pointed out, that each case should be decided on its individual merits.[58]

The power to ban processions was first implemented when the BUF proposed a march through the East End to Trafalgar Square on 4 July 1937. The police anticipated troubles owing to the strength of anti-Fascist opposition and thought the situation justified intervention. Upon recommendation from the Commissioner, the Home Secretary agreed that all public processions through the East End areas with a large Jewish community were to be banned for six weeks.[59] The ban was extended for another six weeks in August, thereafter for the maximum period of three months, and was successfully renewed until 1940. This regulation did not, however, prevent the Fascists from organizing meetings in the East End and holding processions through other districts.

The march on 4 July 1937, which had prompted the ban, was eventually arranged to lead from Kentish Town to Trafalgar Square. It was permitted by the police despite petitions from various organizations urging the Commissioner to prohibit it. The rally, attended by some 3400 Fascists, was supervised by a police force of 108 mounted officers and 2275 on foot. Some 5000 anti-Fascists assembled at Kentish Town, another 5000 at Trafalgar Square and a further 2000 in the vicinity of Trafalgar Square. The meeting, although constantly interrupted by booing and cheering, was orderly, but afterwards fights broke out between Fascists and anti-Fascists. Twenty-eight persons, mostly anti-Fascists, were arrested for assaults, obstructing police and using insulting language.[60]

The BUF planned another march through the East End for 3 October 1937. It also fell under the ban of processions through that area, and was transferred instead to South London. This march, organized to celebrate the fifth anniversary of the BUF, was the last occasion when violent street-battle scenes took place. It only attracted 3000–3500 supporters, while the opposition mobilized a crowd estimated at 40,000–50,000 people with the declared object of staging a second 'Battle of Cable Street' and stopping the Fascists' march. The police diverted the route and tried to cordon off a passage-way for the Fascists, which induced the anti-Fascist crowd to turn against the police, while the Fascists actually passed through. Barriers were erected and missiles of broken cement, stones and bottles were thrown. The police, employing a total of 2663 officers, batoned the crowd to restore order. Several people were knocked down, forty-one policemen were injured and 186 persons charged with obstructing and assaulting police, possessing offensive weapons and using insulting language.[61]

The Public Order Act, then, did not prevent the outbreak of disorder as a matter of course, nor did it halt Fascist or anti-Fascist activities. Least of all did it affect the anti-Semitic agitation of the Fascists which continued to occupy police officers under the order issued six months prior to the passing of the Public Order Act. Fascists continued to sell their literature and to hold numerous indoor and street-corner meetings. They were deprived, however, of their uniforms, without which they appeared much less impressive and lacked the appeal of organized discipline. They were also effectively deprived of their most successful propaganda asset, provocative marches through the East End, where they had been able to draw upon local resentment against Jews and thus actually materialized the dichotomous political situation they were constantly propagating. Most important, the Public Order Act demonstrated the consensus among all democratic factions to defend the traditional concept of law and order against any attempt to usurp political power by totalitarian propaganda techniques, and to victimize one section of the population. It thus symbolized the state authorities' firm intention to assert their political leadership, even if some civil liberties had to be sacrificed.

On balance, police interference seems to have influenced the anti-Semitic campaign only marginally. This was due not so much to a lack of determination on the part of those responsible for drafting the directives not to tolerate anti-Semitic agitation, but to a certain indolence on the operational level to enforce their authority. This antagonism seems to reflect accurately the dual structure of the police which, conceived as an unpolitical executive, receives its instructions from political principals, and has to perform its functions within the limitations of its number of recruits, its financial resources and the conditions of a highly politicized environment, which preclude the possibility of strictly neutral police behaviour.

7   Anglo-Jewry

When anti-Semitism emerged in Britain after World War I, there was no need for Anglo-Jewry to set up a formal organization which would face the problem on behalf of the community. In 1790, a 'Board of Deputies' had been established, incorporating representatives of both sections of the community, Ashkenazim and Sephardim. During the fight for emancipation, this body had emerged as the representative spokesman for Anglo-Jewry. In 1836, it received statutory recognition as an authority entitled to certify Jewish places of worship eligible to hold marriage registers. The 'deputies' were elected representatives of the established synagogues – Orthodox, Reform and Liberal – and of some lay institutions such as Jewish Friendly Societies or the Association of Jewish ex-servicemen. Although as a voluntary association the Board never had official powers, and could not claim to represent the entire community, it came to be regarded as the only authoritative political institution of Anglo-Jewry, whose most prominent activity was to safeguard the civic rights of Jews living in Great Britain.[1]

By the end of World War I, however, Anglo-Jewry did not speak with a unanimous voice. The immigration of some 150,000 East European Jews between 1881 and 1914 had entailed a division of the community, with the old, established, westernized group advocating the rapid integration of Jews into British life, while the new, orthodox community resisted assimilation. The dichotomy between the two became apparent over the issue of Zionism. Those who identified with their host society considered any form of Jewish nationalism opposed to the principle of emancipation. To the pious East European Jews, on the other hand, who were not yet rooted in their new environment, a settlement of Jews in Palestine meant the fulfilment of an age-old dream.

A further issue causing dissension within Anglo-Jewry emerged with Hitler's advent to power, which posed the question of how Anglo-Jewry should react to Jew-baiting in Germany. The spontaneous response of Jews all over the world was an appeal to boycott German goods and services, which was launched in March 1933.[2] Under the self-appointed leadership of Captain Webber,[3] English Jews supported the campaign dedicated to 'help extinguish the fire of persecution at its source'. While the *Jewish Chronicle* encouraged the boycott, suggesting that the cry of 'Perish Judah' should be answered with a mighty 'Jewry, awake!'[4] the Board of Deputies refused to sanction it and was content to express its protest against the defamation and persecution of Jews in Germany. It was not until November 1934 that it passed a motion 'that no self-respecting Jew will handle German goods or utilize German services'.[5] Despite this lack of concord among Anglo-Jewry, the boycott was frequently considered an agreed 'Jewish policy'. The *Daily Express*, for example, anticipating the evaluation of the campaign in the Fascist press, gave the issue much publicity in a front-page article entitled 'Judea Declares War on Germany':

All Israel is rising in wrath against the Nazi onslaught on the Jews. . . . 14 million Jews, dispersed throughout the world, have banded together as one man to declare war on the German persecutors of their co-religionists. . . . The Jewish merchant prince is leaving his counting-house, the banker his boardroom, the shopkeeper his store, and the peddlar his humble barrow, to join together in what has become a holy war to combat the Hitlerite enemies of the Jew.[6]

While the impact of the boycott campaign was over-estimated and the unanimity of world-Jewry exaggerated, the fact that the boycott was endorsed by many non-Jewish critics of the Hitler regime was also ignored. C. Attlee, W. Churchill and other MPs championed the effort when they challenged the Home Secretary in Parliament as to why the Police had ordered a withdrawal of posters calling for a boycott of Germany and German goods. They were instructed that the posters were an irritant likely to 'inflame feeling' and to cause breaches of the peace by anti-Semitic agitators[7]

Most of those who sponsored the boycott campaign also identified with the ostensibly non-party, non-religious 'British Non-Sectarian Anti-Nazi Council to Champion Human Rights', the British branch of a world-wide propaganda movement opposing the NS regime. In 1935, the Council reorganized itself as 'Focus for the Defence of Freedom and Peace', in which Churchill assumed the most prominent rôle. This loosely organized group, which intended to convince the government and the public of the aggressive intentions and the profound immorality of the Hitler regime, advocated an uncompromising policy vis -à-vis Germany. Financed by a few influential Jews, it operated informally, but effectively, and assembled a galaxy of staunch anti-appeasers—among others Violet Bonham-Carter, Walter Citrine, Comm. Locker-Lampson, Archibald Sinclair, Wickham Steed, Robert Vansittart and Robert Waley-Cohen, Vice-President of the Board of Deputies.[8]

The exaltation of anti-Semitism in Germany and the emergence of the phenomenon in England confronted Anglo-Jewry with a dilemma other communities had faced before: should it rally in self-defence, a course German Jewry had taken in response to the activities of anti-Semitic parties in the 1880s and again during the 1920s, or should it refrain from taking public action and remain passive, a policy organized French Jewry had preferred during the Dreyfus Affair?[9] The question presented itself in terms of the successful integration of the Jewish community into the host society: any effort to unify the heterogeneous Jewish community in order to organize a defence campaign implied the revitalization of the fading Jewish identity and a public display of one's Jewishness, both of which contradicted the prolonged efforts to prove that Jews were worthy of emancipation, that their assimilation progressed steadily and that their Jewish identity had become subsidiary to their respective nationality.

Although Anglo-Jewry appeared to be a self-confident minority which had retained its communal institutions, such as the Chief Rabbinate, the Board of Deputies and a weekly paper, the *Jewish Chronicle*, it proved reluctant to take public action when confronted with open hatred. In 1920, disconcerted by the sudden vogue of anti-Semitic publications, it set up a Joint Press Committee, which included representatives from the Board of Deputies, the Anglo-Jewish Association, the B'nai B'rith and the Jewish Historical Society. Its efforts to counter attacks on Jews were limited to the publication of a few pamphlets refuting the stock arguments that Bolshevism was Jewish and Jews were undermining their host societies, and to informal contacts asking individuals who employed these allegations to reconsider their ill-informed judgements. From 1925 onwards it noted a continued diminution in the number of anti-Semitic references, a tendency that was reversed in 1933.[10]

The new wave of anti-Semitism was at first interpreted as a campaign 'conducted by agents working under direct instructions from abroad'.[11] Neville Laski,[12] a representative of the Sephardic community and President of the Board, as well as other Jews of his social ranking and background, perceived the anti-Semitic agitation not as an outburst of latent hatred, but as an imported propaganda drive. Perturbing as it was, it was not considered serious enough to require a new strategy in defence of Jewish rights. This assumption, which *a priori* excluded the possibility that anti-Semitism could ever develop as a home-grown movement in Britain, disregarded the fact that even if the ideology had been imported – which was not unequivocally true for the movements under consideration – it could be exploited by genuinely British movements and could generate hostility amongst a large section of the community.

Conforming to the general policy of appeasement, which was motivated by the priority of 'safety first', the Board proved extremely reluctant to combat anti-Semitism. Just as the Jewish community trusted a few prestigious leaders to safeguard its interests, the Board never wavered in its reliance upon the state authorities to deal with any anti-Jewish incidents. Firmly convinced that traditional British tolerance and liberalism would neutralize scattered attempts to stir anti-Semitic feelings, it perceived no need to demand special protection for the Jewish minority. Still conscious of being a tolerated, rather than accepted, section of the population, it avoided questioning the image of an ostensibly harmonious symbiosis. Indicative of this attitude was the Board's reaction to the parliamentary debate on anti-Semitism: without further discussion, it expressed its appreciation of the Home Secretary's statement that Jew-baiting would not be tolerated in England, and professed sincere gratitude to the members of the House who had raised the issue.[13]

The unshattered sense of security displayed by the majority of established Jewish leaders, of whom only a few personally experienced living conditions and anxieties in the East End, was not shared by the spokesmen of the communities immediately concerned. On 26 July 1936, in opposition to the passivity of the Board of Deputies, the Jewish Labour Council convened a conference to form an effective defence organization to counter the anti-Semitic agitation by the Fascists. There were 131 delegates present, representing 87 Jewish organizations: synagogues, Friendly Societies, Trade Unions, and Zionist organizations. The newly appointed Jewish People's Council (JPC) immediately began to challenge the Board's inactivity. According to what had been expressed at the foundation conference, it maintained that anti-Semitism could not be separated from the movement that propagated it and that Fascism, a political ideology fundamentally opposed to democratic rights and civil liberties, posed the real threat to the community.[14]

The JPC pointed out that the survival of Jewry throughout its diaspora had depended upon religious freedom and that the Jews had consistently opposed dictatorship and tyranny. Since Fascism was seen as equivalent to the destruction of civil rights, it was considered not enough to isolate the anti-Semitic issue, but necessary to combat Fascism as such in cooperation with like-minded groups. A conference held on 15 November 1936, which was attended by 163 delegates representing 91 organizations, endorsed this approach. J. Jacobs, a member of the executive committee of the JPC, pointed out that the traditional policy of negotiating the position of Jewry under any given government would be obsolete in the case of Fascism:

> If Fascism reaches power in this country there will be no question of discussing with the Government about the Jews – the Jews will either be dead or in concentration camps.[15]

From its inception, the JPC waged an active campaign against Fascism. It organized a petition against the Fascists' march through the East End on 4 October 1936, a petition which obtained nearly 100,000 signatures, allegedly within 48 hours. It collected information on Jew-baiting and hooliganism, and staged protest meetings against the anti-Jewish activities of Fascist organizations, in particular the BUF. JPC deputations visited mayors and lobbied the Home Office to ban Fascist marches. It also pressed for the passing of a Political Uniforms Act as well as a Racial Incitement Act, which would make it an offence to publicize in private or in public, orally or in writing, 'words calculated to bring any racial community into public hatred or contempt'.[16] The JPC's most important endeavour, however, was its campaign to evoke a collective response against Fascism, propagating the following slogans:

The streets cannot be surrendered to the fascist hooligans!
Refuse to be intimidated by Fascist terrorism!
Continue to protest at fascist racial incitement![17]

Although it stressed the fact that it was politically neutral and did not identify with any one political party or grouping, the JPC in practice collaborated mainly with left-wing bodies, the groups that agitated for a determined public opposition against Fascism, such as the National Council for Civil Liberties, Trades Councils, Workers' Circles and the Communist Party. At the same time, it accused the Communist Party of endeavouring to make political capital out of the antagonism between Fascists and Jews.[18] The JPC persistently argued that the issue was not one between Fascists and Jews, but between Democrats and Fascists. It did not appeal to the pride and honour of Jews asking them to stand by their Jewishness and to defend their legally acquired rights, but insisted that there existed no specifically Jewish problem, and that the particular Jewish concern was only incidental to the fight against Fascism. Time and again it repeated that

the Fascist attack upon a section of the population, the Jews, is a prelude to the attack upon the liberties of the whole people. Anti-Semitism is, therefore, as much the concern of non-Jews as of Jews.[19]

Although the JPC attacked anti-Semitism as a menace to society at large, its very foundation and the decision to combat Fascism were, in fact, motivated by sectional concerns, even if the general analysis of anti-Semitism conceived the opposition against Fascism as a necessity transcending communal interests. Thus, the JPC justified its own existence by reproaching the Board of Deputies with inactivity. In its political campaign, it associated in particular with the active 'Ex-Servicemen's Movement Against Fascism', a further ostensibly non-political, non-partisan body which in practice was predominantly Jewish. The JPC claimed to voice Jewish sentiments, called upon all Jewish organizations, synagogues and lay institutions to strengthen its campaign, and asked the Jewish people to place confidence in its policy, stressing that 'the coordination of all forces within Jewry is the paramount need of the moment'.[20]

The Board of Deputies vigorously condemned the 'unauthorized activities of the so-called Jewish People's Council which, in approaching Government departments and municipalities, had assumed functions which only the Board was entitled to exercise',[21] and used all its influence to discredit this body. The Board contacted the BBC and *The Times*, both of which had reported about the JPC's efforts to further a cooperative resistance against organized anti-Semitism, and asked them to give no more publicity to JPC activities.[22] It refused to send delegates to the meetings organized by the JPC, and appealed to Jewish societies to boycott the JPC conference on anti-Semitism which was held on 15 November 1936. It was announced that at the same date and time a meeting would be held under the auspices of the Board, to which all Jewish organizations were invited to give their support.[23] President Laski reiterated the Board's position in a letter to the Home Office, and succeeded in stigmatizing the JPC as a body which commanded no respect in 'responsible Jewish quarters'.[24]

The Board's opposition to the activities of the JPC was not only a matter of jealously claiming sole authority for the affairs of Anglo-Jewry, nor was it a mere disagreement over strategy. Whereas the JPC argued that the campaign against anti-Semitism could not be waged from a merely philanthropical point of view, but had to involve a minimum of political commitment and had to oppose the very ideology of which anti-Semitism was a significant part, the Board maintained that as a body of Anglo-Jewry it represented communal, not political, interests. Pointing out that 'there is Fascism in Italy under which 50,000 Jews live in amity and safety', President Laski insisted that a neutral attitude had to be preserved and that 'the Jewish community, not being a political body as such, should not be dragged into the fight against Fascism as such'.[25]

There can be no doubt that the JPC responded to a widespread feeling among London Jewry that it was neglected by its official leaders, and that its particular grievances were ignored by the Board, whose President on one occasion remarked that East End Jewry 'should not imagine it is the whole of the Anglo-Jewish Community'.[26] One observer, who attended a Jewish meeting in the East End, reported to the Board comments suggesting that wealthy British Jews gave financial support to Fascist organizations and that the Board was 'rolling in money'.[27] Yet it was not only the increasing alienation from the community and the ensuing loss of authority that eventually moved the Board to organize some defence work. Some deputies also criticized the lack of leadership and pressed the Board to take action.

At the Board meeting of 24 May 1936, Sir Robert Waley-Cohen, Vice-President, proposed setting up a special *ad hoc* committee for the purpose of defending Jewry against the campaign of calumny. The appeal was discussed, but President Laski opposed it, urging the assembly not to

> exaggerate the nature of that crisis, to create feelings of panic and to destroy the confidence that could properly be placed in a devoted band of people who had been placed in the direction of affairs.[28]

At the July meeting of the Board Mr Turner-Samuels, representative for Newcastle, openly complained about the agonizing inactivity of the Board's officers. His argument was given much publicity in the following report in the *Jewish Chronicle*:

> Why, he asked, should they not fight anti-Semites? What were they to be afraid of? For three-and-a-half years the phrase 'Trust Us' had been used. There had been nothing else at that Board on the subject except a creeping paralysis. . . . They would never satisfy the Jewish people of this country unless they did something practical for their protection.[29]

At last the official institution of Anglo-Jewry decided to end its ambivalence on the question of determined resistance against the anti-Semitic campaign. At the Board meeting of 19 July 1936, the President recommended 'that a Co-ordinating Committee be formed to unify and direct activities in defence of the Jewish communities against attacks made upon it'.[30] This committee, which met for the first time on 26 July 1936, was composed of a few distinguished leaders of Anglo-Jewry, among them President Laski, Sir Robert Waley Cohen and Lionel Cohen, both vice presidents, and Gordon Liverman, treasurer of the Board. A special office was rented for the work of the committee, and a permanent organizing and press secretary was appointed. The committee held monthly meetings to discuss its strategies and the progress of the campaign, and submitted regular reports on its activities to the Board. It was re-named 'Jewish Defence Committee' in November 1938.

The defence campaign organized by the Board of Deputies consisted of four elements: indirect pressure upon Government officials to consider the interests of the Jewish community; apologetical propaganda intended to enlighten the public about peculiarities rooted in Jewish history and religion; self-criticism to reduce objective causes of anti-Semitism; urgent appeals to Jewry to abstain from provocative meetings so as to avoid getting involved in disorder.

The indirect campaign focusing on informal contacts was a continuation of the policy the Board had practised for some time, in particular in consultation with ecclesiastical bodies. When one deputy drew attention to the fact that the *Protocols* were being circulated by a British publishing company, he was told by the President that the matter 'would be considered with the very valuable legal resources which were available to the Board'.[31] Similarly, Laski 'undertook to approach representatives of the chief political parties in this country on the subject'[32] when the BUF's intention to contest the London County Council elections in 1937 became public. In May 1938, he reported that he had met Sir Walter Citrine, with whom he discussed the alleged Fascist penetration of the Trade Unions. Laski reassured the delegates at various meetings of the Coordinating Committee that he was in constant touch with Sir Russell Scott, Permanent Under-Secretary of State for Home Affairs. At the meeting of 15 July 1937 he mentioned that he had had a number of interviews with the Home Secretary and the Commissioner of the Metropolitan Police, which 'had been a considerable factor in the more stringent enforcement of the Public Order Act'.[33] In June 1938 Laski again informed the committee of his contacts with the Commissioner and added 'that there was no doubt whatever in his mind . . . that the Commissioner was most strongly anti-Fascist and in entire sympathy with the views they had laid before him'.[34]

The extent and impact of these semi-official consultations are difficult to assess since they were never described in great detail. The report on defence activities for November/December 1938, for example, only mentions that, investigating the financial sources of anti-Semitic organizations, 'the Chairman and the Secretary of the Board, as a result of certain conversations, have been given the advantage of certain contacts of somewhat unusual character'.[35] Evidence in the police files suggests that Neville Laski, to whom such confidential negotiations were usually entrusted, carried considerable weight with the authorities, and that he had access to high-ranking politicians and civil servants, which was not the case with the JPC. Laski was, however, careful not to infringe the mutual trust he had established and repeatedly advised the committee not to alienate the responsible officials by unreasonable demands.

The most conspicuous efforts the Coordinating Committee undertook to defend the Jewish community against anti-Semitic calumnies lay in the propaganda campaign addressed to the Gentile population. This traditional Jewish response against attacks from the host society disregarded the irrational character of anti-Semitism, and betrayed a naive belief in progress and tolerance. It was based on the assumption that, to prevent anti-Semitism from gaining ground, it was sufficient to enlighten the public about Jewish culture and traditions, and to refute anti-Semitic allegations by contrary evidence. Typical of this approach was an investigation under the direction of Cyril Burt, instigated at the Board's suggestion by the Jewish Health Organization, to investigate the comparative intelligence and attainment of Jewish and non-Jewish school children. This project was the result of an unfavourable report by Karl Pearson in the *Annals of Eugenics*.[36] Inspired by the same principle of spreading apologetical propaganda, a special Jewish Lecture Committee was formed in 1933. It supplied Jewish lectures to non-Jewish societies such as Adult Schools, Rotary Clubs, Peace Pledge Unions and Cooperative Guilds, which were addressed on topics like 'Jewish Beliefs', 'Jewish Home Customs', or 'The Jew in Europe'. Under the auspices of this committee 160 lectures were delivered in 1935, 224 and in 1936, 247 in 1937 and 197 in 1938.[37]

The campaign organized by the Defence Committee and a further sub-committee, the London Area Council, was intended to meet different purposes. In order to avoid creating a 'Jewish problem' where it did not exist, it did not aim at stirring goodwill towards the Jewish community in a widespread propaganda campaign. Instead, in themes as well as location, it followed up Fascist activities, thus operating its campaign strictly as an anti-defamation crusade. The object was again to combat racial hatred by an appeal to reason, quoting facts and statistics in an effort to disprove the standard accusations of anti-Semites. For this purpose the Board, following the initiative taken by the Friendly Societies' Association, trained speakers, mostly inexperienced volunteers, to address open-air meetings. Short guide-lines were prepared by the press officer of the Board, arming speakers with arguments against the most frequent anti-Jewish statements,[38] to inform the public about Jewish history and religion[39] and to demonstrate the complete identification of Anglo-Jewry with British culture, history and politics.[40]

The open-air meetings at street-corners and parks following the meetings of anti-Semitic organizations were conducted on a large scale. The first meetings convened by the Coordinating Committee, held in August and September 1936 in North and East London, were attended by an average audience of 400–500 people, but already during 1937 it was observed that 'its meetings have been comparatively few and attended by audiences to whom its policy made little appeal' numbering on average only 30–50 people. During 1938 a total of 788 meetings were held on 89 different spots but again their propaganda effect was limited since they attracted only small audiences, frequently numbering only a dozen people.[41] According to the conception of these meetings, their appeal depended entirely on the Jew-consciousness stirred by anti-Semitic propaganda. As soon as their opponents lost public attention, the anti-defamation campaign became obsolete.

While the street-corner campaign was intended to reach the hostile Gentile public, prominent Board officers also addressed a few large meetings of sympathetic organizations to evoke their support for the Board's defence campaign. Again, Neville Laski took the most prominent position. He was invited to speak at the National Liberal Club in reply to a previous talk by Oswald Mosley, and addressed various ecclesiastical societies and business associations on general philosemitic topics, such as 'The Jewish Contribution to Civilization'.

A further element of the Board's anti-defamation campaign was to correct the negative images of 'the Jew' in writing. Within the first year of its activities, the Coordinating Committee circulated some 1,000,000 leaflets, which by the end of 1938 exceeded the 2,000,000 mark. Most of them were, like the lectures, meant to enlighten the public on their Jewish fellow-citizens, stressing in particular the patriotism of Jews. In this context, special attention was given to the perennial argument of anti-Semites, that the Jews had shirked military service and had cleared profits while the nation bled – an allegation that was countered by statistics of Jewish casualties and lists of decorations Jews had won during the war.[42]

A further task of the Coordinating Committee was to attend to the non-Jewish press. Its practice of supplying the press and the BBC with information on the Jewish community and its anti-defamation campaign seems to have met with sympathetic response. A summary of the committee's activities for 1938 stated that nearly a hundred letters were sent to the press each month, of which about 85 per cent were printed.[43] Letters to the editor of anti-Semitic nature, particularly with regard to the influx of German-Jewish refugees, were answered by the press officer. To avoid giving the impression of irksome special pleading, the Board used the names of Jewish and non-Jewish supporters, who agreed to stand as signatories. In the same vein, some standard diction-aries were asked to reconsider their entry 'Jew' and 'to jew', defined as 'usurer' and 'to cheat, defraud'. On this issue, however, the Board failed to score a success, since the respective editors insisted that this meaning had to be included in the entry, as it represented a possible usage of the words in question, and not a value judgement by the editors.[44]

The third aspect of the defence campaign of established Jewry, that of self-criticism, was a strategy continuously advanced by Jewish leaders whenever the community was under attack. It represented the typical answer of Jews who had totally assimilated to their environment, but did not deny their Jewish origin and felt embarrassed whenever their co-religionists 'misbehaved' according to the standard criteria of the host society. Already the reform Jews during the enlightenment had readily supported the arguments advanced by their reform-minded Christian contemporaries, that an improvement of their civil status would entail their moral betterment. As enlightened Jews they agreed that a re-education of their community was necessary to disperse common stereotypes and to live up to the expectations placed upon their emancipation. In England, the established community had offered the same concept as a solution to the anti-Jewish reaction following the influx of East European Jewish immigrants in the 1890s, and it revived the policy under the pressure of anti-Semitic agitation in the 1930s, adapting it to the fact that it was no longer the foreign appear-ance but the behaviour of immigrants that was an irritant to the English public.

At the meeting of the Coordinating Committee on 10 December 1936, President Laski suggested setting up a sub-committee 'to deal with such social conditions as sweatshops, bad employers, landlords and price-cutting in the East End'. A sub-committee appointed to consider such 'internal causes' for anti-Semitism suggested at their meeting on 24 May 1938 that a permanent committee should be set up for the following purpose:

1 To make the Community conscious of the effect of individual malpractices on the good name of the Community, and to obtain the cooperation of all elements in Anglo-Jewry in the elimination of such practices.
2 To work in London and outside through appropriate bodies or committees with similar functions by the investigation of individual cases of such practices, and to take such steps as may be fitting to check their continuance.[45]

In November 1938, M. G. Liverman, the Secretary of the Defence Committee, submitted a memorandum to the Board of Deputies, in which he placed great emphasis on the urgent need to analyse objective reasons for anti-Semitism:

I submit that the time has passed for us to pretend that we are a perfect community and to ignore the fact that not a day goes by without anti-Semitism being created by Jews themselves. I have on my desk as I write a batch of trade papers. A casual glance at these will demonstrate how a new generation of unethical Jewish traders are by bankruptcy, due to complete irresponsibility and lack of principle, causing hardship over a wide field and manufacturing anti-Semitism at high pressure. The textile trade in this connection is well known but it may be worth mentioning one before me not so frequently quoted – namely the tobacconist trade.[46]

'Vigilance Committees' were created in various towns and trades to institutionalize the desired self-criticism on cut-price tactics and unfair trading. They followed up complaints about Jewish landlords accused of extorting rent, neglecting to provide elementary repairs or requesting their non-Jewish tenants to pay their rents on Sundays. The most frequent complaints were brought forward by Trade Unions and private individuals against Jewish employers accused of imposing unfair trading conditions on their employees in regard to wages and hours. Another source of resentment emerged from an alleged preference for Jewish immigrants seeking

employment with Jewish firms, which was said to cause re-
dundancies among British employees.[47]

Anglo-Jewry was particularly apprehensive regarding the
influx of German-Jewish refugees, which enhanced the 'Jewish
question' among the population. In December 1938 the Defence
Committee agreed to publish a bi-lingual brochure in English and
German, of which 150,000 copies were distributed, entitled *While
You are in England. Helpful Information and Guidance for Every Refugee.*
This booklet was intended not only to offer information on practical
questions and bureaucratic problems, but to serve also as a 'code,
so to speak, of conduct for refugees to adopt while staying in this
country'.[48]

Apart from the fact that the self-criticism imposed by the Board
was liable to be vilified by opponents as self-denial and an attempt
to appear more English than the English, it showed a remarkable
submissiveness to the anti-Semitic campaign, in that it denied the
Jewish community the right to individuality of its citizens. While
the society at large was assumed to be naturally composed of good
and bad individuals, law-abiding citizens and criminals, Jews were
asked to behave in a uniformly immaculate fashion and to conform
to the bourgeois ideals revered by their official leaders. The postulate that members of the Jewish community – irrespective of their
social background and education – could not afford to 'misbehave',
because it would stigmatize the whole community, in fact accepted
the point reiterated by anti-Semites, that Jews retain an exceptional
position among other societies.

At a special meeting of the Defence Committee held on 13
February 1939, Professor Brodetsky rightly pointed out that 'the
fact that the actions of some Jews were regarded as anti-social did
not necessarily produce anti-Semitism'.[49] Although 'misbehaviour'
of Jews reinforces negative stereotypes and this facilitates the
reception of anti-Semitic propaganda, absence of such experience
does not alter the traditional cliché. 'Normal' behaviour of Jews,
complying with that of the average citizen, is considered exceptional by prejudiced observers. On the other hand, they interpret
bad behaviour as evidence for somebody's Jewish origin. This was
confirmed by the fact that the Board, when investigating complaints against particular persons, sometimes found that the
offender was not Jewish, or that the charges were unfounded.

Like the plan to counteract the anti-Semitic agitation by stating
'the truth' in terms of facts and figures, the practice of self-criticism

represented a well-intended but ingenuous effort to defend Jewry against anti-Semitism. Both ventures reveal the dilettante *ad hoc* character of the defence campaign, the lack of a theoretical analysis of anti-Semitism, and the failure to understand its general significance as a problem of Gentile societies, in which the Jews figure as targets, not as the cause of the attack.

The fourth aspect of the defence campaign led by the Board, that of urging the community to abstain from Fascist meetings, was promoted in agreement with the state authorities. This plea was supported by the argument that much of the abuse and disorder that occurred at Fascist meetings was due to the presence of opposition, while the agitators frequently found it difficult to gather sufficiently large audiences to stage successful meetings once the Jews stayed away. This policy too was rooted in the consistent effort of the established leaders of Anglo-Jewry to behave inconspicuously as a community, and the Board used all its authority to discourage the Jews from taking action, asking them to place confidence in the Board, which was entrusted to safeguard Jewish interests. Characteristic of this appeal was a joint letter by Chief Rabbi J. H. Hertz and President Laski to the *Jewish Chronicle* in which they expressed their conviction that participation by Jews in brawls with Fascists 'brings discredit upon the Anglo-Jewish community and can only be harmful to the general cause which we all have at heart'.[50]

Of the Board's campaign to combat anti-Semitism, the constant appeals to Jews to stay away from Fascist meetings was the most unrealistic and least successful aspect. When the Board requested the *Jewish Chronicle* to refrain from giving any publicity to Fascist activities, the editor pointedly argued that these events were of considerable news value to the readers of the paper and could not be suppressed.[51] Occasionally the lack of contact with the man in the street was criticized within the Board itself,[52] but on the whole it failed to comprehend the real sense of fear that harassed East End Jewry, and proved unable to prevail upon the community to trust its leadership in this crisis: The dilemma with which Jewry was confronted was judiciously summed up by B. L. Q. Henriques, Warden of a Jewish settlement in the East End, in a letter to *The Times*:

If they [i.e. the Jews] keep away from Fascist meetings they allow the slanders and lies told about them to circulate unanswered. If they do attend abuse produces counter-abuse and provocation achieves its purpose. No self-respecting Englishman of the Jewish religion can listen to the speeches without bursting with indignation. . . . So high are the incensed passions of the most law-abiding Jewish citizens that it is becoming impossible to-day to hold them in restraint. They are getting beyond listening to being told to leave it to others to defend them against the un-English and unsportsmanlike attack of the Fascist Party. Indeed, what are they to do under the circumstances? They are so on edge that they are ready to clutch at any straw.[53]

The straw that offered active resistance against the Fascist campaign was the extreme Left. The liberal leaders of the Jewish community naturally disapproved of their co-religionists' apparent political radicalization, and sought to exert a moderating influence. They considered Jewry's move to the left a temporary phenomenon, and tried to excuse it by blaming it upon the Fascist agitation, which was said to elevate ethnicity as a decisive factor in local politics. Thus it was claimed that East End Jews 'contrary to the political views of the vast majority of them . . . are being so terrorized as to be forced into the ranks of Communism'.[54] Rose L. Henriques, chairman of an East End Girls' Club, argued the same case in a circular letter sent to the mothers of absentee girls. Urging them to be 'loyal English Gentlewomen of the Jewish Faith' and to satisfy themselves where their children were spending the evenings, she informed them that 'a great many Jewish girls have joined Communist clubs, not because they are Communists, but because they feel that the Communists were the only people who were trying to fight the Fascists.'[55]

Given the prominence of the issue in the political campaign in the East End, partisanship at the grass-roots level was certainly influenced, often even determined, by the acceptance or rejection of anti-Semitism. While panic-stricken Jews supported the Communists as the only activist anti-Fascists, non-Jewish residents who resented the Jews were attracted by the only anti-Semitic party – both frequently irrespective of their political beliefs. It was, for example, observed that some BUF supporters were Trade Union members, and four of the party's prospective parliamentary candidates were former members of the Communist Party.[56]

Although the resistance against Fascism was clearly the most important factor accounting for East End Jewry's political radicalization, its growing ethnical awareness was not the only reason for supporting the CPGB. While the apparent militancy of the Left offered a far more satisfying response than the placidity displayed by the Board, its general political message appealed to many East End Jews because it integrated the discontent generated by class-consciousness and the Jew-consciousness arising from anti-Semitism into a coherent ideology. At the same time the idea of fighting anti-Semitism by opposing Fascism, and defeating both permanently by working towards an idealized socialist society, removed the stigma of being preoccupied with paltry self-defence, and allied Jewry to a seemingly progressive movement, advocating peace and social reforms.

The theoretical concept of perceiving anti-Semitism as a means of diversion from disquieting social issues and class-conflicts, which was promoted by the Communist Party, not only suited those Jews who, because of their political inclinations, had joined the CP during the 1920s. It also appealed to those hitherto unpolitical members of the community, who now felt alienated from the Board of Deputies and the established leaders of the community. This antagonism was increased by the fact that it was not only based on class-divisions among Anglo-Jewry, but also on a generation-conflict, with the dissatisfied and genuinely agitated young 'hot-heads' impatiently challenging their elders for a more determined resistance against anti-Semitism.[57]

The split among Anglo-Jewry thus appears to have been more fundamental than a mere disagreement over apt strategies to defend the community against anti-Semitic attacks. The question of self-defence merely epitomized and deepened the rift between the 'old' community, which was devoted to the concept of assimilation as it had developed in the age of liberalism, and the 'new' community, which remained sceptical as to the practicability of idealistic concepts and either turned to Zionism as an alternative to assimilation, or to Socialism as a viable form of liberation from ethnic as well as economic bonds. Under the pressure of anti-Jewish agitation, the two factions that shared the view that Anglo-Jewry's future lay in Britain, and that anti-Semitism was only a temporary issue, agreed to reconcile their disagreements and to combine their efforts.

The JPC from its inception had urged Jewry to unite in its struggle against Fascism and anti-Semitism, and had demanded that it should combine with other groups menaced by Fascism, so as to strengthen the campaign in defence of democratic freedom and help to create a popular front. The Board, on the other hand, had been reluctant to cooperate with the JPC, which it considered 'dangerous because it was opposed to Fascism, and not anti-Semitism *per se*, had allied itself to communist and left-wing organizations and was acting as though the Anglo-Jewish community were an *imperium in imperio*'.[58] Under the impression of anti-Semitic legislation in Germany and Italy, the Board revised its attitude that Jewry as a community had no business to oppose Fascism in principle, and eventually agreed that 'the resistance to and the fight against anti-Semitism is coextensive with the fight for democracy'.[59] Pressed in particular by Friendly Societies, who argued that 'the time is long past when Jewry could afford to be divided,'[60] the Board began to negotiate a common platform with the JPC. It insisted, however, that the anti-defamation campaign had to be non-political in the sense that Anglo-Jewry could not yoke itself to any one particular party, and had to avoid 'anything which savours of a Jewish vote or a Jewish party or a Jewish attitude to any political problem'.[61] For the same reason, an appeal was launched 'to Conservative Jewish speakers to come forward', as soon as it was discovered that speakers volunteering for the defence campaign were mostly members of the Labour Party.[62]

After both factions had agreed to a mutually satisfying platform, implying total detachment from party politics, a further obstacle prevented them from merging: the Board, not recognizing the JPC as a peer, requested its total liquidation, while the JPC insisted on the right to nominate representatives to the Coordinating Committee and the relevant sub-committees. This refusal to permit a body, which had successfully challenged its authority, to participate in the common effort to master a critical situation, further curtailed the Board's influence within the community. Its anachronistic obduracy stimulated the criticism of those who claimed that the Board was not a democratic body, because the deputies were elected on a congregational basis, and demanded the secularization of the institution. Since these suggestions aimed at the formation of a definite Jewish pressure-group, they were strongly resented by the assimilated section of the community, whose Judaism was merely a religious bond, and who insisted that 'our duty as citizens must override our sentiments as Jews'.[63]

Anglo-Jewry's reaction against anti-Semitism in England above all illuminates the effect of successful integration, namely a marked loss in the minority's sense of identity. As Jewishness ceases to be an obvious disadvantage, the incentive to seek strength in unity evaporates, and the former solidarity of the oppressed is replaced by competition and a diversification of interests. In the case of Anglo-Jewry, the political and social assimilation of the 'old community', and its successful integration into British society, had reached such a degree that its pretence to formal leadership in other than religious questions had become obsolete.

The anti-Semitic agitation briefly retarded the process of disintegration and revitalized the Jew-consciousness among the assimilated sections of the community. It manifested itself first and foremost in charity: spontaneous fund-raising campaigns to help German-Jewish refugees, and reluctantly-launched appeals to support the anti-defamation campaign at home, for which £4000 was raised by the Manchester Furniture Trade, £2370 by the West End Gown Trade and £1400 at a meeting addressed by President Laski in Birmingham.[64] The generous contributions to relief-funds constituted an effort to satisfy the moral obligation as Jews without impairing the social position achieved as Englishmen by identifying personally with those Jewish communities under attack.[65]

Claiming on the one hand to represent the whole community, denying on the other that there existed anything like 'organized Jewry' lest this could reinforce anti-Jewish arguments, the 'old community', which in the inter-war years still dominated the Board of Deputies, found itself compelled to take action if it was to retain as much as a semblance of authority. Its prolonged hesitancy to defend the community when it was challenged by anti-Semitism at home accelerated its decline of prestige among the masses of Jewry, a process which had set in with its anti-Zionism, followed by its failure to endorse the boycott campaign against Nazi Germany on behalf of Anglo-Jewry. In all three arguments the leaders of the 'new community', who resented the timid attitude that Jews must not defy anti-Semitism, distinguished themselves as the future leaders of Anglo-Jewry.

The defence activities of Anglo-Jewry in their entirety expose most convincingly the myth constantly advanced by anti-Semites, that Jewry constitutes a closely knit corporate entity. Far from sympathizing with the local resentment against Fascism, the leadership of Anglo-Jewry in fact proved deeply alienated from those it claimed to represent. Far from being subservient to their 'financial masters', who allegedly paid the Jewish mob to turn out against Fascism, East End Jews entered a political alliance that not only signified their antagonism to Fascism, but also to their nominal leaders.

8 The Radical Left

The activities of Mosley's Blackshirts and other Fascist groups in the East End induced the formation of various *ad hoc* movements standing for democratic freedom against budding Fascist dictatorship. Thus, a Council of Citizens of East London was formed in the autumn of 1936 under the presidency of the Archbishop of Canterbury. It included representatives from various political parties and religious bodies, and stated as its objectives 'the restoration of the former conditions of tranquillity, good feeling, peace and good-will and order between Jews and Gentiles'.[1] Similarly, an East London Anti-Fascist United Committee was founded in 1936 by East London branches of the Labour and Independent Labour Party, Socialist Leagues, Trade Unions and Jewish working class organizations.

Apart from such local demonstrations of sympathy and general expressions of indignation, the democratic parties did not formulate a policy on the question of anti-Semitism. When commenting upon the political developments in Germany, anti-Semitism was usually explained as a by-product of German history and traditions, where Jews offered themselves as a convenient scapegoat for the diversion of discontent. Occasionally, some champions of the anti-Nazi movement even showed impatience with the prominence given to the 'Jewish question'. At a conference on 'The Grave Nazi Menace' one delegate, Dr H. Dalton, pointed out:

> There has been, I think, slightly excessive emphasis upon the fate of Jews in Germany, terrible as it has been and continues to be. But let us not forget the vast mass of Gentile trade unionists, Socialists and Pacifists, who have been subjected to atrocity and murder. . . . Many millions of the best and purest Aryans have suffered from having held the wrong opinion.[2]

155

With regard to Jew-baiting in Britain, members of the Labour Party and the Liberal Party of the constituencies particularly affected showed their apprehensive observation of the developments by exposing Fascist anti-Semitism in Parliament. Their official policy reduced itself to urging Jews to abstain from provocative meetings so as to avoid giving the Fascists untoward publicity. The prevalent attitude clearly was that political anti-Semitism was a passing phenomenon, incapable of mobilizing a substantial following among the English public.

By contrast, the Communist Party of Great Britain (CPGB) waged a more aggressive, active campaign against Fascism and anti-Semitism. During the 1920s, it had established itself as a loyal subject of the Comintern, faithfully conforming to the current policies laid down by Moscow. Hampered by successive waves of 'red scare' propaganda, it failed to make any headway. Apart from the general strike, when it temporarily succeeded in attracting new recruits in support of its militant attitude, its membership throughout the decade remained at an average of some 3000 supporters.[3] By the end of the 1920s, the CPGB had failed to install itself as the spokesman of the working-class or the unemployed: with a relatively large proportion of Jews and Irish among its small membership, and an imported ideology, it was discredited as a thoroughly un-British phenomenon, lacking any roots in the traditional political culture.

However negligible in absolute figures, the comparatively prominent involvement of Jews in the early history of the CPGB corresponds to the radical tradition among Russian-Jewish immigrants who had settled in the East End.[4] The devastating living conditions these Jews were confronted with, and the fact that many refugees had belonged to the radical intelligentsia in Russia facilitated the reception of socialist propaganda. Although the radical potential amongst these Jews gradually eroded in concordance with their assimilation and an improvement of their standard of living, the pro-Bolshevik sympathies harboured by many of the politically active immigrant Jews explain their support for the CPGB. Small as it was, their partisanship during the 1920s derived from a firm belief in the revolutionary doctrine and was not linked to any specifically Jewish interests.[5]

The serious economic crisis which affected the Western world in 1929, and the apparent inability of the capitalist systems to conquer poverty and unemployment, caused an increasing politicization of the population at large – both those who were directly threatened by the crisis as well as the well-to-do who suffered from 'social guilt' facing the alarming impact the slump had on other sections of the community. Fascism presented one alternative to those who were disillusioned with the existing system, Communism another. In their propaganda methods, both were remarkably alike: they envisaged a universal ideology to cure the world of all evils, each claimed to stand for progress and the common good, and both appealed to the sentiment of the masses by employing flags, songs and marches as symbols of unity and action.

The CPGB, which numbered some 20,000 members by the outbreak of World War II, at the most equalled the BUF in membership. Still failing to flourish as a distinctive working-class movement, it succeeded in attracting a large number of intellectuals and idealists, which lent it a sudden respectability and fashionableness. Their sympathies for the CPGB were not so much founded on an approval of the objective 'For Soviet Britain' than on the support for the party's resistance against Fascism. Since the established parties refused to sponsor a 'popular front', the CPGB was the only political organization promoting a combined effort to combat 'Fascism, the open terrorist dictatorship of the most reactionary, most chauvinist and most imperialist elements of finance capital'.[6] The additional pledge to defend 'the preservation of democratic institutions and civilization against Fascist barbarism'[7] ensured the sympathy of people from a wide political spectrum who shared an acute awareness of the menace of Fascism. Their identification with the radical left was only temporary, defined in negative terms as an alliance against Fascism and war. As the history of the Left Book Club exemplifies, severe splits occurred after the appeal for a popular front had become obsolete, particularly over the question of whether or not to support the war effort and over the attitude towards Russia after the German-Soviet pact of non-aggression.

One element of continuity between the old and new membership of the CPGB was provided by the fact that again many of its recruits were Jews, to whom the threat of anti-Semitism provided an additional stimulus to identify with a party that opposed Jew-hatred as part and parcel of a reactionary ideology. Right-wing propagandists quickly exploited this fact not only in their campaign against German-Jewish refugees, but also in their efforts to thwart the anti-appeasement propaganda conducted by Jews. Lady Astor, for example, rebuked the Jews for their anti-Germanism and warned them 'not to allow themselves to be got at by the Communists as has too often been the case in the past'.[8]

Although many Jews supported the CPGB's anti-Fascist campaign, it would be a mistake to characterize the CPGB as one of the 'champions of the Jews in the anti-Fascist cause'.[9] Analysing anti-Semitism as a problem typical of capitalist societies, the CPGB was in fact less concerned about the lot of unfortunate Jews than about the principle involved. Opposing Nazi anti-Semitism, an article in the *Daily Worker* pointed out:

> We condemn it even more on behalf of the human race from which it attempts to exclude the Jews than on behalf of the Jews whom it seeks to make a scapegoat for all the ills humanity is suffering in consequence of the collapse of the capitalist system.[10]

The CPGB stressed the importance of the fight against anti-Semitism and maintained that 'it is vital to develop solidarity between Jewish and all other workers in London and to give attention and assistance to Jewish organizations',[11] but it did not treat Jew-baiting as a separate issue of special importance. In concordance with Marx's subsumption of the 'Jewish question' under the general analysis and criticism of bourgeois society, the CPGB perceived anti-Semitism not as an ethnic or religious, but as a socio-political issue, as a vehicle manipulated by capitalists 'to divert the attack upon the capitalist class as a whole into an attack upon a section only of that class – the Jewish section'.[12]

The fact that the opposition against anti-Semitism was solely based on the rejection of its socio-economic implications was stated unequivocally by the writer who contributed one of the few publications on the 'Jewish question' sponsored by the Left Book Club. Actually appealing to anti-Semitic anti-Fascists, he declared: 'Hate the Jew, if you must, but do not allow your hatred to make you the victim of the Fascist who, on the plea that he also hates the Jew, makes you his accomplice in worse crimes.'[13] Displaying a fanaticism only comparable to that of his political opponents, the same author went on to explain that Fascist attacks on Jews were not criticized *per se* as too high a price to be paid for the achievement of a better society, but because the promised objectives were false pretence:

If Fascism really meant the end of the class struggle, then the humiliation and destruction of sixteen million Jews would be worth while, for the ultimate benefit to humanity would transcend that of a small minority of people who would scarcely be missed.[14]

Since Fascist Jew-baiting affected in particular the poorer strata of Anglo-Jewry, Communist identification with the Jewish cause fitted in with the party's general political aspirations and did not pose a dilemma of class expediency. While it would have been inopportune for the Left to come out against the anti-Semitism that accompanied the immigration of large numbers of Jews during the 1890s, which was feared to affect the labour market, in the 1930s the support for East End Jewry was unproblematic, in that it did not conflict with the interests of the working-class at large. Yet when the two were not mutually compatible, working-class interests were given priority.

The boycott movement against Nazi Germany, for example, was not supported by the CPGB. Keeping out imports from a serious trade rival, it was argued, would reduce competition on the retail market and thereby raise prices in Britain. At a meeting of Captain Webber's boycott movement in the East End, leaflets were distributed addressed to 'fellow workers', which alluded to the organizers of the meeting as wealthy capitalists who could well afford to boycott German goods. 'We must think in pennies and shillings', it was pointed out, 'and if German goods are cheaper by so much, we are forced, whether we like it or not, to buy German'.[15]

The objection against the 'buy British' implication of the boycott movement was strengthened by the fact that it placed emphasis on individual behaviour as opposed to mass action, which was the strategy of the Left. Jews were admonished not to 'let the timid reactionaries in the Jewish community persuade you to try to separate your just and necessary self-defensive measures from similar measures in defence of revolutionary Socialism and Communism'.[16] The so-called leaders of British Jewry, it was alleged, were themselves Fascists and therefore afraid of working-class solidarity directed against Fascism in general. Not only German goods were stained with Jewish blood, it was argued, 'no less are the goods turned out in the East End sweat-shops stained with Jewish blood'.[17]

To recruit the support of East End Jews, the CPGB unmistakably took advantage of the antagonism within Anglo-Jewry. Rejecting the concept of racial or religious unity over-riding class-differences, the Communists stressed the fact that the only conducive alliance was one inspired by economic and political objectives. 'Jewry is not united and indivisible any more than Gentile society is united and indivisible,' it was declared. 'The real union is and must be, of all those who are exploited within the capitalist system.'[18] To East End Jews, the proposition that the 'main enemy is the large capitalist of the West End, who exploits the East London workers through the medium of small capitalists, who themselves are being pressed down by the large capitalists'[19] explained both the lack of sympathy among their upper-class co-religionists as well as the eruption of hatred from their Gentile neighbours.

The theme of capitalist Jews exploiting working-class Jews was not only developed with regard to minor issues, such as an increase in kosher meat prices,[20] but in particular with reference to Palestine. Zionism was rejected as a Jewish version of nationalism, an inadequate attempt to find shelter from anti-Semitic outbursts in a territory of their own, where all the vices of capitalist societies would be duplicated. Time and again it was repeated that only a society which had surpassed the epoch of class-struggles could bring peace for the Jews, and the reactionary policy of Zionism was contrasted with what was considered a model solution of the 'Jewish problem': the treatment of Jews in the Soviet Union, where Jews allegedly were fully integrated members of the state, enjoying the same rights and duties as other citizens.

In its publications on the 'Jewish question' the CPGB always praised the Soviet Union for having liberated Jews side-by-side with other oppressed sections of the population. Ignoring contrary evidence, apologists quoted Stalin's dictum that 'in the Soviet Union anti-Semitism is regarded as a form of cannibalism',[21] and cited Russian Jews maintaining prominent positions to prove that Jews had achieved equal status. From the definition that anti-Semitism was a form of class struggle, therefore a phenomenon of pre-communist societies, it was deduced that it could not exist in the Soviet Union. The uncritical reasoning employed to confirm the postulate becomes apparent in the following argument:

Jew hatred is a product of the class struggle. . . . Only the abolition of the class struggle can end it. In that case it is clear that anti-Semitism can only return in Russia if Socialism is destroyed.[22]

Whereas Zionists were denounced as Jewish Fascists, puppets of British imperialism, who intended 'to suppress the emancipation movement of the Arab people and of the Jewish workers',[23] the Soviet Birobidjan project was praised as a valid territorial solution to the 'Jewish question'. It was stressed that Jews had to be given a choice between total assimilation and preservation of their national identity and culture – both understood as secular entities reflecting 'a higher type of Jewishness, an integral part of the new society'.[24] Most young Russian Jews, it was pointed out, had 'won their freedom from superstition as well as from capitalism' and had realized that 'Judaism is just as much dope as Christianity'.[25]

The CPGB's change of attitude on the preservation of the national identity of Jews epitomizes the mitigation of its dogmatic treatment of anti-Semitism, which accompanied its intensive campaign for a popular front and its specific appeal to the Jewish minority from 1936 onwards. It accentuated the humanitarian aspect of Jew-baiting, and expanded its pledge to fight for the economically depressed by specifically incorporating ethnic and religious categories into its platform. This realignment was embedded in a general civil liberties campaign which called for an active defence of the *status quo* against the menace of Fascism:

Fascism means the stirring-up of racial and religious antagonism, and the suppression of all religious creeds which do not fit in with the Fascist campaign for war and profits. . . . All those who wish to maintain the best traditions of British freedom of thought and speech, Catholics, Protestants, Jews, should join together in a united people's opposition to the reactionary creed of Fascism.[26]

The definite effort to mobilize Jewish sympathies for the CPGB was a direct outcome of the BUF's increasing emphasis on anti-Semitism. Until 1935, Mosley was attacked for being anti-democratic and pro-capitalist. Anti-Semitism was only discussed in general terms, mostly with reference to its function in Nazi Germany. It was not until organized incidents of Jew-baiting such as defilement of synagogues, assaults upon individual Jews and damage of Jewish property demonstrated the Fascists' instrumentalization of anti-Semitism that Mosley was accused of following Hitler's example in trying to turn the Jew into a scapegoat of capitalism.[27] It was only then that the CPGB propagated the slogan 'Jew and Gentile Unite', whereas before the fight against Fascism had been put forward as a working-class cause.

While the political ideology that claimed to transcend racial strife as well as economic exploitation appealed to those Jews whose class-consciousness was enhanced by the experience of anti-Semitism, the CPGB's appeal for 'the unity of all the anti-Fascist forces in the East End, Jewish and non-Jewish, Communist and non-Communist'[28] also attracted those who were less politicized and perceived anti-Semitism above all as a disconcerting attack upon Jewry. Jewish middle-class East Enders, for example, had little reason to reject Fascism unless it endorsed anti-Semitism, when they became willing to support whoever took up the Fascist challenge.[29] After the BUF concentrated its campaign on the 'Jewish question', the Communists, who coordinated and organized the various anti-Fascist elements, succeeded in enlisting the support of politically uncommitted Jews, who came to look upon them as their only ally in the fight against Fascism.

Supplying both an appropriate message as well as a popular strategy, the CPGB provided the organizational transmission to turn the emotional antipathy against Fascism into political action. Reservations about particular components of its policy were, for the time being, outweighed by the urge to join the anti-Fascist ranks. Under the impact of anti-Semitism then, ethnicity, together with such factors as status and age, assumed some importance in determining the party affiliation of Jews. After the termination of the anti-Fascist campaign it became apparent that to a large extent this had only been a temporary alliance, since the CPGB rapidly lost its support among Jews: in 1945, the CPGB candidate, P. Piratin, a well-known Jewish anti-Fascist, polled 5075 votes in Stepney (47.6 per cent), enough to enter Parliament. After that in general exceptionally favourable year for the CPGB, the party's turnout in Stepney declined continually until 1955, when it reached the level it had maintained before the anti-Fascist campaign, namely 2888 votes (7.6 per cent).[30]

In opposition to the Labour Party and the Board of Deputies, who recommended avoidance of Fascist meetings, the Communists sought their opponents in the streets. Propagating slogans like 'No room in the streets or parks for the Fascist gangsters' they called on members and sympathizers to rally at BUF meetings, as a result of which the anti-Fascist crowd usually outnumbered the Fascist supporters many times over. The most impressive demonstration of the strength of the anti-Fascist opposition occurred on 4 October 1936, when some 100,000 people turned out to stop Mosley's BUF from marching through the East End. After attempts to get the procession banned or diverted had proved unavailing, the CPGB and the ILP, supported in this instance by sections of the Labour and Liberal Party as well as by Jewish and Gentile religious organizations, appealed to the population to support a counter-demonstration in the streets through which Mosley intended to march. Owing to this opposition, Mosley's parade had to be diverted. The actual 'Battle of Cable Street' was fought mainly between anti-Fascists and police, who tried to clear the streets. It is indicative of the local support for the anti-Fascists that of the eighty-three persons arrested all but one came from London.[31]

The explicit object of anti-Fascist agitation, apart from displaying numerical strength, was to disturb Fascist meetings. Roaring down Fascist speakers, shouting 'We want Mosley dead or alive' and singing the Internationale, they frequently succeeded in preventing the speaker from obtaining a hearing. The pattern of agitation was described in a Special Branch report on the BUF's Trafalgar Square Rally on 4 July 1937, which is characteristic of the events at outdoor meetings:

> Sir Oswald's appearance on the plinth was the signal for boos and jeers from the anti-fascists awaiting him in the Square. This pandemonium continued throughout his speech and he was at times audible only to those standing quite close to him.[32]

Like the Fascists, the Communists attracted hooligan elements who were not concerned with political issues, but to whom the identification with one camp offered an opportunity to release their aggressions. One CPGB member noted with regret the recruiting of 'a new class of individuals . . . with a turn for violent language and a yearning for violent action'[33] – evidently a sequel to the increasing militancy in the campaign. These supporters, some of whom were said to have eventually joined the BUF, certainly discredited the anti-Fascist front, whose favourite slogans were to expose 'Blackshirt Brutality' and 'Mosley Thugs'. Violent actions from anti-Fascists, who frequently threw missiles of broken concrete, bottles and stones at their opponents, not only alienated the police, but supported Mosley's claim that the BUF was a martyr for free speech and British traditions, particularly since BUF members – at least after Olympia – were strictly forbidden to carry offensive weapons and were searched before they boarded the vans that took them to mass-rallies. By contrast, the police on one occasion received information that the Young Communist League issued truncheons and knuckledusters before demonstrations.[34]

The police were well aware of dissimilarities within the anti-Fascist movement. The Commissioner's report for October 1937, for example, noted that marches and meetings in the West End were conducted in an orderly manner and attracted largely respectable people, while hooligan elements, said to include many Jews, were observed to be prominent in the East End. The report in particular mentioned 'a lower type of foreign Jew', which was considered to be far more anti-police than anti-Fascist.[35]

The vast majority of people arrested for offensive behaviour in connection with mass-demonstrations were Jews. Sociologically they represented a fair cross-section of East End Jewry, men of lower middle and working-class background, which indicates the unifying impact of anti-Semitism on those Jews affected by the campaign. Their outstanding pugnacity suggests that they personalized the political battle, which many perceived as a fight between anti-Semites and Jews, rather than treating it as a conflict between contradictory ideologies, Fascism and Communism. Their militancy further points to a lack of confidence in both the state authorities and the Jewish communal leadership, which was due to the fact that East End Jews practically lived in a ghetto which resembled more the world they came from than the country that was now their home. Their aggressiveness, sheltered in a more general campaign, seems to have been as much an outcome of their insecurity as non-integrated aliens as an indication of their extreme sensitivity regarding anti-Semitic onslaughts.

Although the CPGB deliberately adjusted its propaganda to enlist the support of East End Jews, it did not revise its position that opposition to Fascism was an epochal necessity irrespective of its anti-Semitic dimension. Similarly, socialist contemporaries, who objected to the mechanical uniformity of opinion in the CPGB and did not subscribe to the bondage of Moscow, analysed anti-Semitism only in the context of general socio-political developments, as a diversion from factual problems. The linkage between anti-Semitism and vested interests, Jewish and non-Jewish alike, was pointed out by Harold Laski, a staunch advocate of a popular front, when he expressed his concern about the 'steady growth of anti-Semitism in the East End':

> Only a war in which we are anti-German can save us from some kind of Fascism. . . . The same cause which prevents action is that which paralyses us over Spain, disarmament, and foreign policy; panic and vested interest. . . . There is nothing a business civilization will not to do keep its property. Even rich Jews will risk Fascism in the hope of buying themselves off rather than strengthen the working-class cause.[36]

The problem of anti-Semitism was largely ignored by one of the most active and popular anti-Fascist organizations, the Left Book Club. Launched as a political propaganda enterprise in March 1936, the Club was also an educational establishment. During its first year it enlisted 39,400 members, and reached a peak in April 1939 with 57,000 members.[37] In November 1936, its monthly journal *Left Book News* published an article by the secretary of the National Council for Civil Liberties on anti-Semitism in the East End, which recorded the incidents of Jew-baiting that had occurred recently. In August 1937, the Club's only contribution on anti-Semitism that appeared in its subscription scheme was published. According to the review of the book in the Club's newsletter, it tackled 'one of the subjects that members of the Left Book Club have most frequently asked shall be included'.[38] The author treated the problem from the orthodox Communist point of view and explained the 'comparative mildness of the Jewish question' in Britain and the United States by the fact that in these countries the class struggle was not yet very mature. He expected an accentuation of anti-Semitism in correlation to growing class antagonism, when it would be manipulated as a deflection from social tensions.[39]

A more active campaign against anti-Semitism, mirroring a less theoretical, rather sensational approach to the subject matter, was conducted by the National Council for Civil Liberties (NCCL). It was founded in 1934 to promote the rights of individuals and to oppose racial, political and religious discrimination. The NCCL claimed to be a non-political body, and listed a galaxy of distinguished contemporaries as Vice-Presidents – among others the Dean of Canterbury, A. Bevan, V. Gollancz, G. Lansbury, H. Laski, K. Martin and B. Russell. The police looked upon it as a spearhead of the Communist Party, with subterranean connections through its secretary, Ronald Kidd, who was followed by Special Branch detectives when present at anti-Fascist rallies.[40]

The NCCL did not devote itself exclusively to an anti-Fascist campaign, but also to questions of civil liberties overseas, rights of asylum and civil rights under emergency decrees. The fact that it did not indiscriminately support the Jewish cause transpired when it rejected the JPC's plea for a Racial Incitement Act, arguing that such legislation would support the claim of anti-Semites that Jews sought special favours under the law. Pointing out that the existing legislation was sufficient to stop racial or religious insult or incitement, it objected in principle to the introduction of further legislation which could be used to suppress freedom of speech and freedom of expression.[41]

In its campaign against anti-Semitism, the NCCL did not advocate a revolutionary doctrine, and stressed the factual consequences of Jew-baiting rather than its theoretical implications. It focused on a passive policy, collecting data of anti-Semitic incidents, and transmitting such information to the press and MPs, trying to induce the proper institutions to proceed against the growing anti-Semitism, and to uphold liberal-humanitarian traditions against anti-democratic ideologies. The NCCL also maintained a panel of legal advisors, solicitor and barrister members who offered their services free of charge where principles of civil liberties were involved.[42]

Supporting the demand for a united front against 'Fascism, which threatens to destroy democracy and civilization',[43] the NCCL naturally found ready supporters among left-wing groups, but it also attracted radical liberals and idealists standing for human rights. On 25 April 1937 it convened a conference on Fascism and anti-Semitism together with the JPC. This was attended by 310 delegates representing 190 Jewish and non-Jewish organizations – Trade Unions, Cooperative Guilds, Left Book Clubs, Labour Party, Liberal Federations and religious societies. After many representatives had expressed their concern about the anti-Semitic agitation in England, which had led to breaches of the peace, personal assaults and damage of property, the conference passed a resolution condemning anti-Semitic propaganda and racial incitement, arguing that the attack upon the Jews was the prelude to a general infringement of democratic liberties. The conference also proposed to delegate a deputation to the Home Secretary, asking him 'to enforce the existing law to prevent the continuance of racial incitement and anti-Semitic propaganda'.[44]

The alleged alliance with the CPGB discredited the NCCL like the JPC with the state authorities, and hampered its activities from the outset. When Kidd asked the Home Secretary to receive a deputation including various MPs, the Dean of St Paul's, and Mr A. M. Wall, Secretary of the London Trades Council, his request was refused. Instead, he was encouraged to submit a statement in writing recommending specific proposals that the Delegate Conference felt should be implemented by the police. It was pointed out that the Home Secretary was fully aware of the importance of enforcing the law against incitements to disorder and of protecting all sections of the population against intimidation, assaults and damage of property, and that he was 'satisfied that the Metropolitan Police as a body are fully alive to their responsibilities in this matter and carry out their arduous duties in a spirit of complete impartiality'.[45]

The refusal to receive a deputation on behalf of the NCCL and JPC is indicative of the ostentatiously unpolitical attitude maintained by the Home Office with regard to anti-Semitism in Britain. While it cooperated with the Jewish Board of Deputies, a religious rather than a political institution, it objected to consulting representatives of organizations which were 'at least as concerned with combating Fascism as with fighting anti-Semitism'.[46] The sensitivity of the issue, arising from the principle that the right of free speech had to be preserved also for the Fascists, was clearly recognized by the counsellor who considered the request:

> For the Government to receive a deputation from organizations, one of whose main objects is to combat Fascism qua Fascism, would be open to misinterpretation and might give rise to serious embarrassment, both to the Government and to the Board of Deputies of British Jews who have hitherto refused to lend countenance or support to the Jewish People's Council.[47]

The negative bias against the NCCL as an organized anti-Fascist body was also reflected in the executive's reaction against specific complaints. Individual allegations of police partiality were taken seriously and referred by the Home Office to the Commissioner, requesting him to comment upon the indictments.

Correspondents who drew attention to the display of anti-Semitic posters in the East End were assured that the police were instructed 'to take appropriate action in all cases coming to notice where the character of posters displayed would be likely to lead to a breach of the peace'.[48] The responsible officers, when questioned about the incidents, confirmed that strict orders had been given regarding Jew-baiting, and that 'definite action will be taken whenever the circumstances warrant it'.[49] Reports from the NCCL, on the other hand, were considered to be one-sided and divorced from public interests.

The prejudice against the NCCL was reinforced by its constant allegations that the police were being increasingly used 'for purely party political purposes and for the suppression of minority opinion which is objectionable to the authorities'.[50] Conversely the executive considered its attacks an unjustified, deliberate vilification of the police force as such. While the NCCL campaign evidently stimulated critical reflection among some sections of public opinion,[51] the Commissioner of the Metropolitan Police dismissed it as a troublesome, self-important, 'self-constituted body with no authority or statutory power' whose activities had no public backing whatsoever.[52] The latter argument, it seems, was not wholly justified, since the NCCL received many letters of protest when its policy was not endorsed by its supporters. This was the case when it opposed the decision to release Oswald and Diana Mosley from their wartime detention: on this occasion, thirty-five members, including Harold Nicolson, resigned because they considered the NCCL's policy biased and not in concordance with the principles of civil liberty.[53]

More effective than its representations to administrative bodies was the NCCL's cooperation with the press, particularly the *News Chronicle* and *Daily Herald*, which gave its reports full publicity and continuously supported the anti-Fascist campaign. NCCL observers attended Fascist meetings and recorded anti-Semitic language, anti-Jewish behaviour and incidents of anti-Fascist police discrimination. Based on such eye-witness reports, which were supplemented by complaints from individuals, memoranda were compiled on the partiality of police, anti-Jewish disturbances and manifestations of prejudice, which were subsequently communicated to the press. Drawing attention to a multitude of particular cases, which could have been easily overlooked in view of the general news about the dispute between Fascists and anti-Fascists, the NCCL persistently revealed the anti-Semitic character of the IFL and BUF. Even if it was only a small section of British society that noted its reports, it seems to have rendered an important contribution to discrediting the Fascist groups.

In comparison with the Board of Deputies, the NCCL operated on a very limited financial basis. Its published balance sheet for 1938 lists an income of £1638 0s. 2d. of which the largest share, £1226 13s. 10d., came from subscriptions and donations. By July 1934, 424 societies were affiliated, which were required to pay an annual subscription of between 10s. and £2.–.–. The total expenditure for the year 1938 amounted to £1585 13s. 1d. of which salaries, £747 8s. 11d., were the largest item, followed by rents, £194 3s. 2d. and literature, £128 19s. 2d. These figures confirm the impression that the NCCL, although supported mainly by left-wing bodies, operated quite independently on a very narrow budget.[54]

Compared to the defence activities of Anglo-Jewry, the motley anti-Fascist Left, embracing not only Communists but civil liberty champions of various shades, mounted a far more successful opposition against Fascist anti-Semitism. The widespread criticism of Hitler and the Nazi regime fertilized its impact when attacking Fascist organizations at home, and its growing militancy was often excused as permissible in the resistance against well-organized Fascist groups, who were determined to squash all opposition on their ascent to power. Although the anti-Fascist movement defined its identity in terms of opposition against a self-contained visible enemy, and was a viable force only as long as its antipode existed, its activities had a lasting impact on the political culture: proven 'right' by historical events, the radical Left's persuasive appeal for a popular front against totalitarianism and its relentless fight against Fascism were acknowledged and it became of increasing significance. Its fight against anti-Semitism, however, had been only one aspect of a much wider campaign, and it evaporated after the anti-Fascist crusade had come to an end.

Conclusions

Before evaluating the impact of organized political anti-Semitism in England between the two world wars, it should be recalled that anti-Jewish prejudices persisted in 20th century Britain as part of the Christian cultural tradition. Social discrimination against Jews was not unusual, and adverse stereotypes of 'the Jews' were mirrored and passed on in folklore and literature – even in nursery rhymes such as the following:

> Jack sold his gold egg
> To a rascally Jew,
> Who cheated him out of
> The half of his due.
>
> . . .
>
> The Jew got the goose
> Which he vowed he would kill,
> Resolving at once
> His pockets to fill.[1]

As xenophobia assumed greater significance during times of exceptional external or internal pressure, latent anti-Jewish attitudes surfaced in particular during times of crises. This became apparent in the years following World War I and the Russian revolution in the widespread, diffuse scare of the 'Jewish peril', which was blamed for the unrest in India, Ireland and at home. The theme of an international Jewish conspiracy was exploited by sections of the press, and the anti-Jewish propaganda definitely caused a more acute 'Jew-consciousness'. Since it focused largely on international rather than domestic policy and was neither developed into a coherent political ideology nor systematically instrumentalized by any power élite, it remained without political significance.

170

The anti-Semitism propagated by Fascist groups during the 1930s differed not in substance but in function from the Jew-hatred of earlier years. It served no longer merely as a 'safety valve' to release social tensions, or as an explanatory model to neutralize objective problems by attributing them to a scapegoat, the Jew, but became the central justification for the Fascists' claim to power. Jewry had been depicted before as the omnipotent antipode of civilization, and had been accused of manipulating the mass-media, cultural establishments, international finance and politics contrary to British interests, but the attempt to base an entire political campaign on the messianic promise to turn the tide of history by solving a hypothetical 'Jewish question' was a novelty in British politics.

In the context of modern German history, the two manifestations of anti-Semitism outlined above have been contrasted as 'bourgeois' and 'fascist' anti-Semitism – the former a vague protest-ideology, the latter an instrument of total power, the practical implementation of a dualistic *Weltanschauung*.[2] The difference, it seems, was not one of content, but one between theory and practice. The charges levelled against Jews have remained the same ever since the emergence of modern anti-Semitism: what changed were the general political conditions, which rendered them particularly acceptable at certain times. Emphasizing the necessity of a 'final solution' to the 'Jewish question', they only drew the logical conclusions from the understanding that Jews represented the incarnation of all evil, and cultivated this into a systematic theory of history.

The analysis of the various concepts of solutions to the 'Jewish problem' as developed by different organizations in Britain confirms the contention proposed in the introduction, that anti-Semitism as a political ideology contains an inherent totality. It exemplifies what British public opinion largely failed to understand when explaining – and thereby exonerating – Nazi anti-Semitism as a corollary of Germany history, Germany's socio-economic system, or the prominent influence of Jews in German public life: the recurring pattern of a progression from ostracism to expulsion to physical destruction clearly shows that the 'final solution' was no singular German aberration, but a potential inherent in the Manichean ideology. This is not to say that it is an inevitable climax of anti-Semitism: its implementation depends on specific historical circumstances. But, as the theoretical reflections of

British Fascists showed, it presents a conceivable *ultima ratio* to subdue the enemy on whose defeat allegedly depends the salvation of the world.

In the analysis of German anti-Semitism, it has been observed that anti-Semitism is both a result and a symptom of economic depression.[3] The same was true for England, where anti-Semitism became apparent during the 1920s and 1930s, two decades of fundamental social and economic crises and political reassessments. Fascist agitators did not invent anti-Semitism, but responded and exploited the latent prejudice, which manifested itself in a bitter 'us and them' ideology: the imagination of an organized Jewish conspiracy dominating British politics, economics and culture quickly 'explained' the complex changes the 'war heroes' witnessed when returning home. 'International Jewish profiteers' became a convenient scapegoat for those who felt disillusioned and deceived. By imagining themselves as the victims of an omnipotent anonymous antagonist, they found a pattern of identification that relieved them of personal responsibility and any sense of failure. This escapist perception of history closely corresponded to a retrospective outlook, characterized by an indiscriminate glorification of the past.

Although the rise and decline of anti-Semitism appears closely related to economic cycles, the crystallization of xenophobia during periods of depression is only significant in presenting a potential object of manipulation. Its lack of inner dynamics becomes apparent with regard to anti-Semitism in England, where the latent prejudice against the Jews surfaced after World War I, subsided during the years of increasing stability and prosperity during the second half of the 1920s, and reappeared again during the crisis of the early 1930s, but did not reach a climax until 1935–6, when it became the central propaganda instrument of the BUF. Only when exploited by this party, which functioned as the political intermediary necessary to generate a mass-movement, did anti-Semitism threaten to become an important element in British political life.

What is crucial then for the development of anti-Semitism is the combination of socio-economic conditions predisposing large sections of the population towards the reception of propaganda which diverts attention from real deprivations to a mythical adversary, and the presence of agitators channelling the diffuse discontent against Jews. Propagating the slogan 'Perish Judah' as the equivalent to 'Britons Awake', they preluded violent excesses against individual Jews, the tangible representatives of the abstraction of a universal antipode. Sheltered in the anonymity of movements which relieved individual members of personal responsibility, and incited by the propaganda of their 'leaders', those who responded to anti-Semitic slogans found an outlet for their subjective sense of frustration and powerlessness by committing acts of vandalism in Jewish areas.

The active anti-Semitic nucleus qualified to provide the leadership in an anti-Semitic campaign in Britain constituted only a small, albeit vocal, minority. Enterprises like the 'Britons', the 'Nordic League' and similar fringe groups were little more than clubs of fanatical anti-Semites cultivating a pathological Jew-hatred. Their anti-Semitism was symbolic for a total lack of critical analysis in the perception of political events, a profound pessimism and a reactionary anti-intellectual and anti-modern *Weltanschauung*. Their crude cult of race was linked to a primitive 'back to nature' campaign, particularly apparent in their veneration of homeopathics and the great emphasis placed on abstinence and austerity. Thus we find the same patterns of prejudice in England as elsewhere.[4]

If, despite a congenial leadership truly dedicated to the cause, an anti-Semitic message that lacked nothing in quality to serve as a perfect umbrella-ideology to unite the nation against an outsider and a widespread dislike of Jews, anti-Semitism failed to become a relevant political force in England, the reasons have to be sought not in any presumptive inadequacies of organized anti-Semitism, but in its lack of historical tradition in England. At a time when the 'Jewish question' was an important issue in central Europe, in England Disraeli, a baptized Jew 'proud of his origins to the point of megalomania'[5], had accomplished an outstanding political career. Here the emancipation of Jews, once completed, was not questioned, and Anglo-Jewry was never again treated as a separate entity.

What hampered the anti-Semitic campaign further was its lack of respectability. Whereas in Germany men like Treitschke, Wagner or Fichte had lent anti-Semitism a certain fashionableness amongst the educated middle-class, it had little ostentatious élitist support in England. This can also be observed from the image of Jews in literature, a medium which both reflects and reinforces common stereotypes: in contrast to 19th century German fiction, where Jews continued to represent negative types, they were humanized and demythologized in English literature, where Jew-villains were balanced by Jew-heroes.[6]

Whereas the flourishing cultural symbiosis with Jews irritated the German nation, which lacked self-confidence after the trauma of defeat, the English national culture absorbed foreign elements without suffering from an identity-crisis. Being a country which had for a long time administered a minority policy not only with regard to the Jewish community, but other ethnic and religious minorities such as the Catholics and the Irish, the heterogeneousness of the nation was officially accepted and justified. Even prejudice manifested itself in this pluralistic context, with popular resentment directed not only against Jews but against a variety of 'outgroups' such as blacks, Indians or immigrants in general.[7]

Unlike Germany, Britain never developed an ethnocentrism based on a romantic nationalism, but enacted the doctrine of moral cultural and racial superiority in colonial rule. Jews therefore were only one, and by no means the most important, group suited as a negative object of identification against which British supremacy could be defined. At the same time, authoritarian patterns of behaviour, known to facilitate the reception of anti-Semitic propaganda, were projected into the power structure overseas, which deflected the submissiveness to a hierarchical *Obrigkeit*, as it is required in the military, from the mother country. Thus the colonial tradition largely immersed potential anti-Semitic support – an assumption which is confirmed by the fact that many of those attracted to anti-Semitic parties were ex-servicemen or people who had previously lived in the colonies.[8]

Stereotypes, it has been argued, are not derived from the object of prejudice, but are the product of Gentile societies, which create clichés by imposing 'typical' Jewish appearance and behaviour on Jews. Deviations from the accepted concepts are interpreted as exceptions, not as a challenge to the validity of these images: individuals are gauged against the stereotype and subsequently qualified as typical or a-typical. While such preconceived judgements and expectations influence individual behaviour towards Jews and facilitate the reception of anti-Semitic propaganda, the relation of myth and truth is not wholly insignificant for the success or failure of modern political campaigns. The fact that in Britain, unlike in Weimar Germany, Jewish influence did not dominate any section of public life such as finance, journalism or the cultural scene, certainly discredited the plausibility of anti-Semitic accusations.

Where many Jews maintained influential posts, a propaganda campaign waged by the mass-media could exaggerate the political weight of Jewry. In England this remained too abstract an issue to mobilize massive support. Significantly, anti-Jewish hostility became most marked when the prominent involvement of Jews gave rise to suspicion, as was the case in the Bolshevik revolution or the responsibility of Jewish ministers for Indian affairs. Similarly, the arrival of German-Jewish refugees caused considerable irritation among the population. 'Jews are news',[9] contemporaries observed, and both government officials and relief organizations were afraid that the widespread hostility against 'refujews' could lead to an outburst of anti-Semitism.[10] Typical of the resentment against Jews, and the attitude that they were not totally blameless for their ill-treatment in Germany, was the following comment:

The Jews are neither quite a nation nor quite a religion. They are something of each. Consequently they are hard to fit into a world of nations. They are an anomaly. 'Mixed with every race, but lost in none', they are an undigested particle which causes disorder.[11]

By and large, the impact of the anti-Semitic campaign remained limited to where it was directed against an identifiable body of foreigners, as was the case in Jewish settlement areas like the East End. The high degree of centralization of Anglo-Jewry in a few urban centres sustained the localization of outbreaks of violence directed against Jews, while the lack of prominent Jewish influence in inter-war Britain hampered the attempts to turn the 'Jewish question' into an issue of over-riding national importance. During the 1930s, the growing resentment against Nazi Jew-baiting further curtailed the effect of organized anti-Semitism in Britain.

Although in theory an integrative ideology appealing to all sections of the population, Fascist anti-Semitism was widely condemned owing to its element of rowdyism and mob violence. While subtle anti-Jewish biases were silently tolerated, the widespread negative attitudes against Jews might have facilitated the reception of a political package including anti-Semitic planks. East End Jew-baiting, however, alienated rather than mobilized political support. This was particularly relevant for the lack of active support from the politically influential radical right, which had been instrumental in the anti-Bolshevik crusade. Defensive in its own pursuit of power, it had blamed the 'subversive machinations' on the despised Jews, but rather in the form of a whispering campaign than in an organized political crusade. Sympathizing with Hitler's anti-Communism and patriotism, the 'appeasers' emphasized that Germany's anti-Jewish policy was not Britain's concern. They were equally anxious, however, not to become identified with a lower-class movement, conducting an activist anti-Semitic campaign.

The acceptance and persistence of fairly rigid class barriers in Britain precluded the success of an equalizing *Volksgemeinschaft* ideology. While the outcome of World War I, generally perceived as a national humiliation, stimulated a mass psychosis in Germany, Britain did not suffer from any comparable experience. Such changes as occurred were gradually assimilated and did not constitute any dramatic disruption in national affairs, leaving a vacuum that could be filled by arousing racial hatred. While it encountered indifference rather than positive support, anti-Semitism alone proved inadequate as a means of achieving political power. Not yet encumbered by the experience of genocide, dislike of Jews was treated as a private opinion. Attempts to end this 'freedom of opinion' by exalting hatred of a particular group in a dogmatic crusade were rejected as they conflicted with the concept of pluralism, a fundamental principle in the English political tradition.

For an assessment of the impact of political anti-Semitism in England it is irrelevant to speculate about the chances of an anti-Semitic campaign conducted at the right time, unimpaired by the adverse publicity discrediting the Hitler regime, or to discuss whether the economic slump affected Britain less than other countries. The difficulty of launching a new movement where the political culture was governed by a two-party system was aptly pointed out by Harold Nicolson who observed after having resigned from the Mosley movement:

The English mind functions only in a groove: get it out of that groove and it flops into panic distaste. . . . I believe that if we ever have communism in this country, it will creep in disguised as left wing Socialism and in all the bombazine of St. Stephen's. And I also believe that if we ever have fascism in this country, it will creep in disguised in the red white and blue of patriotism and the young conservatives.[12]

Much the same seems to have been true for anti-Semitism, which was tolerated under the cloak of liberalism. It usually encountered indifference and only caused resentment when it disturbed civil peace. Implemented less conspicuously – as in the discrimination by the Foreign Office, which remained practically closed to Jews – it caused little resentment indeed.

In England, the anti-Semitic campaign was a passing phenomenon that changed neither the attitude of the English society towards Jews, nor the self-assessment of Anglo-Jewry. The reactions against it were pragmatic *ad hoc* measures which illuminate the patterns of response both from the host society as well as the minority under attack, but they did not affect the course of history. It would be wrong, however, to deduce from this 'negative conclusion' that *ipso facto* English anti-Semitism was insignificant. Limited though it was, it provides a self-contained case for the study of anti-Semitic myths, the instrumentalization of anti-Semitism in political campaigns, the personality pattern of prototype anti-Semites, and the function of prejudice in modern society.

Notes

Full bibliographical details are given the first time any book is mentioned. Thereafter an abbreviated title is given.

Introduction

1. For a summary survey of research on anti-Semitism see R. Rürup, 'Zur Entwicklung der modernen Antisemitismusforschung' (1969), repr. in R. Rürup, *Emanzipation und Antisemitismus* (Göttingen, 1975) pp. 115–25.
2. It is a strange paradox that the anti-Semitic charge that Jews could never escape their identity as Jews, and could never become loyal citizens of Judaic persuasion, reappears as Jewish myth in etiologies of Jewish history, which is often described as unique with reference to *Numbers* XXIII, 9, where Jews are described as 'a people that dwells alone'. Cf. for example Y. Herzog, *A People That Dwells Alone* (London, 1975) p. 175.
3. R. Rürup, 'Die "Judenfrage" der bürgerlichen Gesellschaft und die Entstehung des modernen Antisemitismus' (1974), and T. Nipperdey and R. Rürup, 'Antisemitismus – Entstehung, Funktion und Geschichte eines Begriffs' (1972), both repr. in R. Rürup, *Emanzipation und Antisemitismus*, pp. 74–114. While I share Rürup's qualitative definition of anti-Semitism, I do not agree with his opinion that it was a distinctive phenomenon of the 1870s. The reactionary demand for an 'emancipation from Jewry' is already expressed in J. G. Fichte, *Beitrag zur Berichtigung der Urteile des Publikums über die Französische Revolution* (1793), in the 'Hep! Hep!' movement of 1819, and in early *völkisch* writings. Cf. C. Abramsky, 'A people that shall dwell alone', *New York Review of Books*, XXI (December 1974) pp. 22–4.
4. For a more general definition, cf. A. Silbermann, 'Zur Soziologie des Antisemitismus', *Psyche*, XVI, pp. 252–3.
5. Cf. M. v. Brentano, 'Die Endlösung – ihre Funktion in Theorie und Praxis des Faschismus', in H. Huss and A. Schröder (ed.), *Antisemitismus* (Frankfurt, 1965) pp. 40–1, 48–51.
6. H. Rosenberg, *Grosse Depression und Bismarckzeit* (Berlin, 1972) pp. 88–117.
7. For the emergence of political anti-Semitism, cf. R. S. Levy, *The Downfall of the Anti-Semitic Political Parties in Imperial Germany* (New Haven, 1975). P. Massing, *Vorgeschichte des politischen Antisemitismus* (Frankfurt, 1959). P. G. Pulzer, *The Rise of Political Anti-Semitism in Germany and Austria* (New York, 1964).

8. For a summary survey of 19th-century racialism, cf. M. D. Biddis, 'Racial Ideas and the Politics of Prejudice 1850–1914', *Historical Journal*, XV (1972) pp. 570–82 and L. L. Snyder, *The Idea of Racialism* (Princeton, 1962). For the reception of H. S. Chamberlain in England see C. Holmes, 'Houston Stewart Chamberlain in Great Britain', *Wiener Library Bulletin*, XXIV, nr 2, n.s. nr 19 (1970) pp. 31–6, and L. Poliakov, *The Aryan Myth* (London, 1974) pp. 318–20.

9. Karl Pearson, in his anti-Semitism not representative for the British Eugenics Society, asked for a restriction of alien immigration on grounds of safeguarding a 'superior breed of men'. Cf. K. Pearson and M. Moul, 'The Problem of Alien Immigration into Great Britain, Illustrated by an Examination of Russian and Polish Jewish Children', *Annals of Eugenics*, I (October 1925) pp. 5–127.

10. For a history of Jews in medieval and early modern England see C. Roth, *History of the Jews in England*, 3rd edn (Oxford, 1964).

11. U. R. Q. Henriques, 'The Jewish Emancipation Controversy in 19th Century Britain', *Past and Present*, XL (July 1968) pp. 126–46, suggests that British society tends to compel ethnic minorities to abandon their religious and cultural identity in exchange for political and social equality. It seems to me that Anglo-Jewry assimilated less because of the pressure from the host society than because its assimilated lay leadership provided a catching example of successful integration into Gentile society.

12. For the emancipation of Jews in England, cf. H. S. Q. Henriques, *The Jews and the English Law* (Oxford, 1968). V. D. Lipman, 'The Age of Emancipation', in V. D. Lipman (ed.), *Three Centuries of Anglo-Jewish History* (Cambridge, 1961) pp. 69–106.

13. H. Katz, 'The Party Loyalties of European Jews' and O. Seliktar, 'The Political Attitudes and Behaviour of British Jews', *Jewish Political Behaviour* (Survey Research Centre University of Strathclyde, Glasgow, 1974) argue that Jewish political behaviour is determined more by the degree of religious observance than by class and social status, with a marked preference for Conservatism among orthodox Jews irrespective of their social composition. This does not seem to be consistent with the observation that lower-class immigrants from Russia who entered Britain after 1880 combined strong Labour-bias with religiosity. Correspondingly, Jewish radicals wrote for Jewish workers in Yiddish and refrained from an anti-religious campaign.

14. Cf. V. D. Lipman, *Social History of the Jews in England 1850–1950* (London, 1954) pp. 85–103. Also A. Cohen, 'The Structure of Anglo-Jewry Today', in V. D. Lipman (ed.), *Three Centuries*, pp. 169–85.

15. W. J. Fishman, *East End Jewish Radicals 1875–1914* (London, 1975).

16. Ahad Ha'am to Prof. Klausner, 1908, quoted in A. Cohen, 'The Structure of Anglo-Jewry Today' in V. D. Lipman (ed.), *Three Centuries*, p. 174.

17. *Jewish Chronicle* 12 August 1881, quoted in W. J. Fishman, *East End Jewish Radicals*, pp. 67–8. A currently conducted research project on the sociology of Sheffield Jewry by the Board of Deputies suggests that there was a high intermarriage-rate between new immigrants and daughters of established Jewish families, which indicates that the resentment against the immigrants soon diminished.

18. On the anti-alien agitation see B. Gainer, *The Alien Invasion* (London, 1972);

J. A. Garrard, *The English and Immigration* (London, 1971); L. P. Gartner, *The Jewish Immigrant in England 1807–1914* (London, 1960).

19. J. H. Richardson, *From City to Fleet Street* (London, 1927) pp. 216–17 suggests that the Metropolitan Police feared anti-Semitic riots in this context.
20. J. Banister, *England Under the Jews* (London, 1901) p. 10.
21. ibid., p. 39.
22. W. S. Churchill to D. Lloyd George, 26 December 1918, quoted in M. Gilbert, *Winston S. Churchill*, IV, 1917–1922 (London, 1975) pp. 176–7.
23. J. H. Hertz, *Anti-Semitism* (7 October 1922, Central Synagogue Pulpit nr 8) pp. 7–8.
24. Board of Deputies of British Jews, *The New Anti-Semitism* (London, 1921) p. 2.

Chapter 1   The Myth of a Jewish World Conspiracy

1. The concept of a 'state within the state' was brought up against Huguenots in France around 1600 and transferred to Jesuits, Freemasons and Jews in the 18th century. The latter became a target when the question of Jewish identity and loyalty was raised in the context of Jewish emancipation. For a history of the slogan see J. Katz, 'A State Within A State', repr., in J. Katz, *Emancipation and Assimilation* (Westmead, 1972) pp. 47–76.
2. *Hansard*, 4th series, 1905, CIL. 155.
3. For precursors and a history of the *Protocols* see N. Cohn, *Warrant for Genocide* (London, 1967), J. Gwyer, *Portraits of Mean Men: A Short History of the Protocols of the Elders of Zion* (London, 1938), L. Wolf, *The Jewish Bogey and the Forged Protocols of the Learned Elders of Zion* (London, 1920).
4. N. Cohn, *Warrant for Genocide*, pp. 103–7, concludes that the *Protocols* were fabricated some time between 1894 and 1899. De Waldeck, an *emigré* officer of the Russian Imperial Guard, maintains that General Orgewsky, a member of the secret police, had acquired a copy of the *Protocols* already in 1884 and passed it on to General Tchérevine, head of the *Okhrana*, who placed it in the archives. Rachkovsky, an agent of the *Okhrana*, later traced the pamphlet and handed a copy to Nilus who edited the *Protocols* for the first time. De Waldeck to the Paris Office of the *Morning Post*, 9 September 1921. Uncatalogued MS Special File VII (Gwynne Papers). Although, as Cohn pointed out, the text of the forgery suggests the second half of the 1890s as their most probable time of origin, it seems not altogether unlikely that they were conceived already under Tsar Alexander III when the anti-Jewish agitation was much more intense than under his successor and when the *Okhrana* had just been set up and presumably used all its imagination to instigate anti-Jewish riots.
5. Parliamentary debate 14 February 1917, *Hansard*, 5th series, 1917, XC, 717.
6. *Russia Nr 1*, A Collection of Reports on Bolshevism in Russia, abridged edn of parliamentary paper (London, 1919) p. 67, Rev. B. S. Lombard to Curzon, 23 March 1919.
7. 'Russian Kaleidoscope. Orderly Elements Gaining the Ascendant. The Influence of the Jews', *Morning Post*, 7 August 1917.
8. A. White, *The Hidden Hand* (London, 1917).
9. MS WHI 110 (White Papers): anonymous postcard to A. White c/o Grant Richards Ltd, 25 November 1918.

10. PRO Cabinet papers, series 24, vol. 67 (thereafter CAB 24/67): Sir Basil Thomson, fortnightly report on pacifism and revolutionary organizations in the United Kingdom, and morale in France and Italy nr 24, 21 October 1918.

11. CAB 24/78: Political Intelligence Department Foreign Office, The Aims and Strategy of Bolshevism (Russia/023), 12 April 1919. Cf. R. H. Ullman, *Intervention and the War* (Princeton, 1961) and *Britain and the Russian Civil War* (Princeton, 1968).

12. CAB 24/78: B. Thomson, Report of revolutionary organizations in the United Kingdom nr 1, 30 April 1919.

13. *Horrors of Bolshevism*, repr. from *The Times*, 14 November 1919 (London, n.d.) p. 1. Similarly *The Facts about Bolshevism*, compiled from the accounts of trustworthy eye-witnesses and the Russian press by C.E.B. (London, 1919).

14. *Weekly Dispatch*, 22 June 1919, quoted in M. Gilbert, *Churchill* IV, p. 903.

15. G. Pitt-Rivers, *The World Significance of the Russian Revolution* (Oxford, 1920) p. 29.

16. ibid., p. 25.

17. CAB 24/78: Fortnightly report 30 April 1919.

18. *The Story of Bolshevism. A Warning to British Women*, National Publications n.d. [1918], p. 4.

19. CAB 24/73: Memorandum Secretary of State for War, 8 January 1919, forwarding a letter from Mr H. Pearson, Chief Manager of A. Nevsky Cotton Spinning and Weaving Mills, 2 January 1919.

20. *Russia* nr 1, p. 48.

21. ibid., p. 68: Rev. B. S. Lombard, Chaplain to the British Forces, to Curzon, 23 March 1919.

22. ibid., p. 79, quoted as 'Memorandum by Mr B——'. The same passage appears – not as a citation – in Thomson's memorandum 'The Progress of Bolshevism in Europe', 28 January 1919. CAB 24/75.

23. C. Abramsky, *War, Revolution and the Jewish Dilemma* (London, 1975).

24. W. S. Churchill, 'Zionism versus Bolshevism', *Illustrated Sunday Herald*, 8 February 1920.

25. L. J. Maxse, 'The Key to the Mystery', *National Review*, XXXII (October 1898) pp. 277, 283. For his uncompromising attitude he was complimented upon as an 'able champion for the persecuted' in private letters of approval. MS 446.790, 293, 514, 797, 863 (Maxse Papers).

26. L. J. Maxse, 'The Second Treaty of Versailles', *National Review*, LXXIII (August 1919) p. 819. Similarly ibid. (May 1919) pp. 365–6.

27. CAB 24/61–90: fortnightly reports on revolutionary organizations in the United Kingdom, *passim*. The reports in the beginning included reviews of revolutionary movements abroad which were later covered in separate memoranda, hence different titles and numberings.

28. MS WHI 113 (White Papers): A. White to Sir Isidore Spielmann, 6 April 1922.

29. MS WHI 112 (White Papers): A. White, 'The Jews in India' (n.d.). Similarly Lord Winterton, *Orders of the Day: Memoirs of Fifty Years in the House of Commons* (London, 1953) p. 112.

30. Cf. *Conspiracy against the British Empire*, Report of a meeting held at the

House of Commons on 1 March 1921 by the Duke of Northumberland, Lord Sydenham and others, 2nd edn (n.d.).

31. According to I. Sieff, *Memoirs* (London, 1970) p. 105, the *Protocols* were better known than the Balfour declaration among officers in the Middle East. Cf. also C. Weizmann, *Trial and Error*, I (Philadelphia, 1949) p. 218.

32. *The Jewish Peril. Protocols of the Learned Elders of Zion* (London, 1920) p. ii. The preface of this edition is dated 2 December 1919. The book was published in January 1920.

33. MS uncatalogued, File nr 1 (Britons): Eyre and Spottiswoode Ltd to F. D. Fowler, The Britons, 22 June 1920, 17 September 1920.

34. MS uncatalogued, stapled file 'Shanks', File nr 1 (Britons): various correspondence and draft agreements. Confirmed by MS uncatalogued, Box B (Gwynne Papers): R. H. Cust to H. A. Gwynne, 11 February 1920. According to passing remarks in these documents, Shanks was born in Moscow, a son of an English merchant and his Russian wife, whose family was of French-Jewish origin. G. Shanks was said to have been employed at one time in the Russian Mission in Kingsway, and later at the Conservative Party's Chief Whip's Office. The CP, however, has no record of him as a member of the Central Office Staff.

35. MS uncatalogued, Box B (Gwynne Papers): R. H. Cust to H. A. Gwynne, 11 February 1920.

36. MS uncatalogued, File nr 1 (Britons): various correspondence. Owing to the destruction of their premises during World War II the firm cannot confirm this figure.

37. MS uncatalogued, File nr 1 (Britons): various correspondence. This verifies a hitherto unconfirmed account in the American anti-Semitic *Highland Post*, 17 May 1936, quoted in T. Gaster, 'Elders of Zion', *Universal Jewish Encyclopedia*, IV, p. 58.

38. MS uncatalogued, Box F (Gwynne Papers): Memorandum on the Jewish Question. H. A. Gwynne to Lady Bathurst, 27 January 1920.

39. Quoted ibid.

40. ibid.

41. MS uncatalogued, Box H (Gwynne Papers): W. Tyrell to H. A. Gwynne, 4 February 1920.

42. MS uncatalogued, Box B (Gwynne Papers): C. W. C. Oman to H. A. Gwynne, 24 February 1920.

43. MS uncatalogued, Box B (Gwynne Papers): P. E. Wright to H. A. Gwynne, 14 March 1920.

44. MS uncatalogued, Box B (Gwynne Papers): R. E. Emery to H. A. Gwynne n.d.

45. MS uncatalogued, Box H (Gwynne Papers): E. Saunders, 'An indictment of the Jews – Or a Reactionary Extravaganza?', 19 January 1920.

46. MS uncatalogued, Box F (Gwynne Papers): Peacock to Lord Bathurst, n.d.

47. According to the division of shares of royalties, the articles were written by Ian W. Colvin (37 per cent), N. F. Grant, the foreign editor of the *Morning Post* (19 per cent), H. A. Gwynne (13 per cent), W. Faulkner (11 per cent) and two further members of the *Morning Post* staff, H. W. Allen (10 per cent) and D. S. Meldrum (3 per cent). The remaining shares were due to Mrs Webster.

48. Anon., *The Cause of the World Unrest* (London, 1920) pp. 251–2. The notion of a 'formidable sect' was a familiar catchword at the time, used by Churchill in the parliamentary debate on 6 November 1919 to describe Lenin's international allies.

49. *The Times*, 8 May 1920. W. Laqueur, 'The Hidden Hand – A British contribution', appendix to W. Laqueur, *Russia and Germany* (London, 1965) pp. 311–14, attributes this article to Robert Wilton, *The Times* correspondent in Russia, who vigorously opposed democratic and revolutionary movements. Wilton's sister was married to one General Fanshawe, grandfather of M. Raslovleff, who passed Joly's *Dialogues* to P. Graves.

50. L. Wolf, *The Jewish Bogey*, repr. *The Myth of the Jewish Menace in World Affairs* (New York, 1921).

51. *The Times*, 16, 17, 18 August 1921, repr. as pamphlet *The Truth About the 'Protocols'. A Literary Forgery* (London, 1921).

52. MS uncatalogued, File 'Protocols' (*The Times* Archive): M. Raslovleff to P. Graves, 12, 13 July 1921; P. Graves to W. Steed, 13 July 1921. Although it bears the imprint 'Geneva 1864', the book was first published in Brussels and smuggled into France for distribution. Cf. N. Cohn, *Warrant for Genocide*, p. 73.

53. MS uncatalogued, File 'Protocols' (*The Times* Archive): memorandum of agreement between P. Graves and M. Raslovleff, 2 August 1921.

54. MS uncatalogued, Box B (Gwynne Papers): H. A. Gwynne to J. Millén, 20 December 1920.

55. Lord Sydenham of Combe, *The Jewish World Problem*, repr. from *Nineteenth Century and After*, November 1921 (London, n.d.) p. 2.

56. Lord Alfred Douglas, *Complete Poems* (London, 1928) p. 131.

57. *Cheiro's World Predictions*, 2nd edn (London, 1931, 1st 1928) p. 151.

58. *The Times*, 27 October 1924. The Board of Deputies approached Curzon supplying detailed information on the inaccuracy of his statement, but Curzon died before a reply was received. Board of Deputies, *Annual Report* 1925 (London, 1926) pp. 32–4.

59. Board of Deputies, *Annual Report 1926* (London, 1927) p. 40.

Chapter 2   Social Discrimination and Militant Hooliganism

1. Quoted in *Jewish Chronicle*, 26 September 1930.

2. *Jewish Chronicle*, 28 July 1933.

3. MS JSM 210/111–12 (Middleton Papers Labour Party): R. Davies to J. S. Middleton, n.d. [May 1933]. Also *Jewish Telegraphic Agency*, 10 May 1933.

4. *Jewish Chronicle*, 2 June 1933.

5. ibid., 10 June 1932, similar remarks reported ibid., 4 August 1933, 11 August 1933.

6. *Daily Dispatch*, 17 October 1932, similarly *East Anglian Daily Times*, 2 March 1934, quoted in A. Sharf, *The British Press and Jews under Nazi Rule* (London, 1964) p. 194.

7. *Jewish Chronicle*, 6 January 1933. Cf. ibid., 9 September 1932.

8. ibid., 27 June 1930, 9 January 1931, 9 September 1932. Reports of anti-Jewish discrimination in employment also in *Manchester Guardian*, 17 May

1937; *Reynolds News*, 22 May 1938; *Daily Worker*, 5 October 1939.

9. *Jewish Chronicle*, 9 January 1931, 18 December 1931, 7 April 1933. Reports concerning discriminatory advertisements and practices also addressed to NCCL MS DCL 27.4, 37.4, 41.8 (NCCL) January 1937, 26 October 1938, 7 June 1943, 11 August 1943, 21 August 1943.

10. *Jewish Chronicle*, 14 March 1930.

11. *News Chronicle*, 9 September 1936, 8 October 1936; *Jewish Chronicle*, 16 February 1935; *Daily Herald*, 8 October 1936; MS DCL 43.4 (NCCL) 13 August 1943.

12. Board of Deputies, *Annual Report 1922* (London, 1923) pp. 30–1.

13. *Jewish Chronicle*, 3 June 1932, 1 July 1932, 21 September 1934; *The Times*, 14 September 1934; *Manchester Guardian*, 13 November 1934; MS DCL 37.4 (NCCL) 2 August 1936, 26 August 1937.

14. *Jewish Chronicle*, 1 May 1931, similarly 12 July 1935.

15. ibid., 1 January 1932, 19 February 1932.

16. *Hansard*, 5th series, 7 April 1930, CCXXXVII, 1785. Also Board of Deputies, *Annual Report 1930* (London, 1931) pp. 35–6.

17. Cf. M. Freedman, 'Jews in the Society of Britain', in M. Freedman (ed.), *A Minority in Britain* (London, 1955) pp. 213–23.

18. *Jewish Chronicle*, 9 December 1932, 29 December 1933, 31 August 1934.

19. *Northern Echo*, 9 January 1934, quoted in A. Sharf, *British Press and Jews*, p. 197.

20. MS uncatalogued (Council of Christians and Jews): English Golf Club Union to Council of Christians and Jews, 27 July 1954.

21. H. J. Eysenck, *Uses and Abuses of Psychology* (Edinburgh, 1953) p. 261.

22. Recalled by H. Nicolson, *Diaries and Letters 1930–1939* (London, 1966) p. 327. Cf. ibid., p. 53 and H. Nicolson, *Diaries and Letters 1939–1945* (London, 1967) p. 469.

23. M. Gilbert, *Sir Horace Rumbold* (London, 1967) p. 49.

24. A. Forbes, *Memories and Base Details* (London, n.d. [1922]) p. 320.

25. Cf. V. G. Kiernan, 'Patterns of Protest in English History', in R. Benewick (ed.), *Direct Action and Democratic Politics* (London, 1972) pp. 39–48.

26. *West London Observer*, 26 May 1933, quoted in A. Sharf, *British Press and Jews*, p. 37.

27. MS Coordinating Committee Minutes (Board of Deputies): memorandum G. Liverman (October 1938).

28. *News Chronicle*, 29 February 1936; *Manchester Guardian*, 29 August 1936; *Jewish Chonicle*, 7 July 1939. Insulting words and behaviour also reported in parliamentary debate 10 July 1936, *Hansard* 5th series, CCCXIV, 1562–1634; MS DCL 7.3, 70.1, 74.4 (NCCL): 'Anti-Semitism in East London', 'Disturbances in East London', 'Police discrimination' (1936/7).

29. MS DCL 37.4 (NCCL): S. Volbrecht to NCCL, 4 February 1937.

30. MS DCL 37.4 (NCCL): R. Kidd, report on Fascist meeting, 14 September 1935. Reported in *Jewish Chronicle*, 4 October 1935.

31. *Middlesex County Times*, 30 July 1938.

32. *News Chronicle, Daily Herald*, 29 August 1936. The speaker was fined £2 or seven days' imprisonment for using insulting language. He was sentenced for a similar offence in May 1937. *Daily Herald*, 7 May 1937.

33. *Daily Herald*, 1 November 1938. The speaker, who had previously been bound over for a similar offence, was fined 40s. or one month's imprisonment.

34. PRO Metropolitan Police Files, Series 2, vol. 3109 (thereafter MEPO 2/3109): A. Raven-Thomson at BUF meeting, 12 March 1937.
35. Reported by MP Thurtle in parliamentary debate, 5 March 1936, *Hansard*, 5th series, CCCIX, 1628.
36. MEPO 2/3115: E. G. Clarke at BUF meeting, 23 June 1937. Cf. *Evening Standard*, *Evening News*, 10 July 1937; *The Times*, 13 July 1937.
37. *Daily Herald*, *Manchester Guardian*, 11 August 1936.
38. MEPO 2/3127: monthly reports, April 1939, May 1939, June 1939; *Daily Herald*, 5 April 1939; *Manchester Guardian*, 3 May 1939; MS DCL 37.4 (NCCL): memorandum Council of Manchester and Salford Jews, 24 November 1936. Also *Jewish Chronicle*, 20 May 1932, 24 February 1933, 19 July 1935, 29 July 1938. *Jewish Telegraphic Agency*, 14 May 1932, 4 December 1933. *News Chronicle*, 19 April 1937.
39. R. Skidelsky, *Oswald Mosley* (London, 1975) pp. 381–91.
40. MEPO 2/3080: O. Mosley at BUF meeting West Ham Town Hall, 24 July 1935.
41. *Daily Express*, *Daily Herald*, *Manchester Guardian*, *News Chronicle*, *The Times*, 12 October 1936. *East London Observer*, 17 October 1936. MS DCL 70.1 (NCCL): memorandum 'Anti-Semitism in East London' (n.d.)
42. MS DCL 74.4 (NCCL): memorandum 'Disturbances in East London', August 1937, p. 1.
43. *Reynolds News*, 16 October 1938. This paper tended to exaggerate its reports but decline of trade and picketing of Jewish shops was also mentioned in *The Times*, 17 February 1936; *Daily Herald*, 17 February 1936, 19 February 1936; *Daily Telegraph*, 19 February 1936; *World Jewry*, 21 February 1936; *News Chronicle*, 20 February 1936, 31 July 1936. MS DCL 70.1 (NCCL): memorandum 'Anti-Semitism in East London' (n.d.).
44. MEPO 2/3109: Inquiry regarding protest nr 7 by several MPs, 24 April 1937.
45. MS DCL 37.4 (NCCL): NCCL to Secretary of State for Foreign Affairs, 11 September 1937.
46. MEPO 2/3042, 3043, 3109, 3127: various reports. MS DCL 37.4, 70.1, 74.4 (NCCL): various reports. Also *Daily Herald*, 6 April 1936, 18 May 1936, 26 May 1936; *Daily Telegraph*, 31 March 1936, 8 April 1936, 22 September 1937; *Daily Worker*, 17 June 1938, 25 July 1938; *East London Observer*, 26 December 1936, 14 March 1937; *News Chronicle*, 31 August 1935, 3 September 1935, 6 April 1936, 8 April 1936, 5 May 1936, 7 September 1937, 30 November 1937, 17 September 1938, 15 March 1939; *Star*, 23 October 1936, 17 September 1938; *The Times*, 6 April 1936, 25 September 1936, 23 October 1936.
47. *Blackshirt*, 20 June 1936.
48. MS DCL 37.4 (NCCL): Memorandum 'Jew-baiting' (n.d.) Cf. *Hackney Gazette*, *Daily Herald*, 27 September 1935.
49. MEPO 2/3042: reports from various divisions, June 1936. MS DCL 37.4 (NCCL): Memorandum 'Jew-baiting' (n.d.).
50. MEPO 2/3043: Memorandum 'Jew-baiting' minute John Simon, 31 July 1936 (copy of minutes on HO papers 502, 2735/139).
51. *East London Advertiser*, 3 July 1937, 7 August 1937; *Evening Standard*, 3 August 1937; *Manchester Guardian*, 4 August 1937; *News Chronicle*, 27 July 1937, 26 October 1937.

52. *East London Advertiser, East London Observer*, 22 January 1938.
53. Beaverbrook to Frank Gannett, 9 December 1938, quoted in A. J. P. Taylor, *Beaverbrook* (London, 1972) p. 387.
54. Cf. A. J. Sherman, *Island Refuge* (London, 1973) and A. Stevens, *The Dispossessed* (London, 1975).
55. *Everybody's Weekly*, 17 September 1938, quoted in A. Sharf, *British Press and Jews*, p. 169. Similarly *Sunday Express*, 19 June 1938, 19 July 1938, 13 November 1938.
56. MEPO 2/3109: inquiry regarding protest nr 6 from various MPs, 24 April 1937.
57. This judgement is based on the few cases where complaints of Jew-baiting resulted in an arrest. For a psychological study of East-End anti-Semitism and the sociological stratification of prejudice, cf. J. H. Robb, *Working Class Anti-Semite* (London, 1954).
58. MEPO 2/3042: report Golders Green Station, 19 June 1936.
59. Letter to Hannen Swaffer, repr. in *Daily Herald*, 12 November 1936.
60. Cf. H. Rosenberg, *Grosse Depression und Bismarckzeit* (Berlin, 1967) pp. 95–6.
61. MS DCL 41.8, 43.4 (NCCL): various reports to NCCL in response to an appeal to forward incidents of anti-Semitism (summer 1940).
62. MS JSM/210/173–5 (Labour Party Archive): B. Longstaffe to A. Gould and J. S. Middleton, 19 May 1940.
63. MS Defence Committee Minutes (BoD): specimen circulated at meeting, October 1939.
64. For a comprehensive survey of the literature of a variety of anti-Semitic groups and agitators, cf. H. Blume, 'Anti-Semitic groups in Britain 1918–1940' (Sussex University thesis 1971).

Chapter 3 The Britons

1. MS uncatalogued, File nr 46 (Britons Publishing Company): minutes of meeting, 18 July 1919, the year being corrected in pencil '1918'. The draft of the constitution and the typewritten final constitution both read 'founded by H. H. Beamish 1919.' The foundation of the society was subsequently ante-dated as part of a myth-making to give the impression that it was actually founded during the war. See also *Objects and Membership Form*, ed. Britons (leaflet n.d.).
2. MS uncatalogued, File 46 (Britons): draft constitution item (2), constitution p. 4.
3. *Hidden Hand* I, nr 11 (December 1920) p. 3.
4. *The Times*, 6 December 1919. For bibliographical details of H. H. Beamish see B. A. Kosmin, 'Colonial Careers for Marginal Fascists – A Portrait of H. H. Beamish', *Wiener Library Bulletin XXVII*, n.s. nr 30/31 (1973/74) pp. 16–23.
5. Henry H. Beamish – *Silver Badge Candidate for Clapham* (election pamphlet 1918).
6. *The Times*, 22 June 1918, 30 December 1918.
7. ibid., 27 March 1919. Court proceedings reported in detail ibid., 2 December 1919, 3 December 1919, 4 December 1919, 5 December 1919, 6 December 1919.

8. MS uncatalogued, File 46 (Britons): H. H. Beamish to J. H. Clarke, 16 March 1919.

9. *The Times*, 2 December 1919.

10. *Hidden Hand* I, nr 12 (January 1921) p. 1.

11. ibid., IV, nr 1 (February 1923). Cf. *The Times*, 20 January 1923; *Sunday Times*, 21 January 1923.

12. PRO Foreign Office Papers, series 371, vol. 20739 (thereafter FO 371/20739): Steel to Norton, 16 March 1937.

13. FO 371/20739: Munich Consular Report, transmitted by British Ambassador Berlin to FO, 8 February 1937.

14. MS uncatalogued, envelope Beamish (Wiener Library): H. H. Beamish to one Schepers, South Africa, 11 January 1937.

15. FO 371/20739: extracts of Beamish's lecture delivered on 2 January 1937 in Munich, recorded in Munich Consular Report, transmitted by Ambassador to FO, 8 February 1937. Cf. *Berliner Börsenzeitung*, 18 December 1936; *Daily Herald*, 11 December 1943; *Neue Welt*, 8 January 1937; *Völkischer Beobachter*, 19 December 1936, 23 January 1937, 24 January 1937.

16. MS uncatalogued, File 46 (Britons): H. H. Beamish to J. Dell, then Secretary of the Britons, 3 September 1947.

17. MS uncatalogued, File 46 (Britons): H. H. Beamish to J. Dell, 17 January 1948. Similarly H. H. Beamish to J. Dell, 5 December 1947. Beamish's stationery was decorated with a swastika-symbol headed 'Southern Rhodesia'.

18. J. H. Clarke, *The Call of the Sword* (London, 1917) p. 28.

19. J. H. Clarke (ed.), *England Under the Heel of the Jew* (London, 1918) p. 62.

20. *Hidden Hand*, II, nr 1 (February 1921) p. 4; vol. IV, nr 12 (December 1923) pp. 8–9.

21. ibid., II, nr 6 (July 1921) p. 1.

22. ibid., II, nr 12 (January 1922) p. 2.

23. 'Goy', whose caricatures were also published as postcards, later supplied the Imperial Fascist League with drawings. The latter organization published them in a brochure *The Hidden Hand Revealed* (London, n.d.) which also contained reprints of caricatures published in the Britons' publications. 'Goy', according to personal information from the Britons Publishing Company, was the pseudonym of their executive member, later president, R. T. Cooper.

24. *Hidden Hand*, IV, nr 1 (March 1923) p. 5.

25. Anon. (= H. H. Beamish) *The Jews' Who's Who* (London, 1920) p. 5.

26. *Hidden Hand*, II, nr 2 (March 1921) p. 1.

27. Anon. (= H. H. Beamish) *The Jews' Who's Who*, p. 70.

28. Ibid., p. 13.

29. R. Benewick, *Political Violence and Public Order* (London, 1969) p. 44, implies that the Britons' anti-Semitism is not to be subsumed under the category of 'racial anti-Semitism'. In view of the dominance of racial concepts in their ideology, I cannot agree with his judgement.

30. *Hidden Hand*, V, nr 3 (March 1924) pp. 37–9. Mudge always referred to the 'Nordic Race'. The Britons used the term 'Aryan' mainly in conjunction with the NSDAP, and it did not become a prominent catchword with them.

31. Ibid., V, nr 4 (April 1924) p. 56. The same appeal to 'pride of race' was used by other authors to justify the colour bar.
32. Ibid., I, nr 11 (December 1920) p. 5.
33. Ibid., p. 8.
34. Ibid., II, nr 4 (May 1921) p. 1; nr 6 (July 1921) p. 4; vol. V, nr 3 (March 1924) p. 43. *British Guardian*, V, nr 5 (May 1924) pp. 68–70; nr 10 (October 1924) p. 131.
35. 'The Cuckoo', *Hidden Hand*, I, nr 10 (November 1920). 'The Champion of Truth', *British Guardian*, VI, nr 8 (27 February 1925).
36. *Hidden Hand*, III, nr 11 (December 1922), p. 1. *British Guardian*, V, nr 5 (May 1924) p. 66; nr 10 (October 1924) pp. 135–6.
37. *Jewry Ueber Alles*, I, nr 3 (April 1920) p. 3. *Hidden Hand*, II, nr 3 (April 1921), p. 1.
38. *Hidden Hand*, V, nr 4 (April 1924) p. 56.
39. Ibid., II, nr 2 (March 1921) p. 2. On Liebenfels, cf. W. Daim, *Der Mann der Hitler die Ideen gab* (München, 1958).
40. *Jewry Ueber Alles*, I, nr 1 (February 1920) p. 5.
41. *Hidden Hand*, V, nr 4 (April 1924) p. 51.
42. *British Guardian*, VI, nr 1 (9 January 1925) p. 1.
43. *Hidden Hand*, V, nr 4 (April 1924) p. 51.
44. *British Guardian*, VI, nr 1 (9 January 1925) p. 1.
45. *Hidden Hand*, IV, nr 9 (September 1923) p. 1.
46. *British Guardian*, V, nr 5 (May 1924) p. 69.
47. *Hidden Hand*, IV, nr 4 (April 1923) p. 5.
48. Ibid., II, nr 2 (March 1921) p. 3.
49. Anon. (= H. H. Beamish), *The Jews' Who's Who*, p. 43. Also *Hidden Hand*, IV, nr 5 (May 1923) p. 2.
50. *The Watchman*, 11 July 1924.
51. Anon. (= H. H. Beamish), *The Jews' Who's Who*, p. 41.
52. 'Mr. Beamish Answers A Jew', *Hidden Hand*, II, nr 9 (October 1921) p. 5.
53. *Hidden Hand*, II, nr 4 (May 1921) p. 1.
54. Ibid., IV, nr 4 (April 1923) p. 1. Also Britons (ed.), *Zionism Solved!* (leaflet n.d.). Britons (ed.), *South Africa's Kosher Press* (London n.d.) p. 7.
55. P. de Lagarde, *Deutsche Schriften*, 4th edn. (Göttingen, 1903) p. 391. In 1937 the Polish Government set up a committee to investigate the possibility of settling Polish Jews in Madagascar, after a similar project, conceived in 1926, had been dismissed. In December 1938 G. Bonnet, the French Foreign Secretary, informed Ribbentrop that the French Government considered shipping 10,000 Jewish refugees there. The idea of a Jewish settlement in Madagascar was also mentioned to an English representative of the Anglo-German Fellowship at the Nuremberg Party Rally in September 1935 by the NSDAP ideologist A. Rosenberg. MS 'Notes on Germany and Austria 1932–5' (Lord Mount Temple Papers): memorandum by E. W. D. Tennant, September 1935. On the Madagascar plan cf. *Documents of German Foreign Policy 1918–1945*, series D, vol. IV (London, 1951) nr 372. R. Hilberg, *The Destruction of European Jews* (Chicago, 1961) pp. 260 ff. H. Krausnick, *Anatomy of the SS-State* (London, 1968) pp. 55 ff. L. Poliakov, *Bréviaire de la Haine* (Paris, 1951) pp. 50 ff.
56. *Hidden Hand*, IV, nr 4 (April 1923) p. 1.

57. Britons (ed.), *South Africa's Kosher Press*, p. 7.
58. *Hidden Hand*, V, nr 1 (January 1924) p. 13.
59. Since no membership files of the Britons are available, overlapping membership between this and other fringe organizations can only be documented for some individuals like Beamish, Clarke, Admiral Domvile, Fraser and Mudge.
60. Britons (ed.), *The Conquering Jew* (leaflet n.d.).
61. *Hidden Hand*, IV, nr 5 (May 1923) p. 1.
62. Britons (ed.), *Jewish Bolshevism*. Drawings of Russian leaders with a foreword by A. Rosenberg, dated 1922 (London, n.d.). Previously published in English as *The Gravediggers of Russia*, with a foreword by A. Rosenberg dated 1921 (Munich: Deutscher Volksverlag Dr E. Boepple, n.d.).
63. *Wiener Morgenzeitung* 1 March 1923, quoted in *Hidden Hand*, IV, nr 4 (April 1923) p. 5.
64. K. G. Lüdecke, *I Knew Hitler* (New York, 1937) pp. 213–14.
65. *British Guardian*, VI, nr 9 (6 March 1925) p. 65.
66. Britons (ed.), *The Britons* (London, 1952) lists the prominent members of the society and their careers. Cf. Britons (ed.), *Work and Objects* (leaflet n.d.). Britons (ed.), *Appeal from Sir Barry Domvile* (leaflet n.d.). MS Diary (Britons), *passim*.
67. *Hidden Hand*, I, nr 12 (January 1921) p. 5.
68. J. H. Clarke, *A Patriotic Fund to Fight the Hidden Hand* (leaflet n.d.). MS Diary (Britons): meeting 15 October 1923.
69. MS Diary (Britons): minutes of various meetings.
70. Manufacturers known to have supported the Britons were W. Crick, a Northampton boot manufacturer, vice-president of the Britons 1925–6 and A. Kitson, director of the Kitson Engineering Co. Ltd, author of many articles supporting monetary reforms and 'social credit'.

Chapter 4   Imperial Fascist League
1. On bibliographical details, cf. A. S. Leese, *Out of Step: The Two Lives of an Anti-Jewish Camel Doctor* (n.d.). J. E. Morell, 'Arnold Leese – Fascist and anti-Semite', *Wiener Library Bulletin XXIII*, nr 4, n.s. nr 17 (1969) pp. 32–6.
2. *Fascist*, nr 116 (January 1939) p. 2.
3. A. S. Leese, *Out of Step*, p. 51.
4. *The Times*, 15 August 1936, 22 August 1936, 19 September 1936, 22 September 1936. Immediately after his release Leese reiterated the ritual murder charge in the brochure *My Irrelevant Defence being Meditations Inside Gaol and Out* (London, 1938).
5. A. S. Leese, *Out of Step*, pp. 6, 46.
6. Ibid., p. 48. Cf. *The Times*, 22 September 1936.
7. For the history of the British Fascists Ltd, originally called British Fascisti, see R. Benewick, *Political Violence*, pp. 27–36 and H. Blume, 'A Study of Anti-Semitic Groups', pp. 99–113.
8. IFL (ed.), *The Government of the Future. Fascism – Its Principles* (leaflet n.d.). An amended version was published later under the title *The Government of the Future, Racial Fascism – Its Principles* (leaflet n.d.).
9. *Fascist*, nr 6 (August 1929) p. 4.

10. Ibid., nr 68 (January 1935) p. 2. Also IFL (ed.) *Policy and Organization of the Imperial Fascist League* (London n.d.) p. 4.
11. *Fascist*, nr 31 (December 1931) p. 1. Cf. M. Domarus, *Hitler Reden und Proklamationen I* (Würzburg, 1962) pp. 450–1.
12. IFL (ed.), *The Imperial Fascist League Stands for a New Constitution* (leaflet n.d.).
13. IFL (ed.), *Policy and Organization of the IFL* (London n.d.). IFL (ed.), *The Government of the Future* (leaflet n.d.).
14. IFL (ed.), *Policy and Organization of the IFL*, p. 6.
15. *Fascist*, nr 80 (January 1936) p. 5.
16. Ibid., nr 84 (May 1936) p. 2.
17. Ibid., nr 76 (September 1935) p. 1.
18. Ibid., nr 24 (May 1931)... p. 2. Cf., ibid., nr 73 (June 1935), p. 2; nr 115 (December 1938) p. 2.
19. Ibid., nr 120 (May 1939) p. 3.
20. Ibid., nr 73 (June 1935) p. 2.
21. R. Benewick, *Political Violence*, p. 44. J. E. Morell, 'Arnold Leese', *Wiener Library Bulletin*, XXIII (1969), p. 34.
22. IFL (ed.) *The Imperial Fascist League Stands for a New Constitution* (leaflet n.d.).
23. L. H. Sherrard, 'Yellow English', *Fascist*, nr 5 (July 1929) p. 1. This was the journal's first contribution on racial problems.
24. A. S. Leese, *Out of Step*, p. 50.
25. *Fascist*, nr 73 (June 1935) p. 6; nr 120 (May 1939) p. 2.
26. IFL (ed.), *The Plan of the Jew* (leaflet n.d.), repr. of an article in *Fascist*, nr 26 (July 1931) p. 2.
27. MEPO 2/3069: A. S. Leese to Commissioner of Police, 2 October 1933. For a psychological interpretation of Leese's opposition to Mosley, cf. R. Thurlow, 'Authoritarians and Populists on the English Far Right', *Patterns of Prejudice*, X, nr 2 (1976) p. 17.
28. Cf. M. D. Biddis, 'Myths of Blood', *Patterns of Prejudice*, IX, nr 5 (1975) pp. 11–19.
29. IFL (ed.), *The Hidden Hand Revealed* (London n.d.), contains reprints of illustrations published in *Hidden Hand*, I, nr 11 (December 1920), vol. II, nr 12 (January 1922), and *British Guardian* VI nr 9 (6 March 1925).
30. *The Times*, 22 September 1926.
31. *Fascist*, nr 23 (April 1931) p. 3.
32. Ibid., nr 24 (May 1931) p. 2. In his autobiographical account H. E. Thost, *Als Nationalsozialist in England* (München 1939) p. 250, mentions Lease (*sic*) and the IFL as crusaders against Jewry.
33. *Fascist*, nr 39 (August 1932) p. 2.
34. IFL (ed.), *The Swastika Symbol: What It Means* (leaflet n.d.). Cf. *Evening Standard*, 24 May 1934.
35. MS DCL 40.1 (NCCL): Capt. A. Ramsay, MP (Cons.) quoted in report of meeting of Nordic League, 10 July 1939. Cf. *Fascist*, nr 44 (January 1933) p. 4.
36. J. Barnes, '*Mein Kampf* in Britain 1930–1939', *Wiener Library Bulletin*, XXVII, n.s. nr 32 (1974) pp. 2–10.
37. *Fascist*, nr 51 (August 1933) p. 3. The translator was not named, but it can be assumed that it was Thost.
38. Ibid., nr 37 (June 1932) p. 3. Cf. A. Hitler, *Mein Kampf*, 213th edn (München

1936)p. 316: 'Alle grossen Kulturen der Vergangenheit gingen nur zugrunde, weil die ursprünglich schöpferische Rasse an Blutsvergiftung abstarb.'

39. *Fascist*, nr 64 (September 1934) p. 2. Also ibid., nr 70 (March 1935) p. 7. IFL (ed.), *Race and Politics* (London n.d.) p. 3. IFL (ed.) *Whither the World?* (leaflet n.d.).

40. These contradictions are overlooked by R. C. Thurlow, 'Racial Populism in England', *Patterns of Prejudice*, X, nr 4 (1976) pp. 28–32.

41. A. Hitler, *Mein Kampf*, pp. 334–47.

42. A. S. Leese, *Out of Step*, p. 51.

43. *Fascist*, nr 8 (October 1929) p. 4.

44. Ibid., nr 86 (July 1936) p. 1. Cf. IFL (ed.), *Race and Politics* pp. 6ff.

45. IFL (ed.), *300,000 Jews! What A Lie!* (leaflet n.d.).

46. *Fascist*, nr 63 (August 1934), p. 2. Cf. ibid., nr 120 (May 1939) p. 2. A. S. Leese, *The Mass Madness of September 1938 and its Jewish Cause* (London n.d.).

47. *Fascist*, nr 41 (October 1932) p. 1. Cf. A. Hitler, *Mein Kampf*, p. 70: 'Indem ich mich des Juden erwehre, kämpfe ich für das Werk des Herrn.'

48. A. S. Leese, *Devilry in the Holy Land* (London n.d.) p. 5. Cf. A. Hitler, *Mein Kampf*, p. 356: 'Sie denken gar nicht daran, in Palästina einen jüdischen Staat aufzubauen um ihn etwa zu bewohnen.'

49. *Fascist*, nr 99 (August 1937) p. 2.

50. Ibid., nr 69 (February 1935) p. 2; nr 86 (July 1936) p. 1; nr 104 (January 1938) p. 2. A. S. Leese, *Devilry in the Holy Land*, p. 16.

51. *Fascist*, nr 104 (January 1938) p. 2; nr 110 (July 1938) p. 2.

52. MEPO 2/ 3043: J. Ridout, deputy leader of IFL, cautioned for anti-Jewish language. Commissioner's report to Home Office, October 1936 and November 1936.

53. *Fascist*, nr 120 (May 1939) p. 1.

54. Ibid., nr 109 (June 1938) p. 5.

55. Ibid., nr 69 (February 1935) p. 3.

56. Ibid., nr 64 (September 1934) p. 1.

57. Ibid., nr 67 (December 1934) p. 5. MS uncatalogued, Leese File 11 (Britons): A. Leese to Tony [Gittens], 12 November n.y., ordering 250 cards and envelopes.

58. *Fascist*, nr 97 (June 1937) p. 2.

59. *Gothic Ripples*, nr 6 (11 November 1945).

60. MS uncatalogued, Leese file 11 (Britons): A. Leese to Dell, 20 September n.y.

61. IFL (ed.), *Mightier Yet! Back to Reality* (London n.d.).

62. *Fascist*, nr 88–91 (September 1936–January 1937). The largest single contributions were £10.–.–.

63. PRO 30–69/1/400 (Ramsay MacDonald Papers): Home Office Memorandum on Fascist organizations (February 1934). Cf. *John Bull*, 13 April 1946; *Sunday Referee*, 11 October 1936.

64. *Daily Telegraph*, *Daily Herald*, *The Times*, 18 May 1936. The *Fascist* had praised the very hotel before when, under its previous management, it had refused admittance to Jews. Cf. *Fascist*, nr 62 (July 1934) p. 2. *Manchester Guardian*, *Daily Herald*, 9 August 1934.

65. MEPO 2/3069: Superintendent's report, 18 May 1933. MEPO 2/3043: various monthly reports to Home Office *passim*.

66. Mocatta Collection, uncatalogued (UC London): various stickers. Cf. *News Chronicle*, 31 August 1935.
67. MS Misc. 1933 (Astor Papers): Leese to Lady Astor, 27 February 1933 and 3 March 1933.
68. *Evening Standard*, 24 May 1934.
69. IFL (ed.), *A Message to Tradesmen. Local News! To A Gentile Jester. A Tragic Symphony. To Cyclists and Car Drivers* (leaflets n.d.).
70. *Fascist*, nr. 67 (December 1934) p. 1.
71. MS uncatalogued, Leese File 11 (Britons): A. Leese to Tony [Gittens], 17 October n.y.

Chapter 5   British Union of Fascists
1. For biographical details, cf. O. Mosley, *My Life* (London, 1968) and R. Skidelsky, *Oswald Mosley* (London, 1976).
2. O. Mosley, *Revolution by Reason* (London, 1925) pp. 28–9.
3. PRO 30/69/1/445 (Ramsay MacDonald Papers): Mosley Memorandum, 16 January 1930.
4. O. Mosley, *The Greater Britain* (London n.d. [1932] p. 133.
5. PRO 30/69/1/446 (Ramsay MacDonald Papers): Unemployment Committee Report, 1 May 1930. On the controversy, cf. R. Skidelsky, *Politicians and the Slump* (London, 1967).
6. O. Mosley, *Greater Britain*, p. 50.
7. Cf. L. P. Carpenter, 'Corporatism in Britain 1930–1945', *Journal of Contemporary History*, XI, nr 1 (1976) pp. 3–25.
8. For the concept of Fascism as a generic phenomenon, cf. F. L. Carsten, *The Rise of Fascism* (London, 1967). E. Nolte, *Der Faschismus in seiner Epoche* (München, 1963). H. A. Turner (ed.), *Reappraisals of Fascism* (New York, 1975).
9. *Blackshirt*, 27 April 1934.
10. Ibid., 15 June 1934.
11. Ibid., 2 November 1934.
12. Ibid., 1 April 1933.
13. Ibid., 16 May 1933.
14. MS uncatalogued (Nicolson Papers): H. Nicolson to O. Mosley, 29 June 1932.
15. *Blackshirt*, 4 November 1933.
16. O. Mosley, *My Life*, p. 346.
17. *Blackshirt*, 20 July 1934.
18. Ibid., Cf. *Jewish Chronicle*, 6 July 1934, 27 July 1934.
19. *Blackshirt*, 2 November 1934. Cf. *Daily Express, Daily Herald, Daily Mail, Daily Telegraph*, 29 October 1934, *New Statesman and Nation*, 3 November 1934.
20. *Manchester Guardian*, 1 October 1934; *Blackshirt*, 5 October 1934.
21. MEPO 2/3117: O. Mosley at BUF meeting Southwark Park Road, 1 May 1938.
22. R. Skidelsky, *Mosley*, p. 381.
23. *Jewish Chronicle*, 13 January 1933. Cf. ibid., 30 September 1932, 4 November 1932, 12 May 1933.

24. *Blackshirt*, 16 May 1933.
25. *Action*, 7 November 1936.
26. *Blackshirt*, 12 September 1936.
27. *The Times*, 14, 15, 16 October, 1937. Cf. *Action*, 2 April 1936.
28. *The Times*, 16 October 1937.
29. *Action*, 7 November 1936.
30. O.Mosley,*Fascism, 100 Questions Asked and Answered* (London, 1936) para. 93.
31. O. Mosley, 'Jews and Fascism', in *The Jews* (London: Query Publications nr 2, n.d. [1938]) p. 35.
32. *Action*, 24 July 1937.
33. J. F. C. Fuller, 'The Cancer of Europe', *Fascist Quarterly*, I, nr 1 (1935) pp. 66–81. A. K. Chesterton, 'The Apotheosis of the Jew', *British Union Quarterly*, I, nr 2 (1937) pp. 45–54. A. Reade, 'The Defence of Western Civilization', ibid., vol. III, nr 4 (1939) pp. 52–61.
34. Cf. D. M. Geiger, 'British Fascism as Revealed in the BUF's Press' (New York University PhD thesis 1963). D. M. Geiger, 'Blackshirts as Jew-Baiters', *Wiener Library Bulletin*, XX, n.s. nr 4 (1966) pp. 11–14. W. F. Mandle, *Anti-Semitism and the British Union of Fascists* (London, 1968).
35. MEPO 2/3109: Copy of British Union Song Sheet, 24 April 1937.
36. *Action*, 7 November 1936.
37. A. R. Thomson, 'W. Lewis: The Jews', *British Union Quarterly*, III, nr 2 (1939) p. 87.
38. *Action*, 26 June 1937.
39. Ibid., 17 September 1936.
40. R. Skidelsky, *Mosley*, p. 391.
41. O. Mosley, 'Jews and Fascism', *The Jews*, p. 35.
42. MEPO 2/3109: R. Hargreave at BUF meeting Victoria Park Square, 12 March 1937. For the election results, cf. C. Cross, *Fascists in Britain* (London, 1961) pp. 166–7.
43. MEPO 2/3115: E. G. Clarke at BUF meeting Victoria Park Square, 25 June 1937 and at BUF meeting 23 June 1927.
44. *Blackshirt*, 1 March 1935.
45. O. Mosley, *My Life*, pp. 342, 347–8. In the Camrose trial, one witness claimed that Mosley had checked the proofs of the controversial issue of *Action*. C.f. *The Times*, 15 October 1937. See also R. Skidelsky, *Mosley*, p. 536.
46. MEPO 2/3043: monthly reports, August and September 1936.
47. W. F. Mandle, *Anti-Semitism*, pp. 18–19. C. Cross, *Fascists in Britain*, pp. 126 ff., echoed in A. Cassels, 'Janus: the Two Faces of Fascism', in H. A. Turner (ed.), *Reappraisals of Fascism*, p. 84.
48. MEPO 2/3043: monthly report, August 1936.
49. Ibid., G. Wegg-Prosser to O. Mosley, quoted in monthly report, May 1937.
50. W. F. Mandle, *Anti-Semitism*, pp. 20–3.
51. Cynthia Mosley died on 16 May 1933. In October 1936 Mosley married Diana Freeman-Mitford, daughter of Lord Redesdale. While his first wife remained unsympathetic to Fascism, the second was an ardent admirer of Hitler and, together with her more notorious sister Unity, was frequently present at Nazi events. Cf. D. Pryce-Jones, *Unity Mitford* (London, 1976) pp. 121–49.
52. Cf. J. Jones, *Unfinished Journey* (London, 1937) p. 265.

53. *Blackshirt*, 29 March 1935.
54. O. Mosley, 'The World Alternative', *Fascist Quarterly*, II, nr 3 (1936) pp. 377–95.
55. *Blackshirt*, 31 May 1935.
56. Ibid., 8 August 1936.
57. MEPO 2/3109: British Union Song Sheet, 24 April 1937. Also *Action*, 27 March 1937.
58. *The Times*, 29 July 1937.
59. *Jewish Chronicle*, 17 May 1935. Cf. *Daily Herald*, 11 May 1935.
60. J. Strachey to R. Benewick, 7 April 1960, quoted in R. Benewick, *Political Violence*, p. 151.
61. Cf. above p. 91. To the same effect, I. Ravensdale, *In Many Rhythms* (London, 1953) p. 144, and I. Sieff, *Memoirs* (London, 1970) p. 171.
62. W. F. Mandle, 'The Leadership of the BUF', *Australian Journal of Politics and History*, XXII, nr 3 (1966), pp. 360–83.
63. MEPO 2/4319: SB Sergeant Hunt, 8 June 1934.
64. Ibid., SB Sergeant Rogers, 8 June 1934.
65. Ibid., SB Sergeant Pocock, 7 June 1934. Cf. *Fascists at Olympia* (London, 1934). Parliamentary debate, 14 June 1934, *Hansard*, 5th series, CCXC, 1913–2041.
66. MEPO 2/4319: Superintendent Hammersmith Station to DAC 1, 8 June 1934.
67. MS B. 9. 347–9 (Baldwin Papers): G. Fry to A. S. Hutchinson, 16 January 1935, A. S. Hutchinson to G. Fry, 11 February 1935.
68. O. Mosley, *My Life*, p. 348.
69. FO 371/19453: FO memorandum, 14 December 1935. *Hansard*, 5th series, 1946, CDXXIII, 2140–1. CAB 129/8: report Committee on Fascism, 5 April 1947. On BUF finance see also O. Mosley, *My Life*, pp. 344–50, and R. Skidelsky, *Mosley*, pp. 330, 463–4.
70. PRO 30/69/1/400 (Ramsay MacDonald Papers): Home Secretary, Report on Fascist Organizations, 1 February 1934. Cf. MS MFC 76/1/314 III/11 (Trenchard Papers): Special Branch report, 28 October 1933. See also *Hansard*, 5th series, 1934, CCXC, 2032.
71. *Hansard*, 5th series, 25 July 1940, CCCLXIII, 966–7. Cf. *Jewish Chronicle*, 22 December 1939. CAB 129/8: report on the re-emergence of Fascism, 5 April 1947. See also, R. Benewick, *Political Violence*, p. 110.

Chapter 6   The Forces of Law and Order
1. MS MFC 76/1/314.23 Cat. III/11 (Trenchard Papers): Trenchard to Under-Secretary of State, Home Office, 31 October 1933.
2. PRO 30/69/1/400 (Ramsay MacDonald Papers): Home Office memorandum 'Wearing of Uniforms by Members of Political Organizations', J. Gilmour to R. MacDonald, 1 February 1934.
3. Ibid., minute R. MacDonald, 3 February 1934.
4. PRO 30/69/1/401 (Ramsay MacDonald Papers): J. Simon to J. Gilmour, 16 February 1934.
5. MEPO 2/3112: F. A. Newsam, 11 June 1937 (copy of minutes on Home Office Docket nr 502735/265).

6. CAB 24/250: memorandum by the Commissioner of the Metropolitan Police, 2 July 1934, attached to Home Secretary's memorandum 'Preservation of Public Order', 11 July 1934.

7. MS 1932 (Dawson Papers): R. Barrington-Ward to G. Dawson, 4 May 1934.

8. MEPO 2/3081: Special Branch Report 4 October 1935. Minute Trenchard, 4 October 1935.

9. MEPO 2/3077: Operation Order nr 73, 1 March 1935.

10. MEPO 2/3074: O. Mosley to Sir T. Bigham, 13 September 1934. On police arrangements, cf. MEPO 2/3040.

11. MS MFC 76/1/314.25 III/11 (Trenchard Papers): Trenchard to Under-Secretary of State Home Office, 28 September 1934.

12. *Hansard*, 5th series, 14 June 1934, CCXC, 1932.

13. Cf. parliamentary statements by Home Secretary on 27 February and 5 March 1936. *Hansard*, 5th series, 1936, CCCIX, 634, 1603–11. See also debate on anti–Semitic activities and police conduct, ibid., 1595–1603, and *Hansard*, 5th series, 10 July 1936, CCCXIV, 1563–1603.

14. Immediate action was taken against A. S. Leese who was charged with seditious libel for accusing the Jews of ritual murder. Cf. MEPO 2/3042, 2/3043: monthly report, August 1936.

15. MEPO 2/3043: *aide mémoire* 'Jew-baiting', 16 July 1936.

16. Cf. ibid.: confidential memorandum 22/GEN/76 (A.2), 3 August 1936, and draft (undated).

17. Ibid.: confidential memorandum 'Anti-Jewish Activities', 3 August 1936.

18. *Hansard*, 5th series, 10 July 1936, CCCXIV, 1575.

19. MEPO 2/3104: report superintendent Y-division.

20. MS DCL 7.3, 74.4 (NCCL): 'Police Discrimination' (1937) p. 3, 'Disturbances in East London' (1937) p. 13. Cf. R. Kidd, *British Liberty in Danger* (London, 1940) p. 123.

21. MEPO 2/3043: confidential memorandum, 29 June 1937. Rebuke repeated at Superintendents' Conference, 1 August 1939. Cf. MEPO 2/3127.

22. *News Chronicle*, 21 May 1936.

23. MS DCL 37.4 (NCCL): report of BUF meeting at Victoria Park Square, 12 March 1937.

24. MS DCL 7.3 (NCCL): E. G. Watts, P. Shand to NCCL on 'Arms for Spain' demonstration, 31 January 1939.

25. MS DCL 74.4 (NCCL): M. Battcock to NCCL, quoted in 'Disturbances in East London' (1937) pp. 11–12.

26. MEPO 2/3069: telegram, 14 May 1933, report to Home Office, 15 May 1933.

27. MEPO 2/3115: report of inspector H–division, 12 July 1937. The inspector was cautioned. Clarke was arrested two days later for insulting words and behaviour, in the context of which the shorthand minutes of his earlier speech were examined and action taken against the officer in charge of the previous meeting.

28. MEPO 2/3043: SB report, December 1937 and 1 January 1938.

29. Ibid.: monthly report, July 1938. Cf. also reports for August and September 1938.

30. *Hansard*, 5th series, 14 May 1936, CCCXII, 573–4.

31. MS DCL 7.3 (NCCL): 'Police Discrimination' (1937) pp. 3–4.

32. MS DCL 74.4 (NCCL): collection of statements on Thurloe Square meeting, 22 March 1936, nr 17, nr 25. Similar reports collected after Fascist meeting held on 14 July 1937 in Stepney Green. DCL 75.2.
33. MEPO 2/3089: minute A.L.D., 19 August 1936, copy of minute on Home Office file 648, 133/29.
34. MEPO 2/3087: SB report, 22 February 1936 (Margolis case).
35. Ibid.: minute, 21 February 1936.
36. MEPO 2/3043: monthly report, February 1937 and 12 March 1937.
37. Ibid.: SB report, February 1937. For similar 'cooking' of the final report see ibid., SB report, December 1937, 1 January 1938, draft of Commissioner's report, December 1937, 6 January 1938 and final report December 1937, 11 January 1938.
38. MS DCL 74.4 (NCCL): 'Disturbances in East London' (1937) p. 8.
39. *Hansard*, 5th series, 5 March 1936, CCCIX, 1600. Various reports on anti-Jewish biases of judges in *Free Speech Assembly Bulletin*, nr 20, November 1936, pp. 5–8.
40. MEPO 2/3043: monthly report, February 1938. Cf. *Manchester Guardian*, 6 October 1936.
41. MEPO 2/3078: anonymous letter to Metropolitan Police.
42. MEPO 2/3117: L. R. Stride to Commissioner, 8 September 1937. W. Watts to Commissioner, 8 May 1937.
43. MEPO 2/3048: B. Johnson to Commissioner, 5 July 1937.
44. MEPO 2/3098: P. Game to G. Lloyd, MP, 18 November 1936 .Cf. *Report of the Commissioner of the Metropolis for the year 1936*, pp. 12–13.
45. MS MFC 76/1/314.25 III/11 (Trenchard Papers): Trenchard to Under-Secretary of State Home Office, 28 September 1939. Cf. *Annual Report of the Commissioner of the Metropolis for the year 1934*, p. 50.
46. R. Skidelsky, *Mosley*, p. 240, suggests that the police jealously viewed the BUF as a rival organization. There is little evidence supporting this sweeping judgement.
47. Ibid., p. 416.
48. CAB 24/264: Home Secretary's memorandum to Cabinet, 12 October 1936.
49. Cf. R. Benewick, 'The Threshold of Violence', in R. Benewick (ed.), *Direct Action and Democratic Politics* (London, 1972) pp. 49–63.
50. *Hansard*, 5th series, 26 November 1936, CCCXVIII, 640.
51. During 1937 the Special Branch attended 1741 anti-Fascist as opposed to 1432 Fascist meetings; during 1938, 1391 anti-Fascist as opposed to 1166 Fascist meetings and from January to September 1939, 435 anti-Fascist as opposed to 319 Fascist meetings. Figures compiled from Commissioner's monthly reports MEPO 2/3043, 2/3127.
52. *Church Times*, 30 October 1936. For attitudes of parties and pressure groups see R. Benewick, *Political Violence*, pp. 235–59.
53. CAB 24/264: Home Secretary's Memorandum to Cabinet, 12 October 1936. Cf. I. Simon, *Retrospect* (London, 1953) p. 215.
54. J. Barnes and K. Middlemas, *Baldwin* (London, 1969) p. 931, give the impression that the Prime Minister somewhat reluctantly consented to ban political uniforms, whereas the parliamentary debates suggest that Baldwin regarded the Public Order Bill as an issue of greater importance than did the Home Secretary. There is no reference to the issue in the Baldwin Papers.

55. MEPO 2/3116: O. Mosley to Home Secretary, 5 August 1937.
56. Ibid.: F. A. Newsam to O. Mosley, 7 September 1937.
57. MEPO 2/3110: memorandum DAC 3, 23 April 1937.
58. Ibid.: minutes of meeting, 1 May 1937. Commissioner to DAC 3, 4 May 1937. Cf. T. Jones, *A Diary With Letters 1931–1950* (Oxford, 1954) p. 368.
59. MEPO 2/3048: P. Game to Home Secretary, 16 June 1937, confirmed 18 June 1937.
60. Ibid.: report, 5 July 1937.
61. MEPO 2/3117: operation order nr 124, 30 September 1937. DAC 4 report, 4 October 1937.

Chapter 7 Anglo-Jewry

1. Cf. A. G. Brotman, 'Jewish Communal Organization', in S. Esh and J. Gould (ed.), *Jewish Life of Modern Britain* (London, 1964) pp. 1–17. C. H. L. Emanuel, *A Century and a Half of Jewish History* (London, 1910).
2. B. Krikler, 'Boycotting Nazi Germany', *Wiener Library Bulletin*, XXIII, n.s. nr 17 (1969) pp. 26–32.
3. Captain Webber, whom Chief Constable Sir Francis Griffith considered 'slightly "mental" ', lost his influence within the Jewish community in 1935 after having sacrificed a considerable fortune in the boycott campaign. MEPO 2/3083: memorandum F. Griffith, 24 September 1935. Cf. *Sunday Referee*, 30 June 1935.
4. *Jewish Chronicle*, 24 March 1933.
5. Board of Deputies, resolution passed on 18 November 1934, confirmed 2 October 1935. *Annual Report 1935*, p. 73.
6. *Daily Express*, 24 March 1933.
7. *Hansard*, 5th series, 10 April 1933, CCLXXVI, 2168–70.
8. E. Spier, *Focus* (London, 1963). Cf. D. Aigner, *Das Ringen um England* (München, 1969) pp. 217–27.
9. Cf. M. R. Marrus, *The Politics of Assimilation. A Study of the French Community at the Time of the Dreyfus Affair* (London, 1971). A. Paucker, *Der jüdische Abwehrkampf gegen Antisemitismus und Nationalsozialismus in den letzten Jahren der Weimarer Republik* 2nd edn (Hamburg, 1969). I. Schorsch, *Jewish Reactions to German Anti-Semitism 1870–1914* (New York, 1972).
10. Board of Deputies, *Annual Reports 1919–1933* (London, 1920–34) *passim*.
11. Board of Deputies, *Annual Report 1933* (London, 1934) p. 47.
12. Neville J. Laski (1890–1969), eldest son of merchant Nathan Laski, Manchester, and brother of Harold Laski. President of Board of Deputies of British Jews 1933–40.
13. MS uncatalogued (Board of Deputies minute books): report Law, Parliamentary and General Purposes Committee, 10 March 1936.
14. *Jewish People's Council against Fascism and Anti-Semitism and the Board of Deputies*, ed. JPC (leaflet n.d. [1936]).
15. MS uncatalogued (Parkes Collection): JPC Conference report, 15 November 1936, pp. 3–4. Cf. JPC (ed.), *Report of Activities* (London, 1936). JPC (ed.), *Jewish People's Council and the Board of Deputies* (London, 1936).
16. MS DCL 37.4 (NCCL): draft Racial Incitement Act.
17. JPC (ed.), *We Protest!* (leaflet n.d.).

18. *Daily Worker*, 3 November 1936. See also MEPO 2/3043: SB report, November 1936.
19. MS uncatalogued (Parkes Collection): Conference on Fascism and anti-Semitism, resolution 25 April 1937. Cf. MS DCL 37.4 (NCCL): report on JPC conference, 15 November 1936.
20. MS DCL 37.4 (NCCL): JPC Emergency Resolution and Conference Resolution, 15 November 1936.
21. MS uncatalogued (BoD minutes): Board meeting, 15 November 1936.
22. Ibid.: Coordinating Committee, 25 November 1936. Cf. *The Times*, 8 November 1936.
23. MEPO 2/3043: SB report, November 1936. The attendance at the JPC meeting was estimated at 200 persons.
24. MEPO 2/3112: F. A. Newsam, 11 June 1937.
25. *Jewish Telegraphic Agency*, 16 November 1936 (BoD minutes). For a similar attitude towards non-anti-Semitic Fascist dictatorship among German middle-class Jews, cf. A. Paucker, *Der jüdische Abwehrkampf*, pp. 71–2.
26. *Jewish Telegraphic Agency*, 16 November 1936.
27. MS uncatalogued (BoD minutes): Gellman memorandum on Jewish meeting Philpot Street, 28 June 1938.
28. Laski at Board meeting, 21 June 1936, reported in *Jewish Chronicle*, 26 June 1936.
29. *Jewish Chronicle*, 24 July 1936.
30. Ibid.
31. Ibid., 1 May 1936.
32. MS uncatalogued (BoD minutes): Laski at Coordinating Committee, 26 July 1936.
33. Ibid.: Laski at Coordinating Committee, 15 July 1937.
34. Ibid.: Laski at Coordinating Committee, 21 June 1938.
35. Ibid.: Jewish Defence Committee, summary of activities November/December 1938.
36. Board of Deputies of British Jews, *Annual Report 1937* (London, 1938) p. 40.
37. MS uncatalogued (BoD): Central Jewish Lecture Committee, reports and statements 1937–8 (January 1939).
38. Pamphlet collection (Parkes Collection): Speakers' notes *Jews and the Press*, *Jews and Finance*, *Jews and Bolshevism*, *White Slave Traffic*, *Chain Stores and Price Cutting*, *Protocols*.
39. Ibid.: Speakers' notes *Kol Nidrai*, *Blood Libel*, *Jews in Palestine*.
40. Ibid.: Speakers' notes *Jew as a Patriot*, *Jewish Contribution to English Literature*, *Jewish Contribution to English Drama*.
41. MEPO 2/3043: monthly report, October 1937. MS uncatalogued (BoD minutes): Gellman memorandum on London Area Committee, April 1939.
42. *What the Jews of the British Empire Did in the Great War* (pamphlet n.d.).
43. MS uncatalogued (BoD minutes): Jewish Defence Committee, summary of activities, December 1938. For a less successful campaign conducted by the *Centralverein* in Weimar Germany, cf. A. Paucker, *Der jüdische Abwehrkampf*, p. 59.
44. MS uncatalogued (BoD minutes): secretary's report to Coordinating Committee, February and March 1938. This particular issue is still a subject of argument. Cf. B. Levin, 'J is for Jew', *The Times*, 30 November 1976.

45. MS uncatalogued (BoD minutes): committee report submitted to Co-ordinating Committee, 24 May 1938.
46. Ibid., Liverman memorandum on the work of the Coordinating Committee, November 1938.
47. Ibid.: report of Public Relations Officer, March 1939. For the Trades Advisory Council, set up in 1940, cf. M. Freedman, 'Jews in the society of Britain', in M. Freedman (ed.), *A Minority in Britain*, pp. 217–22.
48. MS uncatalogued (BoD minutes): secretary's report, December 1938.
49. Ibid.: Jewish Defence Committee, 13 February 1939.
50. *Jewish Chronicle*, 12 May 1933.
51. MS uncatalogued (BoD minutes): Coordinating Committee, 15 July 1937.
52. Ibid.: Jewish Defence Committee, 13 February 1939. The dichotomy between 'respectable Jews' and 'East End scum' is impressively conveyed in E. Litvinoff, *Journey Through a Small Planet* (London, 1972).
53. *The Times*, 10 October 1936.
54. Ibid.
55. MS uncatalogued (Parkes Collection): circular letter, 28 October 1936.
56. *Action*, 21 November 1936, 5 December 1936, 20 March 1937, 14 May 1938. Cf. P. Piratin, *Our Flag Stays Red* (London, 1948) p. 18.
57. MS uncatalogued (Mocatta Collection): memorandum M.J.B., 5 December 1934.
58. MS uncatalogued (BoD minutes): Coordinating Committee, 12 November 1936.
59. Ibid.: memorandum to the JPC on the policy of the Board of Deputies, March 1939.
60. Ibid.: resolution passed by Workers' Circle Friendly Societies, Cardiff Branch, 6 April 1938.
61. Ibid.: Percy Cohen memorandum 'Fascist parliamentary candidatures', 23 November 1936.
62. Ibid.: Coordinating Committee, 23 September 1936.
63. N. Laski, *Jewish Rights and Jewish Wrongs* (London, 1939) p. 132.
64. MS uncatalogued (BoD minutes): various reports and balance sheets. The Defence Council's balance sheets for the months March, April and May 1939 stated a total credit of £59,196 7s. 3d. of which £8225 15s. 6d. were donations during that quarter. The current expenditure for the same period amounted to £10,448 8s. 8d., including £8779 10s. 9d. for the campaign and £1118 1s. 4d. Head Office expenses, of which salaries took the largest share.
65. Cf. J. C. Wedgwood, *Memoirs of a Fighting Life* (London, 1940) p. 226.

Chapter 8   The Radical Left

1. MEPO 2/3043: monthly report, October 1936.
2. MS LP/FAS/33/15 (Labour Party): Conference Report 'The grave Nazi menace', 8 October 1936, p. 5.
3. H. Pelling, *The British Communist Party* (London, 1958) p. 192. On this history of the CPGB, cf. P. W. Herrmann, *Die Communist Party of Great Britain* (Meisenheim, 1976). J. Klugmann, *History of the Communist Party of Great Britain*, 2 vols (London, 1968/9).
4. W. Fishman, *East End Jewish Radicals*, pp. 97–225.

5. K. Newton, *The Sociology of British Communism* (London, 1969) pp. 80–3, attributes the Jewish support for the CPGB to the following affinities between Communism and Judaism: learning, social justice, materialism, internationalism. It seems more useful, however, to turn to particular Jewish interests deriving from the political, social and economic conditions and at a given time to explain the particular party affiliation of different sections of the Jewish community.

6. R. P. Arnot. *Twenty Years. The Policy of the CPGB from its Foundation* (London, 1940) p. 48.

7. T. Bell, *The British Communist Party* (London, 1937) p. 166.

8. MS 'Cliveden Set' (Astor Papers): draft letter Lady Astor to the *News Chronicle*, 22 March 1938. This sentence was omitted in the final version which was published in *News Chronicle*, 23 March 1938. Cf. *Herald Tribune*, 1 July 1937, *Manchester Guardian*, 1 July 1937.

9. R. Benewick, *Political Violence*, p. 223.

10. *Daily Worker*, 2 March 1933.

11. CPGB (ed.), *For Unity in London* (London, 1938) p. 26.

12. *Daily Worker*, 2 March 1933. Cf. ibid., 9 May 1935, 16 March 1936, 16 November 1936. Cf. K. Marx, 'Zur Judenfrage' (1844), repr. K. Marx and F. Engels, *Werke*, I (Berlin DDR, 1964) pp. 347–77.

13. G. Sacks, *The Jewish Question* (London, 1937) p. 87.

14. Ibid., p. 85.

15. *Daily Worker*, 28 April 1933.

16. Ibid., 2 March 1933, also 10 June 1933.

17. Ibid., 28 April 1933.

18. Coordinating Committee against Fascism (ed.), *Jews and Fascism* (London n.d. [1935]) p. 16. Similarly R. F. Andrews, *What Lenin Said About the Jews* (London n.d. [1933]) p. 2.

19. *Manifesto to the People of London* (Communist Party London District Congress, April 1937) p. 8.

20. *Daily Worker*, 10 May 1934.

21. Quoted in G. Sacks, *The Jewish Question*, p. 54.

22. Ibid., pp. 60–1. Other apologetical accounts of Jews in Russia in R. F. Andrews, *What Lenin Said About the Jews*. Also *Daily Worker*, 17 July 1933, 20 July 1933, 25 September 1933, 6 July 1934, 29 December 1934, 7 May 1936.

23. *Daily Worker*, 9 June 1934. Cf. ibid., 29 January 1935, 9 May 1935, 7 May 1936, 18 June 1936, 15 July 1938.

24. I. Rennap, *Anti-Semitism and the Jewish Question* (London, 1942)) p. 60. Cf. A. Leon, *The Jewish Question* (2nd English edn. New York, 1970) pp. 263–5.

25. *Daily Worker*, 6 July 1934.

26. Ibid., 2 July 1937. Cf. ibid., 5 October 1936.

27. Ibid., 16 March 1936, 1 October 1936, 16 October 1936, 2 July 1937.

28. Ibid., 3 November 1936.

29. B. Darke, *The Communist Technique in Britain* (London, 1953) p. 45. Examples of both genuine working-class support as well as merely anti-Fascist support for the CPGB among Jews by D. Hyde, *I Believed* (London, 1950) pp. 83, 136.

30. F. W. S. Craig, *Minor Parties at British Parliamentary Elections* (London, 1975) pp. 20 ff.

31. MEPO 2/3043: monthly report, October 1936. The sympathetic press estimated the strength of anti-Fascist opposition at 300,000 people. On 'Battle of Cable Street', cf. R. Benewick, *Political Violence*, pp. 225–31.
32. MEPO 2/3048: SB report Trafalgar Square Rally, 4 July 1937.
33. M. McCarthy, *Generation in Revolt* (London, 1953) pp. 238–9, also p. 156.
34. MEPO 2/3074: Hyde Park Rally, 9 September 1934, telegram, 7 September 1934. Cf. P. Toynbee, *Friends Apart* (London, 1954) p. 21.
35. MEPO 2/3043: Commissioner's report, October 1937.
36. H. Laski to F. Frankfurter, 10 October 1936, quoted in K. Martin, *Harold Laski* (London, 1953) pp. 105–6.
37. J. Lewis, *The Left Book Club* (London, 1970) p. 23.
38. *Left News*, nr 14, June 1937, p. 409.
39. G. Sacks, *The Jewish Question*, p. 40. R. Osborn, *The Psychology of Reaction*, published as the Club's additional book for April 1938, dealt with the psychological factors in the acceptance of anti-Semitism.
40. MEPO 2/3112: copy of Home Office minutes, 25 June 1937. Cf. MEPO 2/3048: SB report Trafalgar Square Rally, 4 July 1937. MEPO 2/3117: SB report Bermondsey March, 3 October 1937.
41. MS DCL 44.2 (NCCL): memorandum 'Legislation in relation to anti-Semitism', n.d. [1937]. At its annual meeting on 27 March 1943, however, the NCCL adopted a resolution calling for legislation against the incitement of racial antagonism. MS DCL 41.8. (NCCL): Anti-Semitism and Fascism, 17 April 1943.
42. NCCL (ed.), *Annual Report and Balance Sheet 1938–9* (London, 1939). Also MS DCL 76.2/A (NCCL): secretary's report of activities, annual conference, 21 February 1939.
43. MS DCL 74.4 (NCCL): R. Kidd, 'Jewish Civil Rights in Britain', speech delivered to international conference against anti-Semitism, Paris, 20 September 1936. Cf. NCCL (ed.), *Fascism and the Jews*, repr. of *New Statesman*, 20 October 1936.
44. MS DCL 44.4 (NCCL): report of conference on Fascism and anti-Semitism, 25 April 1937. Cf. *Jewish Chronicle*, 30 April 1937.
45. MEPO 2/3112: copy of Home Secretary's Private Secretary to R. Kidd, 21 June 1937.
46. Ibid.: F. A. Newsam, 25 June 1937, copy of Home Office minutes 502735/265.
47. Ibid.: The Home Secretary minuted the file 'I agree'.
48. MEPO 2/3088: Home Office to L. Lesser, 30 June 1936, similarly to Rev. A. Mathieson, 24 June 1936. One minute on the first case stated: 'The placard I saw was not offensive in my opinion – it merely said "Our Jewish Aristocracy".' Other posters complained of said 'war means more money to Jews'.
49. Ibid.: SD inspector and superintendent E-Division, 1 June 1936. Cf. MEPO 2/3109: police inquiry into several protests by MPs, 24 April 1937.
50. R. Kidd, *British Liberty in Danger* (London, 1940) p. 123.
51. Cf. *The Times* obituary of R. Kidd, 14 May 1942, describing his *British Liberty in Danger* as 'temperately written, well documented, and in some ways disquieting survey of the threat to personal liberty arising from delegated legislation and other causes.'

52. MEPO 2/3089: Commissioner of Police to Secretary of State, 17 September 1937.
53. MS DCL 41.4 a, b (NCCL): various correspondence.
54. NCCL (ed.), *Annual Report and Balance Sheet 1938–9*, p. 23.

Conclusions
 1. L. Chisholm (ed.), *Nursery Rhymes* (London, 1921) pp. 2–3. Cf. H. Belloc, *Cautionary Tales for Children* (17th impr. London, 1973) pp. 63–8. I. and P. Opie, *The Lore and Language of Schoolchildren* (Oxford, 1967) p. 346.
 2. Cf. I. Fetscher, 'Zur Entstehung des politischen Antisemitismus in Deutschland', in H. Huss (ed.), *Antisemitismus*, p. 30. Also R. Rürup, 'Zur Entwicklung der modernen Antisemitismusforschung' in R. Rürup, *Emanzipation und Antisemitismus*, p. 116.
 3. H. Rosenberg, *Große Depression und Bismarckzeit*, pp. 88–117.
 4. For the susceptibility towards anti-Semitism at a personality level, cf. T. W. Adorno *et al.*, *The Authoritarian Personality* (New York, 1950). S. Freud, *Der Mann Moses und die monotheistische Religion* (Frankfurt, 1964). R. M. Loewenstein, *Psychoanalyse des Antisemitismus* (Frankfurt, 1967, 1st Paris, 1952). J. P. Sartre, *Anti-Semite and Jew* (New York, 1965). Various essays and discussion in *Psyche* XVI (1962) pp. 241–317.
 5. L. Poliakov, *The History of Anti-Semitism*, III (London, 1975), p. 333.
 6. For images of 'the Jew' in English literature, cf. E. D. Coleman, *The Jew in English Drama* (New York, 1968). H. Fisch, *The Dual Image* (London, 1971). B. Glassman, *Anti-Semitic Stereotypes Without Jews. Images of the Jews in England 1290–1700* (Detroit, 1975). E. Rosenberg, *From Shylock to Svengali* (Paris, 1962). J. Strauss, *Le Judaism dans la civilisation Britannique* (Paris, 1962). S. Thompson, *Motif-Index of Folk-Literature*, VI (Cophenhagen, 1958).
 7. Cf. E. Krausz, *Ethnic Minorities in Britain* (London, 1972) pp. 55–86.
 8. Cf. B. Bettelheim, J. Janowitz, *Dynamics of Prejudice. A Psychological and Sociological Study of Veterans* (New York, 1950). See also B. Kosmin, 'Colonial Careers for Marginal Fascists', *Wiener Library Bulletin*, XXVII, n.s. nr 30/31 (1973/4) pp. 16–23.
 9. W. Lewis, *The Jews – Are They Human?* (London, 1939) p. 7. Also H. Martin, *Critic's London Diary* (London, 1960) p. 79. M. Muggeridge, *The Thirties* (London, 1940) pp. 242–3.
10. A. J. Sherman, *Island Refuge*, pp. 88, 157, 180, 216–19.
11. *Evening Standard*, 28 June 1938.
12. MS uncatalogued (Nicolson Papers): H. Nicolson to O. Mosley, 29 June 1932.

Bibliography

A   UNPUBLISHED SOURCES

Astor Papers, Reading University Library: Miscellaneous Correspondence.
Baldwin Papers, Cambridge University Library: Files relating to the British Union of Fascists.
Board of Deputies of British Jews Archive, London: Minute books of the Coordinating Committee, Finance Sub-Committee, Law, Parliamentary and General Purposes Committee, Meetings Sub-Committee 1936–40.
Britons Archive, Chawleigh: Files relating to *Protocols of the Elders of Zion*. Leese Papers, Miscellaneous Correspondence.
Gwynne Papers, University College Swansea: Files relating to V. Marsden and *Protocols of the Elders of Zion*.
Labour Party Archive, London: Files relating to Fascism at home and abroad. J. S. Middleton Papers.
Maxse Papers, West Sussex Record Office, Chichester: Various correspondence to Leo Maxse on 'Jewish Problem'.
Mocatta Library, University College London: Collection of pamphlets and newspapers published by Fascist organizations.
Mosley Secretariat, London: Collection of press-cuttings.
Mount Temple Papers, Hampshire Record Office, Winchester: Files relating to Anglo-German Fellowship.
National Council for Civil Liberties, University Library, Hull: Files relating to anti-Semitism, civil liberties and Fascism.
Nicolson Papers, Balliol College, Oxford: Correspondence H. Nicolson to O. Mosley.
Parkes Collection, University Library, Southampton: Files relating to Anti-Semitism. Jewish Telegraphic Agency Bulletin. Pamphlet Collection.
Public Record Office, London: Cabinet Minutes. Foreign Office Papers. Ramsay MacDonald Papers. Metropolitan Police Files.
The Times Archive, London: G. Dawson Papers. Files relating to *Protocols of the Elders of Zion*. Press-cuttings on Fascism in England.
Trenchard Papers, Royal Air Force Museum, Hendon: Files relating to Fascist agitation in London.
White Papers, National Maritime Museum, Greenwich: Files relating to English race, eugenics, 'Invisible Hand', 'Jewish Question', Jews and journalism.
Wiener Library, London: File 'Beamish'. Pamphlets and press-cuttings. Spector documents.

B   PUBLISHED SOURCES

1. Government Publications and Annual Reports
Board of Deputies of British Jews, *Annual Report*, 1918–40.
House of Commons Debates. *Hansard*, 4th series, vol. CIL, 1905; 5th series, vols. XC, 1917; CCXXXVII–CDXXIII, 1930–46.
National Council for Civil Liberties, *Annual Report*, 1937–9.
Report of the Commissioner of the Metropolitan Police for the Year, 1933–9.
Russia Nr 1, A collection of reports on Bolshevism in Russia. Abridged edition of parliamentary paper (London, 1919).

2. Reference Books
Cook, C., *Sources in British Political History 1900–51*, vols. I, II (London, 1975).
Craig, F. W. S., *Minor Parties at British Parliamentary Elections 1885–1974* (London, 1975).
Hazlehurst, C. and Woodland, C., *A Guide to the Papers of British Cabinet Ministers 1900–51* (London, 1974).
Jewish Encyclopedia, 12 vols (New York, 1965, 1st 1901).
Thompson, S., *Motif-Index of Folk-Literature* (Copenhagen, 1958).
Universal Jewish Encyclopedia, 10 vols (New York, 1939–48).
Wiener Library Catalogue Series, Nr 5 (London, 1971).

3. Contemporary Newspapers and Periodicals
Action, ed. BUF, February 1936–June 1940.
Blackshirt, ed. BUF, February 1933–May 1939.
Civil Liberty, ed. NCCL, n.s. Nr 2 (Autumn 1937) – n.s. nr 10 (December 1939).
Daily Worker, ed. CPGB, 1933–9.
Fascist, ed. IFL, March 1929–September 1939.
Fascist Quarterly, ed. BUF (January 1935–October 1936), ctd as *British Union Quarterly* (January 1937–Spring 1940).
Gothic Ripples, ed. A. S. Leese, 1945–8.
Jewish Chronicle, 1918–39.
Jewry Ueber Alles, ed. Britons (February–June 1920), ctd as *Jewry Ueber Alles or The Hidden Hand Exposed* (July–August 1920), ctd as *The Hidden Hand or Jewry Ueber Alles* (September 1920–September 1923), ctd as *The Hidden Hand or The Jewish Peril* (October 1923–April 1924), ctd as *The British Guardian* (May 1924–June 1925).
Left Book News, ed. Left Book Club (May–November 1936), ctd as *The Left News* (December 1936–December 1940).
New Witness, ed. C. Chesterton, November 1912–May 1923.
The Times, 1918–39.
Press-cuttings of the national and local press collected by the National Council for Civil Liberties and the Wiener Library.

4. Memoirs
Darke, B., *The Communist Technique in Britain* (London, 1953).
Forbes, Lady Angela, *Memories and Base Details* (London, n.d. [1922]).
Henriques, B. L. Q., *The Indiscretions of a Warden* (London, 1937).
Hyde, D., *I Believed* (London, 1950).

Jones, J., *Unfinished Journey* (London, 1937).
Jones, T., *A Diary With Letters 1931–50* (Oxford, 1954).
Litvinoff, E., *Journey Through a Small Planet* (London, 1972).
Lüdecke, K. G. W., *I Knew Hitler* (New York, 1937).
McCarthy, M., *Generation in Revolt* (London, 1953).
Martin, K., *Critic's London Diary. From the 'New Statesman' 1931–56* (London, 1960).
Mosley, D., *A Life of Contrasts* (London, 1977).
Mosley, O., *My Life* (London, 1968).
Muggeridge, M., *The Thirties* (London, 1940).
Nicolson, H., *Diaries and Letters*, 3 vols (London, 1966–8).
Piratin, P., *Our Flag Stays Red* (London, 1948).
Ravensdale, Baroness Irene, *In Many Rhythms* (London, 1953).
Richardson, J. H., *From the City to Fleet Street. Some Journalistic Experiences* (London, 1927).
Sieff, I., *Memoirs* (London, 1970).
Simon, J., *Retrospect. The Memoirs of the Rt Hon. Viscount Simon* (London, 1952).
Spier, E., *Focus. A Footnote to the History of the Thirties* (London, 1963).
Thost, H. W., *Als Nationalsozialist in England* (München, 1939).
Toynbee, P., *Friends Apart* (London, 1954).
Wedgwood, J. C., *Memoirs of a Fighting Life* (London, 1940).
Weizmann, C., *Trial and Error*, 2 vols (London, 1949).
Winterton, Earl C. T., *Orders of the Day* (London, 1953).

5. Brochures, Pamphlets and Contemporary Publications
Allen, E., *It Shall not Happen Here* (London, 1943).
Allen, W. E. D., 'The Fascist Idea in Britain', *Quarterly Review*, CCLXI, nr 518 (1933), pp. 223–38.
Andrews, R. F. (= Rothstein, A. F.), *What Lenin Said About the Jews* (London n.d. [1933]).
Anticipating the Protocols, repr. from *Patriot*, 5 September 1929.
Arnot, R. P., *Twenty Years 1920–40* (London, 1940).
Banister, J., *Alien Reform of the Tariff* (London, 1930).
—— *American Anglophobia* 2nd edn (London, 1929).
—— *The Champions of Our Pauperocracy* (London, 1920).
—— *England Under the Jews* (London, 1901).
—— *Hints to London Editors* 5th edn. (London, 1936).
—— *London's Hyphenated Press* (London, 1924).
—— *The Nasalite Plot Succeeds* (London, 1931).
—— *Our Alien Makers of Revolution* (London, 1925).
—— *Our Alien Press* (London, 1915).
—— *Our Hyphenated Citizens* (London, 1916).
—— *Our Jews and Irish* (London, 1930).
—— *Our Judeo-Irish Labour Party* (London, 1923).
—— *Samuel in the Helpless Lion's Den* (London, 1916).
—— *Why the London Press Favours Alien Immigration* (London, 1913).
Bell, T., *The British Communist Party* (London, 1937).
Belloc, H., *The Jews* (London, 1922).

—— and B. T. B., *Cautionary Tales for Children*, 17th impr. (London, 1973, 1st 1918).

Blakeney, R. B. D., 'British Fascism', *Nineteenth Century and After*, XCVII, nr 575 (January 1925) pp. 132–41.

Bolshevism is not Jewish, ed. Woburn Press (London, n.d.).

The BUF and Antisemitism (n.d.).

British Union of Fascists, *Above Parties – Against Communism* (n.d.).

—— *American Jews Threaten Britain* (n.d.).

—— *Are Communists the Fifth Column for Russia?* (n.d.).

—— *Britain and Jewry* (n.d.).

—— *British Union Policy* (n.d.).

—— *The British Union Stands for Trade Unionism* (n.d.).

—— *Britons* (n.d.).

—— *Conscription* (n.d.).

—— *Constitution and Rules* (n.d.).

—— *The Empire and the British Union* (n.d.).

—— *Introduction to Union Movement Policy and Membership* (n.d.).

—— *May Day Special* (n.d.).

—— *Mosley Right or Wrong* (n.d.).

—— *Objects of the Union Movement* (n.d.).

—— *Pharmacy in British Union* (n.d.).

—— *Pictorial Record 1932–7* (n.d.).

—— *Stop the Flood of Alien Jewish Immigrants* (n.d.).

—— *Trade Unionists! You Are the Victims!* (n.d.).

—— *What Jews did in the War* (n.d.).

—— *Yorkshire Betrayed. British Union Textile Policy* (n.d.).

Britons Publishing Company, *The Britons* (London, 1952).

—— *The Britons. Objects and Membership Form* (n.d.).

—— *The Code of the Jew*, 5th edn (n.d.).

—— *The Conquering Jew* (n.d.).

—— *The Emancipation of the Gentiles from the Yoke of the International Financier* (n.d.).

—— *The English Birthright* (n.d.).

—— *Four Protocols of Zion* (*Not the Protocols of Nilus*) (London, 1921).

—— *Jew World Plot* (n.d.).

—— *The Jew-alition Government* (n.d.).

—— *Jewish Bolshevism* (n.d.).

—— *The Jewish Peril* (n.d.).

—— *The Jews' Ritual Slaughter* (n.d.).

—— *Kol Nidre. The Jews' Immoral Prayer* (London, 1922).

—— *Lord Melchett* (London, 1929).

—— *A Plot for the World's Conquest* (London, 1936).

—— *Secret Societies Unveiled* (n.d.).

—— *South Africa's Kosher Press* (n.d.).

—— *What the Jews Say About Themselves* (n.d.).

—— *Who Made the World War?* (n.d.).

—— *Who Wants War?* (London, 1936).

—— *Why Are the Jews Hated?* (London, 1936).

—— *World Conquest Through World Government. Protocols of the Learned Elders of Zion*, 85th impr. (Chawleigh, 1972).

—— *The World Crash* (n.d.)
—— *Zionism Solved!* (n.d.).
Buchan, J., *The Thirty-Nine Steps* (London, 1915).
The Cause of World Unrest, Intr. by the editor of the *Morning Post* (London, 1920).
Chambers-Hunter, W. K. A., *British Union and Social Credit* (n.d.)
Cheiro (= Hamon, Count L.), *Cheiro's World Predictions*, 2nd edn. (London, 1931, 1st 1928).
Chesterton, A. K., *Apotheosis of the Jew* (London n.d. [1937]).
—— *Oswald Mosley, Portrait of a Leader* (London, 1937).
Clarke, E. G., *The British Union and the Jews*, 3rd edn. (London, 1937).
Clarke, J. H. *The Call of the Sword* (London, 1917).
—— *England Under the Heel of the Jew* (London, 1918).
—— *The God of Shelley and Blake* (London, 1930).
—— *William Blake on the Lord's Prayer* (London, 1927).
Cobbett (pseud.), *Jews and the Jews in England* (London, 1938).
The Conspiracy against the British Empire. Report of a meeting held at the House of Commons on 1 March 1921, 2nd edn (London, n.d.).
Crouch, A. C., *Jews Are News!* (Leicester, n.d.).
Domvile, Sir Barry, *Calling All Britons* (n.d.).
Douglas, Lord Alfred, *Complete Poems* (London, 1928).
The Facts about the Bolsheviks, compiled from the accounts of trustworthy eye-witnesses and the Russian Press by C. E. B. (London, 1919).
Facism, Antisemitism and the Jews, ed. Jewish People's Council against Fascism and Antisemitism (n.d.).
Fascism. Its History and Significance (London. 1924).
Facism. The Enemy of the People, ed. National Council of Labour (London, 1934).
Fascists at Olympia. A record of eye-witnesses and victims, compiled by 'vindicator' (London, 1934).
The First Jewish Bid for World Power, repr. from *Patriot*, 9, 16, 25, 30 January 1930 (n.d.).
For Britain. Truth in War Time (n.d.).
For Unity in London. Communist Party London District Annual Congress June 1938 (London, 1938).
Fry, L., *An Analysis of Zionism* (n.d.).
—— *The Jews and the British Empire* (n.d.).
Gallacher, W., *Anti-Semitism. What it Means to You* (London, 1943).
Gordon-Canning, R., *The Inward Strength of A National Socialist* (n.d.).
—— *The Spirit of Fascism* (London, 1937).
Goulding, M., *Peace Betrayed. Labour's Policy through British Union Eyes* (n.d.).
The Gravediggers of Russia, pref. by A. Rosenberg (Munich, n.d. [1921]).
Gwyer, J., *Portraits of Mean Men. A Short History of the Protocols of the Elders of Zion* (London, 1938).
Hamm, E. J., *Britain Awake! Challenge to the Old Gang*. (n.d.).
—— 'Other concentration camps', *The European*, nr 47 (January 1957) pp. 313–9.
Harlow, P., *The Shortest Way with the Jews* (London, 1939).
Henry Hamilton Beamish — Silver Badge Candidate for Clapham (London, 1918).
Hertz, J. H., *Anti-Semitism*. A sermon preached by the Very Revd the Chief Rabbi 7 October 1922 (n.d.).

Heyward, P., *Menace of the Chain Stores* (n.d.).
Hill, F. D., *'Gainst Trust and Monopoly!* (n.d.).
Hitler, A., *Mein Kampf*, 213th–217th impr. (München, 1936).
Homer, A., *Judaism and Bolshevism*, repr. from *Catholic Herald* October, November 1933 (London, 1934).
Horrors of Bolshevism, repr. from *The Times*, 14 November 1919 (n.d.).
Hutchison, G. S., *Truth. The Evidence in the Case* (London, 1936).
Hyamson, A. M., *Great Britain and the Jews* (Edinburgh, 1918).
Imperial Fascist League, *Agriculture Comes First* (n.d.).
—— *Beware! He is Fooling You!* (n.d.).
—— *British Taxi Drivers!* (n.d.).
—— *Freemasonry* (London, 1935).
—— *The Government of the Future, Fascism – Its Principles* (n.d.).
—— *The Government of the Future. Racial Fascism – Its Principles* (n.d.).
—— *The Hidden Hand Revealed by the 'Fascist' Cartoonist* (n.d.).
—— *The Jew: Past and Present* (n.d.).
—— *A Jew Remains a Jew* (n.d.)
—— *Jewish Press Control. The London Newspapers* (London, 1936).
—— *Local News!* (n.d.).
—— *A Message to Tradesmen* (n.d.).
—— *New Constitution* (n.d.).
—— *No Jews! It Isn't Done that Way!* (n.d.).
—— *Our Jewish Aristocracy: A Tale of Contamination*, 2nd edn. (April 1936).
—— *P. E. P. or Sovietism by Stealth*, 2nd edn (London, 1935).
—— *The Plan of the Jew* (n.d.).
—— *Policy and Organization of the IFL* (n.d.).
—— *Questions of Public Importance* (n.d.).
—— *Race and Politics* (n.d.)
—— *Restoration is Our Policy for Britain* (n.d.).
—— *The Swastika Symbol: What it Means* (n.d.).
—— *To Cyclists and Car Drivers* (n.d.).
—— *To a Gentile Jester of the Variety Profession* (n.d.).
—— *Whither the World?* (n.d.).
—— *Why is there a Conspiracy of Silence on the Brutal Jewish Method of Slaughter of Cattle?* (n.d.).
—— *300,000 Jews! What a Lie!* (n.d.).
Inquire Within (pseud.), *Light Bearers of Darkness* (London, 1930).
It Shall not Happen Here! ed. National Council for Civil Liberties (n.d.).
Jenks, J., *The Land and the People* (n.d.).
Jewish People's Council Against Fascism and Anti-Semitism and the Board of Deputies (n.d. [1936]).
Jewish People's Council: Report of Activities July–November 1936 (n.d.).
The Jewish Peril. Protocols of the Learned Elders of Zion (London: Eyre and Spottiswoode 1920).
Jewish Policy Exposed, ed. W. Joyce (London, 1938).
The Jews. Query Publications, nr 2 (London, n.d. [1938]).
Jews Among the Entente Leaders (London, 1918).
Jews and Fascism, ed. Coordinating Committee against Fascism (n.d.).
Jews and the War. An Answer to Anti-Semites (n.d.).

Jews Must Answer, ed. United Jewish Committee (London, 1942).

The Jews of Britain (London, 1936).

Jews: Some Plain Facts, ed. Woburn Press (n.d.).

The Jews' Who's Who (anon. = H. H. Beamish) (London, 1920).

Kidd, R., *British Liberty in Danger* (London, 1940).

Kitson, A., *The Bankers' Conspiracy* (London, 1933).

Lane, A. H., *The Hidden Hand* (n.d.).

Lansbury, G., *Anti-Semitism in the East End* (n.d.).

Laski, N., *Jewish Rights and Jewish Wrongs* (London, 1939).

Leese, A. S., *Bolshevism is Jewish* (n.d.).

—— *Devilry in the Holy Land* (London, 1938).

—— *Disraeli the Destroyer* (n.d.).

—— *Gentile Folly: The Rothschilds* (London, 1940).

—— *The Jewish War of Survival* (Guildford, 1945).

—— *The Legalised Cruelty of Shechita* (n.d.).

—— *The Mass Madness of September 1938 and its Jewish Cause* (London, 1938).

—— *My Irrelevant Defence Being Meditations Inside Gaol and Out* (London, 1938).

—— *Out of Step: Events in the Two Lives of an anti-Jewish Camel-Doctor* (n.d. [1951]).

Lewis, W., *The Jews Are They Human?* (London, 1939).

Manifesto to the People of London, Communist Party London District Congress April 1937 (London, 1937).

Marsden, V. E., *Jews in Russia* (London n.d. [1921]).

Maxse, L. J., 'The Chameleon of the Rue Nitot', *National Review*, nr 435 (May 1919), pp. 359–81.

—— 'The Second Treaty of Versailles', *National Review*, nr 438 (August 1919) pp. 814–76.

A Modern Pilgrim's Progress by A Fellow Pilgrim (= A. Kitson) (Oxford, 1935).

Mosley, Sir Oswald, *The British Peace – How to Get It* (n.d.).

—— *British Union for British Race* (Southend, n.d.) [1937]).

—— *Fascism in Britain* (London n.d. [1933]).

—— *Fascism: 100 Questions Asked and Answered* (London, 1936).

—— *The Greater Britain* (London n.d. [1932]).

—— 'Jews and Fascism', in *The Jews*. Query Publications, nr 2 (London, n.d. [1938]).

—— *Revolution by Reason* (London, 1925).

—— *Ten Points of Fascist Policy* (n.d.).

—— *Tomorrow We Live* (London, 1936).

—— 'The World Alternative', *Fascist Quarterly*, II, nr 3 (1936) pp. 377–95.

Murchin, M. G., *Britain's Jewish Problems* (London, 1939).

National Council for Civil Liberties, *The Record of a Decade of Work, 1934–45, for Democracy and Civil Liberty* (London, 1945).

——*Report of Conference on Fascism and Anti-Semitism* (London, 1937).

The New Anti-Semitism, ed. Board of Deputies (London, 1921).

Nursery Rhymes, ed. L. Chisholm, (London, 1921).

Osborn, R., *The Psychology of Reaction* (London, 1938).

Pearson, K. and Moul, M., 'The problem of alien immigration into Great Britain', *Annals of Eugenics*, I, nr 1 (October 1925) pp. 5–127.

Pitt-Rivers, G., *The World Significance of the Russian Revolution* (Oxford, 1926).

The '*Red Menace*' to *British Children*, ed. British Fascists (London n.d. [1928]).

Rennap, I., *Anti-Semitism and the Jewish Question* (London, 1942).

Risdon, W., *Strike Action or Power Action* (London n.d. [1938]).

Rudlin, W. A., *The Growth of Fascism in Great Britain* (London, 1935).

Sacks, G., *The Intelligent Man's Guide to Jew-Baiting* (London, 1935).

—— *The Jewish Question* (London, 1937).

The Simple Jewish Worker (n.d.).

Speakers' Notes, ed. Woburn Press (n.d.).

Spencer, H. S., *Democracy or Shylocracy* (London, 1918).

Stewart, B., *The Hidden Hand* (n.d.).

The Story of Bolshevism. A Warning to British Women (n.d. [1919]).

Sydenham of Combe, Lord, 'The Jewish world problem', *Nineteenth Century and After*, XC (November 1921) pp. 888–901.

Thomson, A. R., *Break the Chains that Bind Us* (n.d.).

—— *The Coming of the Corporate State* (London n.d. [1939]).

—— *Slump or Economic Independence?* (n.d.).

To the People of London! Manifesto of London District Congress Communist Party of Great Britain (April 1937).

*The Truth About '*The Protocols*'. A Literary Forgery*, repr. from *The Times*, 16, 17, 18 August 1921.

Valentin, H., *Antisemitism Historically and Critically Examined* (London, 1936).

Virgil (pseud.), *The Invisible War-Maker* (n.d.).

—— *The World's Enemies* (n.d.).

We Protest! ed. Jewish People's Council Against Fascism and Anti-Semitism (n.d.).

Webster, N. H., *Germany and England*, repr. from *Patriot* October 1938 (London, 1938).

—— *Secret Societies and Subversive Movements* (London, 1924).

—— *World Revolution. The Plot Against Civilization*, 6th edn. (Chawleigh, 1971, 1st 1921).

What the Jews of the British Empire Did in the Great War, ed. Woburn Press (n.d.).

White, A., *The Hidden Hand* (London, 1917).

Wolf, L., *The Jewish Bogey and the Forged Protocols of the Learned Elders of Zion* (London, 1920).

World Jewry versus Britain, ed. Union for British Freedom (n.d.).

C   SELECTIVE SECONDARY LITERATURE

Abramsky, C., 'A People that Shall Dwell Alone'. *New York Review of Books*, XXI, nr 20 (December 1974) pp. 22–4.

—— *War, Revolution and the Jewish Dilemma*. Inaugural Lecture delivered at University College, London 28 April 1975 (London, 1975).

Adorno, T. W., Frenkel-Brunswick, E., Levinson, D. J. and Sanford, R. N., *The Authoritarian Personality* (New York, 1950).

Aigner, D., *Das Ringen um England* (München, 1969).

Alderman, G., 'The Anti-Jewish Riots of August 1911 in South Wales', *Welsh History Review*, VI, nr 2 (December 1972) pp. 190–220.

Allport, G. W., *The Nature of Prejudice* (London, 1954).

Antisemitismus. Zur Pathologie der bürgerlichen Gesellschaft, Huss, H. and Schröder, A. (ed.) (Frankfurt, 1966).

Arendt, H., *Elemente und Ursprünge totaler Herrschaft* (Frankfurt, 1955).

Aronsfeld, C. C., 'The Britons Publishing Society', *Wiener Library Bulletin,* XX, nr 3, n.s. nr 4 (summer 1966) pp. 31–5.

Barnes, J. and Middlemas, K., *Baldwin* (London, 1969).

Barnes, J. J., 'Mein Kampf in Britain', *Wiener Library Bulletin,* XXVII, n.s. nr 32 (1974) pp. 2–10.

Benewick, R., *Political Violence and Public Order* (London, 1969).

—— 'The Threshold of Violence', in R. Benewick and T. Smith (eds), *Direct Action and Democratic Politics* (London, 1972) pp. 49–63.

Bernstein, F., *Der Antisemitismus als Gruppenerscheinung* (Berlin, 1926).

Bettelheim, B. and Janowitz, M., *Social Change and Prejudice* (New York, 1964).

Biddis, M., 'Myths of Blood', *Patterns of Prejudice,* IX, nr 5 (September/October 1975) pp. 11–19.

—— 'Racial Ideas and the Politics of Prejudice 1950–1914', *Historical Journal,* XV (1972) pp. 570–82.

Birch, L., *Why They Join the Fascists* (London n.d. [1937]).

Blume, H. S. B., 'A Study of Anti-Semitic Groups in Britain 1918–1940' (University of Sussex Thesis, 1971).

Bracher, K. and D., *Zeitgeschichtliche Kontroversen um Faschismus, Totalitarismus, Demokratie* (München, 1976).

Brentano, M. v., 'Die Endlösung – Ihre Funktion in Theorie und Praxis des Faschismus', in Huss, H. and Schröder, A. (eds), *Antisemitismus* (Frankfurt, 1966) pp. 36–76.

Brotman, A. G., 'Jewish Communal Organization', in Esh, S. and Gould, J. (eds), *Jewish Life of Modern Britain* (London, 1964) pp. 1–17.

Carpenter, L. P., 'Corporatism in Britain', *Journal of Contemporary History,* II, nr 1 (January 1976) pp. 3–25.

Cassels, A., 'Janus: the Two Faces of Fascism', in Turner, H. A. (ed.), *Reappraisals of Fascism* (New York, 1975) pp. 69–92.

Cecil, R., *The Myth of the Master Race. Alfred Rosenberg and Nazi Ideology* (London, 1972).

Cohen, A., 'The Structure of Anglo-Jewry Today', in Lipman, V. D. (ed.), *Three Centuries of Anglo-Jewish History* (London, 1961) pp. 169–85.

Cohn, N., *Warrant for Genocide. The Myth of the Jewish World Conspiracy and the Protocols of the Elders of Zion* (London, 1967).

Cowling, M., *The Impact of Hitler. British Politics and British Policy 1933–40* (London, 1975).

—— *The Impact of Labour 1920–4* (Cambridge, 1971).

Cross, C., *The Fascists in Britain* (London, 1961).

Dawidowicz, L. S., *The War Against the Jews 1933–45* (New York, 1975).

Direct Action and Democratic Politics, Benewick, R. and Smith, T. (ed.) (London, 1972).

Emanuel, C. H. L., *A Century and a Half of Jewish History* (London, 1910).

Eysenck, H. J., *Uses and Abuses of Psychology* (Edinburgh, 1953).

Fetscher, I., 'Zur Entstehung des politischen Antisemitismus in Deutschland', in Huss, H. and Schröder, A. (eds), *Antisemitismus* (Frankfurt, 1966) pp. 11–33.

Finestein, I., 'The New Community', in Lipman, V. D. (ed.), *Three Centuries of Anglo-Jewish History* (London, 1961) pp. 107–23.

Fisch, H., *The Dual Image. A Study of the Jew in English and American Literature* (London, 1971).

Fishman, W. J., *East End Jewish Radicals* (London, 1975).

Foot, P., *Immigration and Race in British Politics* (London, 1965).

Freedman, M., 'Jews in the Society of Britain', in Freedman, M. (ed.), *A Minority in Britain. Social Studies of the Anglo-Jewish Community* (London 1955) pp. 201–42.

Fuchs, E., *Die Juden in der Karikatur* (München, 1921).

Gainer, B., *The Alien Invasion. The Origins of the Aliens Act of 1905* (London, 1972).

Gannon, F. R., *The British Press and Germany 1936–9* (Oxford, 1971).

Garrard, J. A., *The English and Immigration. A Comparative Study of the Jewish Influx 1880–1910* (London, 1971).

Gartner, L. P., *The Jewish Immigrant in England 1870–1914* (London, 1960).

Gaster, T. H., 'Elders of Zion; Protocols of', *Universal Jewish Encyclopedia IV* (New York, 1948) pp. 46–60.

Geiger, D. M., 'Blackshirts as Jew-Baiters', *Wiener Library Bulletin*, XX, n.s. nr 4 (Autumn 1966) pp. 11–14.

—— 'British Fascism as Revealed in the BUF's press' (New York University PhD thesis, 1963).

George, M., *The Hollow Men. An Examination of British Foreign Policy Between the Years 1933 and 1939* (London, 1967).

Gilbert, M., *Sir Horace Rumbold. Portrait of a Diplomat* (London, 1973).

—— *Winston S. Churchill*, IV, 1917–22 (London, 1975).

Ginsberg, M., *Reason and Unreason in Society. Essays in Sociology and Social Philosophy* (London, 1947).

Glassman, B., *Anti-Semitic Stereotypes Without Jews, Images of the Jews in England 1290–1700* (Detroit, 1975).

Graham, A. J., *Fascism in Britain* (Badminton, 1966).

Grego, J., *Rowlandson the Caricaturist*, 2 vols (London, 1880).

Hales, J. W., 'Shakespeare and the Jews', *English Historical Review*, XXXVI (October 1894) pp. 652–61.

Heise, W., 'Antisemitismus und Antikommunismus', *Deutsche Zeitschrift für Philosophie*, IX (Berlin DDR, 1961) pp. 1423–45.

Henriques, U. R. Q., 'The Jewish Emancipation Controversy in 19th Century Britain', *Past and Present*, XL (July 1968) pp. 126–46.

Herrmann, P. W., *Die Communist Party of Great Britain* (Meisenheim, 1976).

Herzog, Y., *A People that Dwells Alone. Speeches and Writings of Yaacov Herzog* (London, 1975).

Holmes, C., 'Houston S. Chamberlain in Great Britain', *Wiener Library Bulletin*, XXIV, n.s. nr 19 (1970) pp. 31–6.

—— 'Immigrants and Minorities in Great Britain', *Patterns of Prejudice*, X. nr 3 (1976) pp. 1–6.

Horkheimer, M. and Adorno, T., '*Elemente des Antisemitismus*', in Adorno, T. and Horkheimer, M., *Dialektik der Aufklärung* (Frankfurt, 1969), pp. 177–217.

Jahoda, M., 'Stereotype', in Gould, J. and Kolb, W., *A Dictionary of the Social Sciences* (London, 1964) pp. 694–5.

Jersch-Wenzel, S., 'Die Lage von Minderheiten als Indiz für den Stand der

Emanzipation einer Gesellschaft', in Wehler, H. U. (ed.), *Sozialgeschichte Heute. Festschrift für H. Rosenberg* (Göttingen, 1974) pp. 365–87.

Jewish Life in Modern Britain. Conference held at University College, London 1 and 2 April 1962, ed. Esh, S. and Gould, J. (London, 1964).

Jones, J. R., 'England', in Rogger, W. and Weber, E. (eds), *The European Right* (Berkeley, 1965) pp. 29–70.

Katz, H., 'The Party Loyalties of European Jews', *Jewish Political Behaviour*, University of Strathclyde Survey Research Centre, Occasional Paper nr 12 (1974) pp. 1–19.

Katz. J., *Emancipation and Assimilation. Studies in Modern Jewish History* (Westmead, 1972).

Kiernan, V. G., 'Pattern of Protest in English History', in Benewick, R. and Smith, T. (eds), *Direct Action and Democratic Politics* (London, 1972) pp. 25–48.

Klugman, J., *The History of the CPGB*, 2 vols (London 1968/9).

Kosmin, B. A., 'Colonial Careers for Marginal Fascists. A Portrait of Hamilton Beamish', *Wiener Library Bulletin*, XXVII, n.s. nr 30/1 (1973/4) pp. 16–23.

Krausnick, H., *Anatomy of the SS State* (London, 1968).

Krausz, E., *Ethnic Minorities in Britain* (London, 1971).

Krikler, B., 'Boycotting Nazi Germany', *Wiener Library Bulletin*, XXIII, n.s. nr 17 (1969) pp. 26–32.

Lagarde, P. de, *Deutsche Schriften* 4th edn (Göttingen, 1903 1st 1885).

Laqueur. W., *Deutschland und Rußland* (Berlin, 1965).

Larsen, E., *First With the Truth. Newspapermen in Action* (London, 1968).

Leon, A., *The Jewish Question. A Marxist Interpretation*, 2nd edn (New York, 1972 1st 1942).

Lewis, J., *The Left Book Club. A Historical Record* (London, 1970).

Lipman, V. D., 'The Age of Emancipation 1815–80', in Lipman, V. D. (ed.), *Three Centuries of Anglo-Jewish History* (Cambridge, 1961) pp. 69–106.

—— *Social History of the Jews in England 1850–1950* (London, 1954).

Lippmann, W., *Public Opinion*, 13th edn (New York, 1950 1st 1922).

Loewenstein, R. M., *Psychoanalyse des Antisemitismus*, 2nd edn (Frankfurt, 1968).

Mandle, W., *Anti-Semitism and the British Union of Fascists* (London, 1968).

—— 'The Leadership of the BUF', *Australian Journal of Politics and History*, XXII, nr 3 (1966) pp. 360–83.

Marrus, M. R., *The Politics of Assimilation. A Study of the French Jewish Community at the Time of the Dreyfus Affair* (Oxford, 1971).

Martin, K., *Harold Laski. A Biographical Memoir* (London, 1953).

Marx, K., 'Zur Judenfrage', in Marx, K. and Engels, F., *Werke I* (Berlin DDR, 1972) pp. 347–77.

Marxisten gegen Antisemitismus, ed. Fetscher, I. (Hamburg, 1974).

A Minority in Britain. Social Studies of the Anglo-Jewish Community, ed. Freedman, M. (London, 1955).

Morell, J. E., 'Arnold Leese – Fascist and Anti-Semite', *Wiener Library Bulletin*, XXIII, n.s. nr 17 (1969) pp. 32–6.

Mullally, F., *Fascism Inside England* (London, 1946).

Newall, V., *The Encyclopedia of Witchcraft and Magic* (London, 1974).

—— 'The Jew as a Witch Figure'. in Newall, V. (ed.), *The Witch Figure* (London, 1973) pp. 95–124.

Newton, K., *The Sociology of British Communism* (London, 1969).

Nolte, E., *Die Krise des liberalen Systems und die faschistischen Bewegungen* (München, 1968).

Opie. J. and P., *The Lore and Language of Schoolchildren* (Oxford, 1967; 1st 1959).

Parkes, J., *Antisemitism* (London, 1962).

—— *The Emergence of the Jewish Problem 1878–1939* (London, 1946).

Paucker, A., *Der jüdische Abwehrkampf gegen Antisemitismus und Nationalsozialismus in den letzten Jahren der Weimarer Republik*, 2nd edn (Hamburg, 1969).

Pelling, H., *The British Communist Party* (London, 1958).

Poliakov, L., *The Aryan Myth. A History of Racist and Nationalist Ideas in Europe* (London, 1974).

—— *Bréviar de la Haine. Le IIIe Reich et les Juifs* (Paris, 1951).

—— *The History of Anti-Semitism*, III (London, 1975).

Pryce-Jones, D., *Unity Mitford* (London, 1976).

Psyche, XVI, nr 5 (1962) pp. 241–317.

Pugh, M., 'Peace with Italy. BUF Reactions to the Abyssinian War 1935–6', *Wiener Library Bulletin*, XXVII, n.s. nr 32 (1974) pp. 11–18.

Pulzer, P. G., *The Rise of Political Anti-Semitism in Germany and Austria* (New York, 1964).

Reappraisals of Fascism, ed. Turner, H. A. (New York, 1975).

Reichmann, E. G., *Flucht in den Haß. Die Ursachen der deutschen Judenkatastrophe*, 7th edn (Frankfurt, 1969).

Robb, J. H., *Working-Class Anti-Semite. A Psychological Study in a London Borough* (London, 1954).

Rosenberg, E., *From Shylock to Svengali. Jewish Stereotypes in English Fiction* (London, 1961).

Rosenberg, H., *Große Depression und Bismarckzeit* (Berlin, 1967).

Roth, C., *A History of the Jews in England* 3rd (Oxford, 1964).

Rürup, R., *Emanzipation und Antisemitismus* (Göttingen, 1975).

Samuel, M., *The Great Hatred* (New York, 1941).

Sartre, J. P., *Anti-Semite and Jew* (New York, 1965; 1st 1946).

Schneider, W., 'Fascism', *Marxism, Communism and Western Society*, III (New York, 1972) pp. 282–302.

Schorsch, I., *Jewish Reactions to German Anti-Semitism 1870–1914* (New York, 1972).

Seliktar, O., 'The Political Attitudes and Behaviour of British Jews', *Jewish Political Behaviour*, University of Strathclyde Survey Research Centre, Occasional Paper nr 12 (1974) pp. 21–44.

Sharf, A., *The British Press and Jews under Nazi Rule* (London, 1964).

—— *Nazi Racialism and the British Press 1933–45* (London, n.d. [1963]).

Sherman, A. J., *Island Refuge. Britain and Refugees from the Third Reich 1933–9* (London, 1973).

Silberman, A., 'Zur Soziologie des Antisemitismus', *Psyche*, XVI (1962) pp. 246–54.

Silberner, E., *Sozialisten zur Judenfrage* (Berlin, 1962).

Skidelsky, R., 'Great Britain', in Woolf, J. (ed.), *European Fascism* (London, 1968) pp. 231–61.

—— *Oswald Mosley* (London, 1975).

—— *Politicians and the Slump* (London, 1967).

Snyder, L. L., *The Idea of Racialism. Its Meaning and History* (Princeton, 1962).

Stevens, A., *The Dispossessed. German Refugees in Britain* (London, 1975).
Straus, R., *Die Juden in Wirtschaft und Gesellschaft* (Frankfurt, 1964).
Sulzbach, *Die zwei Wurzeln und Formen des Judenhasses* (Stuttgart, 1959).
Taylor, A. J. P., *Beaverbrook* (London, 1972).
Three Centuries of Anglo-Jewish History, ed. Lipman, V. D. (Cambridge, 1961).
Thurlow, R., 'Authoritarians and Populists on the English Far Right', *Patterns of Prejudice*, X, nr 2 (1976) pp. 13–20.
—— 'Racial Populism in England', *Patterns of Prejudice*, X, nr 4 (1976) pp. 27–32.
Trachtenberg, J., *The Devil and the Jews. The Medieval Conception of the Jew and its Relation to Modern Anti-Semitism* (New Haven, 1943).
Ullman, R. H., *Britain and the Russian Civil War* (Princeton, 1968).
—— *Intervention and the War* (Princeton, 1961).
Wischnitzer, M., *To Dwell in Safety. The Story of Jewish Migration since 1800* (Philadelphia, 1948).
Wistrich, R. S., 'French Socialism and the Dreyfus Affair', *Wiener Library Bulletin*, XXVIII, n.s. nr 35/6, pp. 9–20.
Zeman, Z. A. B., *Nazi Propaganda*, 2nd edn (Oxford, 1973).

Index